WRITING THE
POPULAR
NOVEL

ALSO BY LOREN D. ESTLEMAN

THE AMOS WALKER SERIES

Retro

Poison Blonde

Sinister Heights

A Smile on the Face of
the Tiger

The Hours of the Virgin

The Witchfinder

Never Street

Sweet Women Lie

Silent Thunder

Downriver

Lady Yesterday

Every Brilliant Eye

Sugartown

The Glass Highway

The Midnight Man

Angel Eyes

Motor City Blue

THE DETROIT SERIES

Thunder City

Jitterbug

Stress

Edsel

King of the Corner

Motown

Whiskey River

THE PETER MACKLIN SERIES

Little Black Dress

Any Man's Death

Roses Are Dead

Kill Zone

Something Borrowed,
Something Black

THE PAGE MURDOCK SERIES

Port Hazard

White Desert

City of Widows

The Stranglers

Murdock's Law

Stamping Ground

The High Rocks

WESTERN NOVELS

Black Powder, White
Smoke

The Master Executioner

The Rocky Mountain
Moving Picture
Association

Journey of the Dead

Billy Gashade: An
American Epic

Sudden Country

Bloody Season

Gun Man

This Old Bill

Mister St. John

The Wolfer

Aces & Eights

The Hider

OTHER NOVELS

Peeper

Dr. Jekyll and Mr. Holmes

Sherlock Holmes vs. Dracula

Red Highway (previously
published as The Oklahoma Punk)

SHORT STORY COLLECTIONS

The Best Western Stories
of Loren D. Estleman

People Who Kill

General Murders

NONFICTION

The Wister Trace

LOREN D. ESTLEMAN

A comprehensive guide to crafting
FICTION THAT SELLS

WRITING THE POPULAR NOVEL

FOREWORD BY JOHN LESCROART

**WRITER'S
DIGEST
BOOKS**

CINCINNATI, OHIO
WWW.WRITERSDIGEST.COM

DEDICATION

To Lois Randall, and to the memory of Georgia Remer, conscientious copy editors of the noble old school, this book is gratefully dedicated. They sanded off the rough edges in my early days; most of them, anyway.

Visit our Web site at www.writersdigest.com for information on more resources for writers. To receive a free weekly e-mail newsletter delivering tips and updates about writing and about Writer's Digest products, register directly at our Web site at http://newsletters.fwpublications.com.

08   07   06   05   04   5 4 3 2 1

Library of Congress Cataloging-in-Publication Data

Estleman, Loren D.
  Writing the popular novel: a comprehensive guide to crafting fiction that sells / by Loren
  D. Estleman.
     p. cm.
  Includes index.
  ISBN 1-58297-287-7 (hardcover: alk. paper)   ISBN 1-58297-288-5 (pbk.: alk. paper)
     1. Fiction—Authorship. I. Title.
PN3365.E73 2004   2004053031
808.3—dc22   CIP

Edited by Kelly Nickell
Designed by Terri Eubanks
Art Directed by Lisa Buchanan
Cover by Nick & Diane Gliebe/Design Matters
Production coordinated by Robin Richie
Author photograph by Deborah Morgan; Image of typewriter keyboard © C Squared Studios/Getty Images; Image of antique typewriter © Ken Reid/Getty Images.

ACKNOWLEDGMENT

I'm indebted to my wife, Deborah Morgan, a skilled writer who is as hard on her own work as she is on mine, for suggestions innumerable that helped to bring shape and substance to this book. Its shortcomings are all my own.

ABOUT THE AUTHOR

Loren D. Estleman has published more than fifty books in the mystery and historical Western genres and mainstream fiction. He has received fifteen national writing awards, including three Shamuses, four Golden Spurs, and three Western Heritage Awards. In addition, he has been nominated for the Edgar Allan Poe Award, England's Silver Dagger, and the National Book Award. His latest Amos Walker detective novel is *Retro*. In 2002, Eastern Michigan University named him an honorary Doctor of Humane Letters. He is also the author of *The Wister Trace*, a scholarly study of the history of the Western novel, and has reviewed books for *The Detroit News*, *The Washington Post*, and *The New York Times*. He lives in rural Michigan with his wife, author Deborah Morgan.

WRITING THE POPULAR NOVEL   by Loren D. Estleman

CONTENTS

F O R E W O R D

I'VE BEEN AN AFICIONADO of the Wyatt Earp legend for most of my life. So in 1987, when I read a glowing review of *Bloody Season*, a then-new book about the gunfight at the O.K. Corral written by Loren D. Estleman, I ran right out and bought it in hardcover. The concise and compelling opening words of the book—"He was dying faster than usual that morning"—drew me into a world that should have been recognizable to anyone who had grown up, as I had, watching television and movie Westerns.

But as the pages flew by, the story with all of its familiar elements—the Earps, the Clantons, Doc Holliday, Big Nose Kate, the shootout itself—underwent what I can only call a spiritual transformation in my own psyche. Suddenly the players in the drama, the streets they walked, the women they loved, the business interests they fought and sometimes died for, all coalesced into a Tombstone, Arizona, that seemed quantifiably and qualitatively different from (not different than, see chapter four) the Old West that I thought I'd known. Somehow, as if by magic, Loren's clean, unadorned prose had created a tangible, real place out of a hackneyed old movie set— a new kind of fictional landscape inhabited not by stick figures dressed in black or white, but by fascinating, complicated, contra-dictory, often violent, sometimes tender, modern human beings.

Magic indeed. The spell Loren had cast was so captivating that I finished the book and immediately turned back to the beginning and started it all over again. Not only was I reluctant to break out of the nearly narcotic trance that *Bloody Season* had induced, but as a fledgling author myself, I wanted—no, I needed, with a poor novice writer's desperation—to understand how Loren had done it.

For done it he surely had. Although set in the 1880s, this was a very modern novel. It was also a genre piece and a literary work (nominated for the Pulitzer Prize no less); above all, it was a popular, commercial, accessible book. I reasoned that if I could get to some sort of intuitive understanding of Loren's technique and approach to artistry, I too might someday be able to make a living putting words on paper. I'm still working on the former, but to my surprise, delight, and satisfaction, the latter has come to pass. And I credit no small part of my own success to the lessons embedded in *Bloody Season*.

So you can do what I did. You can reread the same book five or six times, even going so far as to type individual sections yourself to try and understand the rhythms and pacing, hoping to glean from the experience a few raw gems that you can then cut and polish to your own specifications. Or you can read the book you now hold in your hands, take its lessons to heart, and begin to apply them to your writ-ing today.

Make no mistake: *Writing the Popular Novel* is a book for the serious writer; that is, the person who cares about plot and character and, above all, words and their usage; the person who aspires to make writing fiction his life and livelihood. (If you don't like my gender-specific pronoun, gentle reader, I refer you once again to chapter four.)

The following partial list describes people for whom this book is not intended: It is not for the dilettante. It is not for someone who longs to have written something, so that then she can tell her friends that she's a writer. It is definitely not for you if you're looking for shortcuts to publication, because there aren't any. It's not for you if you don't want to do the work it takes to get your prose clean enough to persuade an actual editor in a real publishing house (i.e., someone who will pay you) to take your book. It's probably not your cup of tea if you don't think or care that there's a difference between its and it's, then and than, persuade and convince; if you can't find the time to actually put words on paper with regularity; if you want Google to do your research for you; if you don't burn to capture your ideas and characters in your own prose; if you don't know or want to know why I'm using semicolons in this paragraph. Finally, if you're intellectually, spiritually, or physically lazy, fugettaboutit.

Writing is work, plain and simple. Getting it right takes thought, commitment, and effort. If you're not ready to deal with that, perhaps you'd find greater happiness doing your book shopping today in the cooking section.

Okay. Are we clear?

But having said all of the above, *Writing the Popular Novel* is an upbeat, practical primer on the art, techniques, and even the business of prose fiction. (If you're appalled that now I've started not just sentences but two paragraphs with the word "but," see chapter four once again. In fact, even if you make the incorrect decision not to buy this book, I urge you to turn to chapter four now and read it in its entirety—won't take you five minutes.) *Writing the Popular Novel* is also very, very funny in many, many places—a distinct plus in a reference work. The "Fiction Facts" at the end of each chapter, all by themselves, are worth the price of admission.

Loren has written and sold more than fifty books and hundreds of short stories in a wide variety of genres and styles. He is a master both at structuring fictional work and using language effectively. In these pages, however, he offers far more than a crash course in the formal techniques all writers should have at their disposal and that elevate his own work to the level of art (although he does that in the most felicitous and entertaining prose style you're likely to run across anywhere). Spend some time with any one of these chapters, and you'll find yourself inside the mind and heart of one of the country's most talented and successful working novelists. The passion for writing and for all the attendant work of the writer's life bleeds out of these pages.

You can stop reading this Foreword (not "Forward") here if you'd like, so long as y'all promise to come back soon, and take a peek at the Table of Contents. Right away, you'll notice the nuts and bolts approach to almost every one of the issues facing the would-be writer. Why fiction anyway? What kind of book should you write? Is genre necessarily opposed to art? How does one go about setting up a workspace? How many pages should you try for at each sitting? What's an outline all about? Computer, pen, or pencil? Conflict. Tense. Point of View. Research. Dialogue. Whose advice should you heed/avoid? What about agents?

These are the daily concerns of every working writer. Loren's personal experience dealing with each of these questions, and his solutions to them, would alone make this book invaluable. But add the experiences of other professionals from every genre—household names from mainstream, romance, mystery, suspense, horror, Western, science fiction—all well represented here by example, and you've got a reference book for the ages.

The single most difficult hurdle I faced at the beginning of my own career was a seemingly inborn prejudice that the writer's life was in fact something to which a "regular guy" like myself could never realistically aspire. After all, I was raised and educated in the suburbs. My parents worked in business jobs and between them knew no authors or agents. My father, a voracious and sensitive reader, counseled me to view writing as a hobby, not a career, so I didn't submit what turned out to be my first published hardcover novel until thirteen years after I'd written it. I didn't even meet another real live author (Dennis Lynds) until I'd published four of my own books!

Perhaps worst of all for any prospective writer, I had had a ridiculously happy childhood, living with parents I loved and siblings I had lots of fun with. Now, assuming that anyone who is still reading these words wants, in some fashion, to become a writer, you know that the absolute worst fate that can befall a future author is to be burdened with a happy childhood. I can't tell you how many times I've wished I were James Ellroy, or Tobias Wolff, or Pat Conroy, or even Anne

Lamott. All these folks, and so many more, had an insurmountable leg up on me. It was hardwired into their birthrights that they could become "real" writers because they'd had traumatic and/or miserable early lives. Talk about twisted, but it often broke my young writer's heart that I hadn't.

So, you'll understand, my career was doomed from the start.

In hundreds of conversations with readers around the country, I learned that my experience, my own feeling not so much of technical inadequacy, but of the impossibility of actually publishing with regularity and becoming a professional writer, is not unique. Few of us grow up surrounded by the literati; most of us trying to break into the business are not exactly embraced by the culture.

In my opinion, the best of the many great things about this book is that Loren's optimism about writing books as a life choice—any style, any genre, just so long as they're good books—is simply infectious. There is no other word for it. Everyone who is willing to put in the time and do the work, even those cursed with happy lives or blissful childhoods, can be in the club.

Publishing is not a closed society, but an open, artistic, fascinating, challenging world (and yes, also a business) that can accommodate nearly endless variety. Fiction is not dead; to the contrary, it's thriving. New writers publish all the time. Great novels, entertaining novels, important novels, popular novels are being written every day, right now. The fiction market is a vibrant and living beast that, in fact, constantly seeks and even demands infusions of new blood.

That's you, dear reader, just as soon as you've finished your book and it's as damn good as it's going to get and you're ready to submit it and start the next one. Because, after all, you want to write popular novels as a career. Don't you?

This book's wonderful contribution is a palpable sense that becoming a published writer of popular fiction is not impossible at all. It isn't easy, of course, but success doesn't come easily in many fields. And there are rules, sure, and matters of taste, judgment, style, form, and—perhaps most of all—imagination. But all this, to the real writer, is the fun stuff; the work actually produces endorphins! If you're a word person and writing's your drug, these are the questions you want to be addressing, the problems you can't wait to work on and solve.

My little caveat paragraph above ought to give you some idea of the kinds of would-be writers who won't benefit from this book. And unfortunately, there is no getting around some of the difficulties you'll encounter in the writing process. Loren doesn't pretend it's all a party. But what he does do is invite you to travel with him down the roads he's walked and take a look at the scenery all around you. Smell the smells, taste the tastes, pay the tolls. You'll find it to be an entertaining and informative voyage to a land that always may have seemed forever just out of your reach. If, at the end of it, you feel like you belong with other authors of popular novels in Estleman country, he's happy to show you in *Writing the Popular Novel* just about everything you'll need to get there on your own.

And that, like it or not, is the way everyone arrives.

—John Lescroart

The Decline and Fall
of Mainstream Fiction
* * *

SOMETHING IS ALWAYS DYING in publishing.

At one time or another, the watchdogs of literature have predict-ed the imminent demise of the Western, the novel, the short story, fic-tion itself; lately even the future of the book as we know it has been called into question. From Sam Johnson's day to Kurt Vonnegut's, this fascination with death has shrouded the critical community in peren-nial widow's weeds.

Without exception, the forecasts have proven false. Following the lead of Larry McMurtry, Cormac McCarthy, and Annie Proulx, the Western is entering its greatest period. More new novels are in pro-duction this year than in any other since Jonathan Swift and Daniel Defoe first made the form popular in the eighteenth century. The short story struggles on in anthologies and specialty magazines, as it did when Edgar Allan Poe was forced to peddle copies of publications containing his work to support himself and his family. Readers' sur-veys support the theory that in times of crisis, a troubled public chooses to escape into the lives of invented characters more exotic and conflicted than ours. And following an early enthusiastic trial, publishers' interest in the loudly trumpeted "e-book," that wireless wonder capable of downloading the works of Shakespeare, Tolstoy, and J.K. Rowling into a portable hand-held format, has slowed down considerably. The book survives in its original low-tech incarnation.

In our time, the only type of fiction that shows definite signs of fading from our culture is the traditional, unclassifiable story variously identified as literary, academic, and mainstream. Plainly put, unless your name is Norman Mailer, Joan Didion, or John Irving—an aging society, for all its merits—if your writing cannot conveniently be defined as suspense, romance, Western, or science fiction, your chances of publishing under a major imprint are about as likely as being struck by lightning while being kidnapped by terrorists on your way to claim your million-dollar lottery check.

As with all trends, this one is governed by the laws of commerce. General fiction is a hard sell.

The phenomenon is fairly new. Until recently, the philosophy in publishing was to publish bestsellers in order to subsidize the books publishers wanted to publish. The relatively modest sales of many Pulitzer- and Nobel-prizewinning books brought prestige to firms forced to subsist on the popularity of the latest fat historical saga, flashy space opera, and slam-bang actioner displayed eye-catchingly in the entrances of bookstores and in the monthly bulletins of the Book-of-the-Month Club.

At that time, legendary moguls named Nelson Doubleday, Alfred A. Knopf, and Harold Macmillan chaired the boards of publishing institutions whose buildings bore their names. Their reputations were built on the enduring reputations of Rudyard Kipling, Ernest Hemingway, Edith Wharton, and other literary lions, and in the early days of their management, books dominated the entertainment industry, with little competition from the early cinema and the radio in the parlor. Publishers could afford to gamble on the work of promising unknowns in the faith that authors of skill and insight would eventually find their audience and assume the thrones left vacant by their celebrated predecessors.

The moguls are gone. Those who have taken their place must compete with blockbuster movies, rock concerts, video arcades, and the ubiquitous Cyclops eye of television for their share of the market. The "synergy" of the instant bestseller transformed almost immediately into a major motion picture, video-game tie-in, and TV series spin-off, and the profits that result, offset the rising costs of production and promotion, and shorten the patience required to wait for next year's Tom Wolfe to catch up with this week's Nicholas Sparks. It matters not at all that Sparks and his crowd couldn't fill out a change-of-address form without strenuous editing; any book that can divert the attention of the average viewer of reality TV is bound to galvanize the staff in Sales.

It can be argued that mainstream fiction benefited greatly from ignorance on the part of its publishers. Proliferating bookstore chains and computer accounting now enable the bean counters in New York to access instant sales figures and learn how well—or how badly—a title in the current catalogue fared during its first two weeks between covers. Anything less than a steep climb up the charts negatively affects the likelihood of the author's next book receiving wide promotion, or possibly even publication.

The tyranny of numbers, and editors' fears for their jobs, force them to stake the company treasury only on sure things. While it's difficult to track the sales history of first novels not easily assigned to a recognizable category, it's easy to do a search on first Westerns, mysteries, romances, and sci-fi chronicles, crunch the figures, and work up a table showing whether a publisher can afford to take a risk on a debut book in one of those genres, and if so, how much it can invest without taking a bath and laying off the creative staff.

Needless to say, such a publishing climate is devastating for the writer who prefers great themes, profound characters, and unresolved conflict over means, motive, and opportunity, or how many light years are involved in piloting a spacecraft to Jupiter. Had the climate existed in 1851, *Moby Dick* might never have seen the light of day; it didn't sell out its original 5,000-copy print run until the 1920s. Under present conditions, it's impossible to determine how much potentially immortal literature is not being published because it took

Herman Melville seventy years to match the numbers of a Stephen King shocker on the day it's released

That's the downside, and no one who loves great reading would disagree that it's very down indeed. The upside is, faced with the same situation in 1924, Charles Scribner's Sons might have looked at *The Great Gatsby*—its enigmatic protagonist with a criminal past, his obsession with a rich married woman, a tragic hit-and-run accident, and a fatal shooting in a swimming pool—seen its potential for suspense and romance, packaged it as a mystery, and without compromising so much as a comma of F. Scott Fitzgerald's vision, managed to do what in fact it failed to do: sell every copy it printed and go back to press. As it happened, not one of Fitzgerald's titles was in print when he died sixteen years later, and he was largely forgotten until his work was rediscovered by academics in the 1960s. At the end of the day, there is something to be said for crass commercialism.

This isn't airy, "What if?" speculation. The quality of genre writing in our time suggests that today's budding Melvilles, Wolfes, Whartons, Hemingways, Kiplings, and Fitzgeralds have fixed their talent and vision on category fiction, building inroads into the reading habits of future generations while staying ahead of this month's rent. They have made genre fiction the mainstream of the twenty-first century.

In the pages to come, I will show why it's no disgrace—far from it—for a writer to follow the lead of Sir Walter Scott, Charlotte Brontë, Nathaniel Hawthorne, and, in a later day, Raymond Chandler, Dick Francis, Ursula K. Le Guin, and hundreds of other literary heavyweights who have taken aim on the broad middle of the popular market and punched holes through the barricades that separate epochs. He or she might not write the elusive Great American Novel; but nothing that is truly great has aspired to that level without first becoming popular.

* * *

Fiction Fact

Ian Fleming named his most famous character after a friend, James Bond. It was the blandest and most unheroic name he could imagine, perfect for a secret agent.

* * *

Better Than Life:
Why Fiction Exists

* * *

LET'S BE HONEST, at least with ourselves; nobody needs us.

Writers of fiction are artists, not craftsmen. Craftsmen are cabinetmakers, glaziers, cobblers—skilled laborers who fashion practical objects for their customers' everyday use. Were they to lay down their tools tomorrow, by the end of a month the world would run out of places to store its pots, pans, and prescriptions, its windows would be open to the elements, and it would be barefoot. Artists paint pictures, compose narratives, carve statues. Were they to abandon their studios tomorrow, rooms would go undecorated and patients in doctors' reception areas would have to talk to one another to pass the time. This is a dreary scenario to be sure, but no one would mistake it for the apocalypse.

Oscar Wilde, himself no mean artist, said, "All art is quite useless." Its disappearance from our culture would not place a single life in jeopardy or threaten the gross national product. By the time its absence was noticed, the details would be too stale to report in a newspaper. If you're still unconvinced, ask yourself which classes are the first to be dropped from the curriculum whenever a school district is forced to cut its budget. Music, art, and literature must in critical times step aside for math, science, and geography.

Why, then, is there art?

Because a bare wall is an offense to the eye. Because the ability to shape cold marble into a semblance of warm flesh is proof that man was not put on earth merely to coexist with the other mammals. Because a paragraph printed on ordinary paper by conventional methods can transport us to the crest of Everest or the hold of the *Bonhomme Richard* without removing us from the comfort of our armchairs. Because without art, existence would be intolerable.

Fiction is our only avenue of escape from the carapace of bone that imprisons our perceptions. It should be better than life, or it has no business being here in the first place.

The above is not a plea for uplifting themes and happy endings, although it would be a refreshing change of pace if Cornell Woolrich and Joyce Carol Oates were to lighten up once in a while. Treachery and tragedy are fully as diverting as probity and triumph. "Better than life" in this context refers to the natural human craving for sense and order, and the responsibility of the writer to satisfy it.

The world cries out for editing. Life is chaotic and absurd, and people are imperfect, unpredictable creatures. There are no beginnings or endings in nature. One episode not only leads to another, but often runs parallel or perpendicular to it, while incidents with the potential to be dramatic and fascinating have an exasperating habit of petering out, their promise unfulfilled and whatever lessons they might contain obscured by their own ambiguity. As intelligent adults, we accept this situation because we're resigned to the wisdom that we can't change it. When it becomes too much to endure, we turn from it to a world that offers reason and delivers closure. This is why reading is so often described as "escape." Simply stated, we expect fiction to make sense because life does not.

The very first rule of writing fiction rejects the basic truth of life: Characters must be consistent. If the matriarch of a powerful family of soda pop manufacturers has been established through three hundred pages as obsessively well organized, she cannot meet her end by getting her feet tangled in one of her own discarded sweaters and falling out her bedroom window. This kind of thing happens to people every day in the world we inhabit, despite evidence of past behavior, but we have left that world for a better one. If it happens here, we will throw the novel or short story out the window after the old lady, and good riddance to them both. In a pilotless universe, we accept confusion because there is no place to file a complaint. In a story, plotted and executed by an individual or individuals in collaboration, we know whom to blame.

And then there is dialogue.

When engaged in conversation, we change tenses in midsentence, snarl syntax, forget the points we set out to make, and arrive at conclusions unsupported by the information we have provided. Our listeners ignore these lapses because we aren't reading from a prepared script, and we have the aid of vocal inflection to convey some sense of what was intended. In cold print, even the most uneducated speakers manage to pass on intelligence with an eloquence that on the street would sound forced. It still comes off that way in some Victorian fiction, composed in an era when writers were under pressure from society to respect the Queen's English, except when framing dialogue spoken by foreigners or members of the lower classes. Today, writers argue with fundamentalist copy editors to preserve redundancies, imperfect grammar, and phonetic spellings in their characters' speech. The effect is more realistic, but still only an illusion of the way even well-bred people speak in casual situations. I'll have more to say on that subject in chapter twelve.

Just as painters and photographers arrange their subjects into a composition intended to lead the eye along a selected path, so a writer creates a pattern that will lead the imagination to a specific conclusion. It may be as simplistic as a moral—"Crime does not pay" is an easy example—or as thought-provoking as a philosophy. This is frequently interpreted as "what the author has to say." It's just as frequently dismissed by writers who insist that all they want to do is entertain. But this, too, is a purpose, and the methods by which it's achieved don't exist in nature.

The most common method is formula. A formula is a predetermined set of characters, plot devices, and scenes employed in telling the story, and in the case of certain writers, in telling them all. Edgar Allan Poe engineered an entire career around stagnant tarns, grim manor houses, psychotic narrators, and the theme of premature burial. By varying the motivations and order, and because he was passionately devoted to his subjects, he managed to tell the same story over and over without trying the patience of generations of readers who have devoured "The Fall of the House of Usher" as eagerly as "The Pit and the Pendulum," "The Black Cat," and "The Cask of Amontillado," notwithstanding their surface similarity. And in so doing, he gave birth to the detective story and science fiction.

His success has been echoed by writers as varied as Louis L'Amour, Barbara Cartland, Mickey Spillane, and John Grisham, all of whom have adhered to a formula and placed themselves among the best-selling writers in history.

"The mixture as before," sniffed one critic, contemptuous of the recurring themes in the work of W. Somerset Maugham; who seized upon the phrase for the title of his next collection of short stories.

Mainstream writers in particular decry the use of formula in genre fiction, referring to it as an unhealthy dependency. They seem to be implying that they themselves are not dependent upon it. Yet they are, and have been since Stone Age man first related the details of an eventful hunt for his captive listeners around the fire.

It's hazardous (not to say pointless) to disagree that William Shakespeare is the greatest writer of all time. Every minute of every day, one of his plays is in production somewhere, and in 2000, *Time* magazine named him the Man of the Millennium. Sigmund Freud acknowledged that he based most of his theories about the human subconscious on the themes to be found throughout the Shakespearean canon. Yet the Bard of Avon was shackled to his formula as surely as the least-remembered penny-a-word pulpster of the ten-cent adventure and detective magazines of the 1930s and 1940s.

Shakespeare's livelihood depended upon royal patronage and the continued goodwill of the fishmongers and loafers who attended his public performances. Had Queen Elizabeth I belonged to the House of York instead of the House of Tudor, it's doubtful that Richard III would have come down to us as the scoundrel Shakespeare made of him, or Henry VIII—her father—as the defender of England. Although he might have been spared the headsman's axe for flattering the first and slandering the second, the playwright would almost certainly have waited in vain for a return invitation to Buckingham Palace and the gratuities that accompanied it. Even his most loyal admirers must concede that Henry's soliloquy at the end of Act V, Scene V, extolling the birth of his daughter ("This royal infant—heaven still move about her"), is a transparent bid for approval from the throne. Being Elizabeth, she could not have failed to see through it. Being human, she could only respond in kind.

At the same time, as part owner and treasurer of the Globe Theater, the Man of the Millennium recognized that it was the pennies forked over by the humble groundlings to sit at the actors' feet that kept the galleries supplied with thatch and paid for the costumes. The simple folk might stare in awe at the crowned heads onstage, but it was Macbeth's rascally gatekeeper, Hamlet's happy gravedigger, and the bawdy barracks gossip of an army of spear-carriers that brought them back sniggering for the next show. Whether Shakespeare suspected or cared that his plays would still be watched and venerated four hundred years later is unknown, but contemporary observers record that whenever the banner went up the staff announcing a new Shakespeare play, most of London crossed the river to attend. The man knew what side his mutton was roasted on.

"No writer ever in any age got a blank check," Raymond Chandler wrote. "He always had to accept some conditions imposed from without, respect certain taboos, try to please certain people. It might have been the Church, or a rich patron, or a generally accepted standard of elegance, or the commercial wisdom of a publisher or editor, or perhaps even a set of political theories. If he did not accept them, he revolted against them. In either case they conditioned his writing."

Fortunately—political correctness, religious fundamentalism, and the Patriot Act to the contrary—the formulas today are dictated by the demands of the marketplace rather than government or social oppression. Chapter two will examine various categories and their requirements. The business at hand is to explain the necessity of following a formula without surrendering to it.

When a writer embraces a genre, he or she has entered into an unwritten contract with the reader. As in all other areas of commerce, a customer browsing in a bookstore has the right to expect that a book advertised as a mystery will raise and answer its own questions, a Western will illuminate the pioneer experience, a romance will bring two hearts together, and a work of science fiction will transport him or her to an exotic universe made plausible by present or future scientific possibilities. If any of these conditions is not met, a reader is lost, and at current book prices the prospects of winning him back are grim. When a cereal box promises raisins in every spoonful and turns out to contain marshmallows instead, a customer has been cheated; and the customer who happens to prefer marshmallows to raisins has been missed. And it's a vexing paradox of business economics that while one satisfied customer does not necessarily lead to many, dissatisfied customers tend to multiply rapidly. Negative word-of-mouth travels at warp speed.

Contempt for the formula, then, is not the answer. But neither is a slavish fidelity to it. Scores of timid writers have sought to avoid alienating their audience by marching straight down the well-hollowed path, never touching the sides or questioning the restrictions established by the limitations of their predecessors. As a result, the veteran reader will forecast the ending within the first fifty pages. While not precisely a guarantee of failure—cynics have insisted for decades that the essence of entertainment is predictability—this approach does nothing to advance the art. Moreover, it's mind-numbing for the artist, who might as well be digging postholes. It's a toss-up in the end who will lose patience first and abandon the effort, the reader or the writer.

This robotic attention to dogma killed the traditional Western. A staple of popular culture since before the invention of the automobile, the Western's dependency on stock characters and familiar situations could not sustain the form following the social and political revolutions of the 1960s and 1970s. The gap went unbridged and the audience lost interest. It fell to the genre-bending work of major writers already well known in the mainstream to salvage this first homegrown contribution to world literature and pilot it into its third century.

The challenge is to respect the formula without surrendering to it. There are as many shootouts in *Blood Meridian* and *A Thousand Acres* as in *Destry Rides Again* and *Riders of the Purple Sage,* but when a bullet finds its mark and a character dies, the life of everyone who knew the victim is changed irrevocably. This was the case in the American West of history, but was often ignored in the West of myth because it was perceived to interfere with the action. Yet it speaks to a generation still reeling from the casualties of Vietnam and the civil rights movement. As a result, books by authors unconcerned with outdated tenets bypass the ghetto of the dwindling Western racks and are shelved in Fiction and Literature alongside Willa Cather and William Faulkner.

As previously stated, the mystery is defined by its pledge to answer the questions it raises in the course of the plot. In its formative years the principal question was, "Whodunit?", and writers from Sir Arthur Conan Doyle to Agatha Christie to Rex Stout have thrilled millions of readers addressing it. Today, thanks to iconoclastic contributions by Dashiell Hammett and Raymond Chandler, and in our own day Sara Paretsky and Dennis Lehane, the question is more often, "Why was it done?" The dark worlds that unfold in the quest for the answer fill pages originally devoted to discussing the various poisonous properties of certain species of blowfish. The investigation depends as much as ever on motives, alibis, and physical evidence, but the author's observations on the subjects of crime, detection, and human relationships in the postmodern world lift the narrative to the plane once reserved for mainstream fiction. Once again, the difference is one of repercussion. The corpse was once a human being, possessed of those flaws and virtues that influence others. It's more than just a piece of a puzzle.

The same can be said of romances, science fiction, and horror, all of which will be dissected later. (We haven't yet pierced the thick hides of the Western and mystery.) Maturity of approach and complexity of characterization have stretched guidelines and raised ceilings almost to infinity.

Almost.

There is a tipping point, beyond which a category book no longer belongs to a category. Once it's passed, it isn't difficult for an editor to declare the story unclassifiable, but it's next to impossible even for an expert to identify the point when he or she is standing on top of it. It's like mixing paint: Blue-green is not green-blue, but there was a moment during the process when it could have gone either way. Publishers prefer their colors primary and their categories unhyphenated. Offer them a mystery-romance or horror-science fiction, and unless you're famous and bankable, they will probably reject it or ask for a major rewrite rather than try to decide how to promote a hybrid. And if the word "literary" rears its egg-shaped head, the manuscript is as good as in the return envelope. Literary novels (even when packaged as literary Westerns or literary detective stories) are perceived to appeal only to the university professors who write them.

In the old days, this wasn't a problem; the boundary lines were rigid and inviolable. But we're celebrating flexibility, not condemning it. Today, the only restrictions the writer must accept are imposed from within. The best way to push the limits without exceeding them is to remember the three Ps:

1. **Plot.** Some stories are driven by character, others by plot. Although both approaches are acceptable, never forget the importance of the character's actions to the story. Ask yourself why this person is doing what he's doing, and whether it adds to understanding his character or to the progress of the plot. It should do one or the other, but it most certainly must bear on the story. Otherwise it's self-indulgent.

    Raymond Chandler, poking a little fun at the formula imposed by the pulp-fiction magazines where he began his career, once wrote: "When in doubt have a man come through a door with a gun in his hand." As he himself said, the effect when overdone "could get to be pretty silly." However, it kept these rough-and-tumble stories from bogging down, and was a surefire cure for the block. It's helped me out of some doldrums. The gun, of course, can be figurative; it can be a bomb or an oncoming car in your character's lane or just an unexpected arrival or discovery. The point is to shift into another gear and wake up your reader. (Hamlet skewering Polonius behind the curtain made quite a different thing of his inner malaise, and opened the door to the bloodshed to follow.)

2. **Pace.** Overlong descriptive passages, navel-gazing introspection, and pointless dialogue slow down the action to no good purpose. But nonstop, edge-of-your-seat action is a cartoon. Find the happy medium and stick to it.

    Take a tip from Hollywood. Moving pictures are expected to move, and so screenwriters and directors insert exterior scenes in moving cars or along strollable beachfront between scenes shot indoors with people talking. This simple formula of varying the action and setting applies to serious drama as well as to slam-bang adventure flicks. If your last chapter opened with dialogue, open the next with a description or introspection, and vice versa. Avoid stagnation, but give your readers a chance to catch their breath.

3. **Paragraphs.** The evolution of the paragraph is the most significant event in the history of fiction. Blame it on MTV and Lara Croft if you like, but attention spans are shorter than they used to be, and dense, impenetrable blocks of print invite neither readers nor editors to enter the world you've created. Victor Hugo once slathered a single sentence over three pages in *Les Miserables,* but if you want to make people less miserable, break it up. On the other hand, short paragraphs stacked end on end are choppy and distracting. Ross H. Spencer, a forgotten private-eye writer of the 1980s, burned out his readership in record time by writing his novels entirely in one-line paragraphs, creating the surging-and-dying effect of a Model T motor refusing to start on a cold morning. His "See Dick Run" style was annoying in the extreme.

    The type and subject of the novel you're writing often dictates the form of your paragraphing. When I write a historical novel that takes place during the nineteenth century, I find my descriptions becoming more voluptuous, and break less often than when I'm writing a novel of contemporary suspense. The intention is to create a subliminal bridge to the prose of Charles Dickens and Henry James, and provide the illusion that the narrator belongs to their world. The readers of this kind of fiction are less likely to lose patience with this leisurely pace than would the fans of, say, a breakneck story of international espionage set in our own time. I would no sooner subject the carriage trade to a Formula I car chase than I would seat a B-2 pilot in a gondola in the Venice of the Doges and expect him not to bolt. This is what formula is all about.

Whether your fiction belongs to either of these extremes or occupies a place closer to the middle, variation is the watchword. Interpose longer paragraphs with shorter ones, and create a pleasing rhythm that does not call attention to itself. Remember, we want people to forget they're reading writing. Paragraphing affects pace, which in turn affects plot, which allows you to respect the formula even as you are subverting it.

* * *

Fiction Fact

Margaret Mitchell wrote the last chapter of Gone With the Wind *first, and didn't write the first chapter until after the book was accepted, ten years later.*

* * *

2

What to Write

* * *

WHEN I DECIDED, at age fifteen, that I wanted to write fiction for a living, I gave no thought to what kind of fiction I wanted to write. I went with my heart, choosing subjects that excited me. My tastes ran toward action and adventure, and since it's more fun to write the kind of thing you like to read, I'm the happier and the more successful for it. To this day, when I question the direction a project is taking, I stop and ask myself if I would buy and read this book. If the answer is no, I either tear apart and rebuild, or scrap the whole thing.

"Do the thing you most want to do." I can't think of advice more pleasant. If you enjoy it, chances are your reader will as well. Bear that in mind when making your selection among the genres that follow.

1. **Romance.** For as long as I can remember, my mother bought and read four to six romance novels each week. She'd been raised on the classics and had read *The Count of Monte Cristo* in the orig-

inal French, but after facing the challenges of the Great Depression, a world war, and rearing two sons, she found her escape in books that swept her away with passion and promised happy endings. I always remember her whenever some stuck-up literary snob dismisses the form as limited and banal. He should make his audience feel so good.

"Novel" in German is *Roman;* and in the early days of the English novels our Teutonic language directed us to define any work of fiction as a romance. Today, romances are love stories, and since they offer transcending, tempestuous affairs of the heart ending in blissful union, the evolution of the term seems natural. The works of Jane Austen and the Brontë sisters and Margaret Mitchell's *Gone With the Wind* are romances by modern definition.

However, if category romance is your aim, the tragic ending of *Wuthering Heights* and Rhett Butler's ultimate abandonment of Scarlett O'Hara are not options. Harlequin Books, the *doyenne* of this highly specialized school of writing, will not consider a manuscript that does not end with its heroine and hero embarking on life's great journey together, optimistic and mutually devoted, and preferably in a clinch. The publishers who have followed its lead, including Bantam, HarperCollins, and Dorchester, apply the same standard. Other guidelines are as rigid. Each publisher maintains several divisions, or "lines"— Harlequin has eight, and Silhouette, which is owned and operated by the same firm, has five, making this publisher the General Motors of romance fiction. Each line carries its particular set of requirements, which to ignore is to be shown the door. More than any other, this market requires studying before submission.

These strictures are not arbitrary. They're based on intense market research and reflect the expectations of the customers who shop the various lines as if they were brand names. And the customer base is huge. By the turn of the twenty-first century, a scant thirty years after Harlequin pioneered the genre, 50 percent of all paperback books sold in the United States were romances, with a North American readership of forty-five million and an annual sales revenue of a billion dollars. Assiduous attention to the demands of its readers has made the romance the eight hundred-pound gorilla of category fiction.

Inflexible guidelines can be exasperating, and if your model is *The Bridges of Madison County,* with its resonant theme of romance deferred for the sake of duty, this is not your market. But its enormous popularity and a constant turnover in talent make it the friendliest place for a newcomer to break into print than any other since the pulp fiction bubble burst in the 1950s. Editors are desperate for new writers, and unlike their pulp predecessors are paying larger advances for first novels than any other category.

Since women comprise most of the readership, women writers dominate the field; but there are a number of male writers working it under female pseudonyms. The protagonists are women, so an ability to write convincingly from the feminine perspective is crucial. Editors and readers will know if you're faking it.

This genre is constantly in cycle. Gothic romances set in castles and dreary old mansions once proliferated, but they wore out their welcome. "Bodice-rippers"—lusty tales laid against historical backdrops with coaches and highwaymen and pirates and titled damsels—quickly became a caricature and lost their franchise. But they may be back. At one time or another, this diverse market has experimented with time travel, frontier subjects, reincarnation, mystery, and romantic comedy, making it more versatile than may seem apparent based on its strict guidelines. The important thing to remember is that the book must remain a love story from start to finish. Once the romance slips into the background, it has become something else and will not fly.

The best news is that writers who have built up a following before reaching that tipping point have managed to break out and become categories unto themselves. Even the most romantically challenged have heard of Barbara Taylor Bradford and Nora Roberts, but research may be required to learn that best-selling suspense novelist Tami Hoag also earned her chops working in the romance trenches. In the meantime, all made their livings while they were honing their skills. In our highly competitive profession, paid apprenticeships are rare.

2. **Western.** The Western is the first and oldest American literary form. It is also the one most savaged by critics. It has been called racist, sexist, jingoist, and subliterary, and at its peak in the 1950s, you could not enter a drugstore or a movie theater or turn on a television set without being confronted by blazing sixguns and Indians in war paint. With the possible exception of the category romance, no other genre has inspired similar loyalty and derision at one and the same time.

    Like romances, Westerns were most popular when the rules of writing them were at their most restrictive. Unlike the romance, the Western's failure to evolve in a time of change doomed it to near-extinction only a few short years ago. For decades, its scope was reduced to that narrow alley of time between the end of the Civil War and the official closing of the frontier in 1890. The heroes were white and aggressively male, and readers expected fast-draw contests, plenty of equestrian action, Indian fights, and dialogue along the lines of, "Slap leather, ya sidewinder!" But if you think including all these things in your manuscript guarantees publication in today's market, you're as ill-prepared as Custer at the Little Big Horn.

    Today's Western is founded on accuracy and authenticity of historical detail. This is not new. The classics—Owen Wister's *The Virginian,* Jack Schaefer's *Shane,* Elmer Kelton's *The Day the Cowboys Quit*—upheld their readers' sensational expectations while adhering to the roughhewn elegance of Victorian America adrift in the wilderness. It was their tenth-carbon imitators who overlooked the dramatic properties of history in their haste to provide action. In so doing, they obscured the mesmerizing reality beneath a superstructure of myth. And their influence was as insidious as it was pernicious. The movie Western, a moribund genre for years, enjoyed a renaissance in the early 1990s following the success of *Lonesome Dove,* the TV miniseries based on Larry McMurtry's best-selling and Pulitzer Prize-winning epic novel, *Dances With Wolves,* adapted by Michael Blake from his book into a box office hit and Oscar winner, and the equally successful and award-winning *Unforgiven.* Their prominence came from their gritty authenticity, which rekindled jaded audience interest in the real frontier; but this message was wasted on producers, who merely saw it as an opportunity to empty their vaults of every hackneyed shoot-em-up script that had been moldering for decades, and released a string of uninspired, old-fashioned features that disappointed viewers and critics and resentenced the Western to life in obscurity.

Had it not been for the continued hard work and prosperity of Larry McMurtry, Cormac McCarthy, Barbara Kingsolver, Jane Smiley, and Annie Proulx, each of whom discovered unmined ore in historical fact, the diminishing returns of post-1960s America would have killed the genre once and for all. Instead, their vision brought a new audience to the Western and, for the first time in its passage, the respect and awe of such prestigious publications as *The New Yorker* and *The New York Times.*

In their hands, good did not always triumph over evil, fascinating characters long assigned to peripheral roles were brought to the forefront, and the exalting, tragic, and spellbinding drama of the American wilderness was exploited to its full potential.

Today's Western is as likely to be told from the points of view of women, Hispanics, Native Americans, and European immigrants as it is by hard-bitten male WASPs with hoglegs on their hips. Often it's told *by* women, Hispanics, Native Americans, and European immigrants; not for reasons of political correctness, but because the story of civilization's conquest of the frontier involved the polyglot influence of many cultures. It may take place as early as prehistoric times and as late as in our own, and it is based on thousands of hours of research. Any hack can work new variations on the formula made famous by Max Brand and Frank Gruber, pulp-school giants now nearly forgotten, but it takes scholarship and dedication to turn over the earth that has drifted over the fascinating reality. But it's there waiting, with stories untold and conflicts enough to nourish entire careers.

Thirty years ago, scores of publishers were buying Westerns on a regular basis. That number has dwindled to a few, but stories of the West told skillfully and with depth of feeling are of interest to prestige houses that would never have considered acquiring frontier fiction in the past. Artistic freedom is now the theme of this market.

3. **Science Fiction.** The narrative of scientific possibility-become-reality is forever in flux, mutating faster than the sinister microbes in Michael Crichton's *The Andromeda Strain*, which influenced NASA to quarantine astronauts who had walked on the moon. From its beginning, very early in the Industrial Age, this category has forced its practitioners to sprint in order to stay ahead of scientific fact. By the middle of the twentieth century, most of the gee-whiz gadgets available to the twenty-fifth-century hero of the collaborative comic strip *Buck Rogers* were commonplace, and well before 1984, the chilling totalitarian surveillance technology warned of by George Orwell in *1984* and Aldous Huxley in *Brave New World* were solidly in place. Both Jules Verne and H.G. Wells, writing by gaslight of journeys to the moon and invasions from Mars, made astonishingly accurate predictions about space travel and the distances between planets that would be supported by calculations made possible long after their deaths. And this book can't contain the number of pages necessary to list all the references made to *Frankenstein* in relation to current experiments in DNA engineering, nearly two hundred years after Mary Shelley first committed the name to paper.

In contrast, much of what Ray Bradbury wrote of Mars in *The Martian Chronicles* in 1950 would be proven faulty by 1970; yet the book remains in print, and continues to delight many thousands of discerning readers.

Bradbury, I must point out, employed information supplied by scientists at the time. But the reason for his enduring success is the same reason generations of readers continue to enjoy Verne's *From the Earth to the Moon* and Wells' *War of the Worlds*—and for that matter, current works by Ursula K. Le Guin,

Michael Stackpole, and Brian W. Aldiss, whose science is based on current evidence—the stories hold up as stories. Readers who couldn't care less if the Milky Way were made of Bluebonnet margarine thrill to the adventures of astronauts marooned on uncharted planets, and science buffs who know the molecular weight of water better than they know the names of their representatives in congress will forgive dissent in thermonuclear theory provided characters are interesting and their behavior consistent. The basic rules of fiction apply here as they do elsewhere.

However, literary license doesn't excuse the writer from the laws of plausibility. Although science fiction and fantasy are often shelved side by side in bookshops and video stores, they are philosophical opposites. Science fiction is directed by what is theoretically possible, while the basis of fantasy is the impossible made plausible. We accept that a hand-held weapon that emits a laser beam can pierce armor, because external logic tells us it can, even though the technology doesn't yet exist to reduce the size of the equipment to a weapon portable enough to hold in one hand. (It may exist by the time you read these words; but by then your science fiction has become scientific fact, and you have ventured into the even more demanding territory of the techno-thriller.) We do not accept that a magic sword wielded by an enchanted knight can breach a castle keep, unless the internal logic of the story makes a convincing case in its favor. In skilled hands, fantasy is not less believable, for all its dependence on wish fulfillment over solid science. But it is not science fiction.

Science fiction is a mother ship, dispatching many drones: space opera, time travel, apocalyptic, pre-apocalyptic, post-apocalyptic, Utopia, Dystopia, parallel universe, etc. The ship itself is bisected into hard and soft science. If hard science is your goal, you have to explain how your time machine works based on Stephen Hawking's researches into the speed of light and Albert Einstein's theory of relativity, not to mention the hardware involved. If you're more interested in having your protagonist *actually* meet Einstein, soft science and a long tradition of time-travel stories will suit your purpose; but only if the market is not oversaturated with time-travel stories at time of submission. Which brings us again to the importance of studying the field.

Even more than with the romance, it's crucial to know what's being written in science fiction and what's been written before. It's an idea-driven market, and if you're banking on your concept carrying the day, you'd better be sure it hasn't already been done to death. Thomas Sullivan, whose oft-reprinted short story "The Mickey Mouse Olympics," about genetics-code cheating in the international Olympic games, has proven eerily prophetic, has said that his first attempt at science fiction, a story in which the Crucifixion is shown to have taken place on a planet other than earth, was returned with a derisive letter from an editor, explaining that this idea had been used so often it was referred to in the trade as a "Shaggy God story." In order to write for the genre, it helps to be a fan, to understand its past and its present and—in true science-fiction tradition—to predict its future.

This form assumes intelligence on the part of the reader, with good reason. Most of its customers score high in standardized IQ testing. They are in the main brilliant and highly educated, with many interests and lively imaginations. They're not easily misdirected. Bear that in mind when you set out to tell a story whose ending they won't write for you three lines after you've begun.

4. **Mystery.** I'm not sure whom I'd rather not compete with on *Jeopardy:* a fan of science fiction or a regular reader of mysteries. They both know all the tricks, and by and large they are experts in more fields than I can count. Prominent mystery readers have included Franklin D. Roosevelt, Mark Twain, Sylvia Porter, W. Somerset Maugham, Maxwell Perkins, John F. Kennedy, and Margaret Atwood, and if any of them were to show up in the green room, I'd walk out and join the line for *Wheel of Fortune* where my chances are at least even.

Illustrious figures tend to possess brilliant minds. It's tempting to suggest they're drawn toward the puzzle element involved in assembling clues, scrutinizing suspects, balancing timetables, and arriving at the correct conclusion before the writer reveals it; in effect playing chess with him and beating him at his own game. But this doesn't explain the popularity of such masters of the modern mystery as Raymond Chandler, Linda Fairstein, and Robert Crais, whose plots are less orderly than the rules of procedure in a board game, and whose characters are far more complex than the die-cut pieces that move around on it. As with the best science fiction, the mystery that continues to challenge and entertain readers who were not yet born when it first appeared is one that provides a story at least as compelling as the central question, one that resonates long after he or she has forgotten whodunit.

Strictly defined, a work of mystery fiction is one that raises and answers its own questions in the course of the narrative. Most often it's a tale of crime, but a crime story is not a mystery if it fails to present a problem whose solution lies at the end of the investigation. Elmore Leonard, one of our premiere crime novelists, has won the Edgar Allan Poe Award for Best Mystery Novel and was named a Grand Master by the Mystery Writers of America, but he is quick to confess that his novels are not mysteries, because the reader is witness to all the criminal activity. In the mystery, *who* committed the crime—chiefly murder, although it hasn't always been so—is the most common question, but often it's only bait to draw the reader into the shadow world imagined by the author. By the last page, the paradoxes and imponderables of life itself may have become more important than the identity of the murderer; but because the question was asked, it's the responsibility of the writer to provide an answer.

The challenge increases in direct ratio to the increasing sophistication of the reader. During the 1920s—that brief, tumultuous decade often referred to as the Golden Age of the Mystery—pinning the murder on the least likely suspect was sufficient to confound all but the most dedicated amateur detective in the audience. But other readers caught on quickly, and presented with a list of possible murderers, made a beeline to the one person who could not possibly have committed the murder. Writers responded with the red herring: a false clue or suspicious character designed to draw attention away from the actual culprit. Needless to say, this too became a recognizable device, and had the mystery continued to evolve in this direction, it's likely the genre would have exhausted all the possibilities and passed out of fashion.

Prohibition rescued the mystery, just as it created a new kind of criminal and financed widespread corruption out of the enormous profits made from the traffic in contraband whiskey. The Depression added desperation. Itinerant bank robbers and battling bootleggers filled America's front pages and newsreels with a kind of real-life crime that made the genteel murderers created by Agatha Christie, Dorothy L. Sayers, and S.S. Van Dine seem quaint and out of date. "Hardboiled" mysteries pitting private detectives and fed-up police officers against gangsters and crooked politicians burst out of the pages of the ten-cent pulp magazines onto the silver screen, obscuring the old formula of crime and detection behind casts of shifty characters and clouds of machine-gun smoke. *Who* took a backseat to the disturbing question of *why:* official cover-up, mob retaliation, or something worse? In the hands of such writers as Dashiell Hammett, Chandler, and Erle Stanley Gardner, mystery fiction read less like *Burke's Peerage* and more like the *New York Daily News.*

The wheel continues to turn. Racketeers in sixteen-cylinder Cadillacs have become as rare as butlers in livery, but crime is more relevant to our daily lives than ever. A mobile society poses a moving target, and few of us can claim not to have been touched by the underworld in some way, whether through direct assault or a weekend burglary. As long as readers remain potential victims, they will continue to be drawn toward a form of literature that exposes the criminal mind and promises justice of a sort. They may wish to plunge into the contemporary outlaw jungles of Margaret Maron and T. Jefferson Parker, or escape from the modern into the historical whodunits of Lindsey Davis and William J. Palmer, where killers skulk behind the columns of the

Roman Forum and prowl the sopping alleys of London's East End; and the more they learn about murder and detection, the more they will want to know. With this natural thirst for knowledge now working for it rather than against it, the mystery is a medium that can be made to say anything.

5. **Horror.** As hinted above, stories of anxiety in an uncertain world attract more readers than they repel. But while the mystery in general promises to lay their fears to rest through the mechanics of justice, horror turns out the lights on them.

Success in this category depends absolutely on the writer's empathy with the reader. When you set out to scare the bejeezus out of someone, you need to know what he fears the most. A miss is as good as a mile, and the remaindering tables of bookstores everywhere are stacked with discounted horror novels that succeeded only in being unintentionally funny.

What frightens you the most? Poverty and death are right up there, if you're an adult. If you're a responsible parent, the thought that something might happen to your children tops the list. When you were a child, fear of abandonment left you exposed to the monsters of mayhem and abduction that crouched beneath your bed and among the dust bunnies. All these fears—vulnerability, outside evil, extinction—stalk us throughout our lives. We dread the unseen. In the daylight, we can avoid unpleasant sights by turning away or closing our eyes. In the dark, closing our eyes only adds to the terror.

Horror straddles two worlds, the corporeal and the supernatural. We have the six o'clock news to remind us that monsters walk the earth in the shape of serial killers, child molesters, and common rapists. With them in place, it hardly seems necessary that we should give thought to a spectral plane populated with vampires, werewolves, witches, and ghosts. Yet the plane exists, if only in our dreams; and as Freddie Krueger warned, no one can protect us there. But then the crucifix that works against Count Dracula promises no protection from Hannibal Lecter. Both types of villain offer unique advantages to their creators.

Like mystery, horror is always raising the bar. The shower slashing in Robert Bloch's *Psycho* drove Americans back to bathtubs, and the shark in Peter Benchley's *Jaws* emptied beaches, but decades of familiarity and a thousand parodies have weakened their effect. However, the voluptuous dread of Bram Stoker's *Dracula* chills readers more than a century after the book first appeared, possibly for Freudian reasons of which Stoker himself may have been unaware. Stephen King, despairing of his ability to shake up an audience desensitized by the casualties of the Holocaust and Vietnam, will, he says, "go for the gross-out" when he fails to frighten by legitimate means. Meanwhile, a new screening of William Peter Blatty's *The Exorcist* thirty years after the movie premiered managed to paralyze a generation that sniggered at *Scream*. Blatty's theme of demonic possession and sudden loss of innocence hurdles decades.

Inevitably, a form that exploits emotions so ruthlessly burns itself out from time to time. The horror market goes cold and hot by turns, and editors with a backlog of, say, vampire stories worry about oversaturating the market and wind up driving a stake through its heart all by themselves. It seems every other cubicle in New York City contains a self-fulfilling prophet looking down both barrels of a thirty-year mortgage. If scaring people is your preference, don't be put off by dire declarations about the form's future. Chances are by the time you have something to show, the dark clouds will have passed; or in this case, grown deliciously darker.

Critics of supernatural horror complain that it's too easy to write because it isn't bound by the laws of nature, as are mystery and science fiction. Yet it must obey the rules of its own logic. If you've established that a werewolf can only be slain by piercing its heart with a silver bullet, and your hero or heroine stops one in full charge by firing an ordinary lead slug into its brain, the reader who has paid attention knows the werewolf will pop right back up, and you've sacrificed your shock effect. If it *doesn't* pop right back up, you've cheated, and have lost that reader for life. You may have fooled him into buying the book, but he won't buy the next and will warn his friends. A crooked used-car dealer will never be as successful as his honest competitor, because he's dependent upon the next unwary customer rather than return business. He'll always remain where he started. The most fantastic story must be realistic, even if it's a reality you made up.

Be your own guinea pig. If something frightens you, it will frighten your readers, provided you're capable of communicating your own fright. This can be as difficult as tickling yourself. A comic rehearsing his act in an empty room has only his instincts to assure him his jokes are funny, but the novice horror writer, like the novice comic, is wise to try out his material on an audience whose reactions he trusts. Ask someone reliable to read your work, or read it to him or her yourself. Often you'll hear things you wouldn't notice if you only read it aloud in private. There's nothing like a little flop-sweat to show you where you went wrong, and better your friends see it than an editor.

These are the five main categories in popular fiction. Decide which intrigues you most. The odds are—arid my advice is—that those you like to read are those you'll choose to write. Select more than one, giving all your muscles a work-out, and no matter how far your dreams carry you, your next book will excite you as much as your first.

* * *

Fiction Fact

When J.K. Rowling wrote Harry Potter and the Sorcerer's Stone, *she typed three separate copies because she couldn't afford copying fees.*

* * *

3

A Clean, Well-Lighted Place
* * *

ERNEST HEMINGWAY—who coined the phrase, "a clean, well-lighted place"—wrote standing up. Marcel Proust composed most of *Remembrance of Things Past* in his bathtub. Edith Wharton worked sitting up in bed. F. Scott Fitzgerald kept track of his chapters by posting them on a wall, in rows like notices on a community bulletin board. Jack Kerouac wrote without interruption by mounting a roll of teletype paper above his typewriter, never pausing to crank in a new sheet. Moss Hart started and finished his first Broadway play sitting on a beach in New Jersey. Legend has it Odin, head of the creative department of the ancient Norse gods, once found inspiration by plucking out his right eye and dropping it into the Well of Wisdom; however, it should be pointed out that Odin was a creature of mythology, and his method should not be tried at home.

The lesson is that each of these remarkable individuals found his or her own best approach, and literature has benefited from them all. There are as many ways to write as there are writers, and there is no wrong way.

One difference between the amateur writer and the professional is the amateur often says, "This is how you do it," while the professional says, "This is how *I* do it." The seasoned veteran knows all too well that his *modus operandi* may not work for everyone, however kind it's been to him or her. That's an important point to consider whenever an unpublished member of your writers' support group insists that you will never be successful until you obtain a particular brand of computer (his brand), program it with *his* preferred type of software, set it up in the northeast corner of a room with adequate ventilation, and write between the hours of 4:00 and 6:00 a.m. without stopping, seven days a week. There is one of these know-it-alls in every group, and it's anyone's guess how many promising writers have been discouraged by his myopic vision, which extends to his criticism of his fellow members' work. You will know him by the way he dominates every conversation and the number of rejections he has drawn without a single sale.

It stands to reason that somewhere, for someone, that equipment, that location, and that schedule have accompanied a stellar career. It's just as reasonable to assume that spectacular results have come from ten minutes here, a half hour there, and the odd two luxurious hours spent crouched over a Big Chief tablet with a well-gnawed No. 2 pencil on a packing crate next to a furnace.

I've never known a writer, successful or otherwise, who claimed to be a born self-starter. Certainly I'm not one. No doubt there are some who are, and I envy them their natural advantages. The rest of us need a kick in the behind. Failing that, we draw up a schedule and establish the habit of maintaining it no matter what.

I started out an awful tyrant, with excellent consequences. For many years, I sentenced myself to a set amount of time in one spot with all the necessary tools at hand. During that time, barring bathroom breaks, I couldn't leave that spot or do anything but write. I had the option of doing nothing, but under no circumstances might I read (except what I'd written or to check a fact), telephone a friend, or get up to oil the swivel on my squeaky office chair. My theory was that sooner or later I'd be forced to write, if for no other reason than to escape going mad; and that eventually something I wrote would be worth saving. Sneer if you like, but that's how we educate our children. We lock them up in a schoolroom for twelve years and don't let them talk to one another or look out the window, in the faith that they'll learn something out of sheer boredom. In most cases it works, while the results of less traditional techniques have been spotty at best.

These days I'm more benevolent. I have my permanent work station, and I average six hours, five days a week, but I often linger over my coffee mornings and blow the quitting whistle early when I'm tired or complacent about what I've accomplished that day. But I've published fifty books and counting, and more than a quarter-century of meeting deadlines (give or take a couple of weeks) assures me I'll make up in pure desperation for the sin of sloth as Judgment Day approaches. However, I do shoot for five clean, type-written pages per day. Some days, unforeseen interruptions or the intensity of the work itself limits me to two pages, but I will heave aside the firmament to produce those two, and on those days when the five come early, I push for more. Discipline has replaced fanaticism, but I'm still a fundamentalist at heart. I owe whatever I've acquired to that early fervor.

Few beginning writers have the luxury of large blocks of time to write. Jobs, family, and social responsibilities take up most of the day, and one or two hours of leisure to pursue one's dream are as rare as a hip dentist. But hours are made of minutes strung together, and in the end no one can tell if they came all in a lump or piece by piece over the course of a year. Writer Thomas Sullivan found that his family obligations and high school teaching position left him only two minutes to write each day, in the school library, before the bell rang announcing his first class. Two minutes is barely time to brush one's teeth, yet Sullivan managed to squeeze at least a paragraph out of those precious moments, day after day. Driving to school, he would be writing in his head, and by the time he sat down with a pencil and pad, the words were in order and ready to record. This situation continued for years, during which he wrote three books, including the critically acclaimed horror novel *Born Burning* and dozens of short stories. He has since retired from teaching and writes full-time, but his output is unchanged. Desperation and inspiration are often one and the same.

Sullivan's regimen combined consistency and discipline. He knew he would be in the same place at the same time every day and so was able to work without distraction. I don't care how busy your day is. You can afford two minutes, and probably a good deal more. Decide when they are—before breakfast, during your lunch break, after dinner—convince friends and family you're beyond reach at that time, strap yourself in, and write. Establish a routine and stick with it. You may not produce much at the beginning, and what you do produce may not be very good. Eventually your writer's imagination will rebel against inaction and start telling a story, if only to amuse itself. With the raw material in place, whipping it into shape will be easier than you think.

Save your energy for writing. Sharpening pencils and drumming together crisp blank sheets can be therapeutic; clearing the dining room table, hoisting your battered Smith-Corona out of its case, and shoveling debris away from the computer will just exhaust you, and the very thought of having to do it will give you one more excuse than you need to avoid writing. Set up a work station and leave it in place. Knowing you can just plop yourself down and create can have an aphrodisiac effect on your performance.

Pick the tools you're comfortable with. Silicone Valley has done a head job on beginning writers, convincing them that any equipment that doesn't involve booting up, logging on, downloading, accessing, and deleting is obsolete, and will prevent your work from being considered seriously by editors. The book you're reading was composed on a manual typewriter with fingers that have never touched a computer keyboard and never will. I've had a comfortable partnership with this machine and its predecessors for many years and millions of words, and I have no incentive to discontinue it. Occasionally, editors ask me to submit my manuscripts with a disc, but they don't insist upon it, and since the technology now exists for a publisher to scan typewritten material directly into the computer, I don't waste time worrying about the day when the request becomes a demand. If you like writing on a computer, you belong to the majority, and I say more power to you and your modem. But you can write just as well with a goosequill, and either type up your final draft or find someone else to type it up when it's finished. It isn't an issue.

Elmore Leonard writes all his best-selling suspense novels in longhand, on unlined yellow legal tablets he has made to his order. Veteran mystery writer Bill Pronzini swears by his electric typewriter. Harlan Ellison, the dean of science fiction authors, uses manual typewriters exclusively, buying his ribbons by the case because they're no longer available in most office supply stores and storing them in his refrigerator to preserve their integrity. Erle Stanley Gardner, creator of Perry Mason, dictated his books orally, as many as five at a time, employing portable recorders and an army of secretaries to put them on paper. Mark Twain, the first name writer to use a typewriter, grumbled about having a machine stand between him and his work (many of his complaints have been echoed by today's writers, applying them to the computer). Henry David Thoreau invented a new kind of pencil because he was dissatisfied with the ones his father made in his factory in Concord. It's hard to imagine a more efficient writing instrument than the lowly No. 2: It's portable, requires no power source, and comes with its own delete feature, handily attached to the end opposite the point. And there is no danger of its being replaced by a jazzy new model five minutes after you purchased it.

If a computer is your choice of poisons, it should not be community property. Declare it off-limits, at least during the hours when you will be sitting in front of it, writing or staring at the screen. Nothing saps the creative juices quicker than having to threaten your spouse or children to give up their seat, or to explain to them why you haven't tapped a key or clicked the mouse in twenty minutes when they could have been destroying aliens or shopping online. If you can afford it, buy another computer for your exclusive use and have a separate telephone line installed.

My wife, mystery writer Deborah Morgan, a computer user, offers this piece of advice, when sitting down to write: "Don't check your e-mail." The same goes for playing Solitaire, browsing on e-Bay, and aimlessly surfing the Net. What begins as a harmless peek will eat up hours. If you're vulnerable to temptation—and we all are, hence all

---

this harping—disconnect the telephone line, unless you intend to use the Web for serious research.

Al Bready, the fictional pulp-writer hero of Tom De Haven's *Derby Dugan's Depression Funnies*, forced himself to meet tough deadlines by soaking his only pair of shoes in the bathtub, thus preventing himself from leaving his apartment before the job was done. Study his example and find the writing method that works best for you, even if you own more than one pair of shoes.

* * *

Fiction Fact

Asked to share the secret of his success, best-selling Western writer Luke Short said: "First I write myself into a corner. Then I write myself out."

* * *

4

Gears and Pulleys

* * *

NEAR THE MIDDLE OF *GET SHORTY,* Elmore Leonard's witty, criminal take on contemporary Hollywood, mobster Bo Catlett, eager to break into the movie industry, imparts this wisdom on writing screenplays to the protagonist, Chili Palmer:

> *"… You have the idea and you put down what you want to say. Then you get somebody to add in the commas and shit where they belong, if you aren't positive yourself. Maybe fix up the spelling where you have some tricky words. There people do that for you. Some, I've even seen scripts where I know words weren't spelled right and there was hardly any commas in it. So I don't think it's too important."*

This is a funny speech; but to any professional writer who's ever been trapped in conversation with a writer wanna-be who doesn't necessarily want to *write,* it's too close for comfort. Just as a celebrated architect's life may seem glamorous until one considers the algebra involved in drawing up a building plan, the writer seen breezing along the cocktail circuit sacrifices most of his or her glitter when it comes to reeling in dangling participles, splicing split infinitives, and riffling through Webster's in search of the proper spelling of *hemorrhage* for the umpteenth time.

True, there are people who "do that for you"; but good, conscientious copy editors are scarce and their numbers are dwindling, and most of them are busy making the work of established authors look better. It's a rare acquisitions editor who can see past mutilated grammar, multiple misspelled words, and clueless punctuation in a manuscript lifted from the slushpile and find gold.

Maxwell Perkins was one. This legendary editor at Charles Scribner's Sons saw past young F. Scott Fitzgerald's horrible spelling and crimes against English usage, snapped up *This Side of Paradise*, smoothed out the mechanical flaws, and introduced one of the most important writers of the twentieth century. Editing *The Sun Also Rises*, Perkins gently corrected Ernest Hemingway's habit of leaving out commas where their presence was needed for comprehension and spent thousands of hours trimming Thomas Wolfe's verbiage so that *Look Homeward, Angel* would not have to be carried away from the checkout counter on a handtruck.

Perkins died in 1947, having in addition discovered James Jones, Marjorie Kinnan Rawlings, and S.S. Van Dine, and so far no editor has appeared to fill his chair. While we're waiting, it serves us best to do for ourselves what under ideal circumstances we might expect other people to do for us. I'm talking about taking a crash course in English Composition.

Hold on; I'm not suggesting we diagram sentences. That was the only subject I failed in English. Although I was fortunate enough to be born with an eye for spelling and a sense for syntax, after publishing more than fifty books and a couple of hundred short stories I still don't know a first predicate from a second, and although I know what a preposition is I can't define it. Most of the designations seem as arbitrary to me as the names of the constellations, and the whole business of drawing angular lines on a blackboard to determine which words go where seems a little too right-brained for the creative mind. So with a nod of apology and appreciation to the late lamented Mrs. Zemke for her untiring efforts to overcome my natural inadequacies, I propose we leave the scientific method to the scientists and move on to the messy business of making sense out of the language of William Shakespeare, Robert Louis Stevenson, and Anne Tyler.

English is a fascinating amalgam of the Latin and Teutonic languages that changed the face of the world two thousand years ago. As with most hybrids, the result is complicated and difficult to explain to the outsider. Understanding it is no picnic for the insider either, and so I'm reducing the subject to a discussion of a few points where mistakes are most commonly made. In so doing, I'm going to borrow from Father Guido Sarducci's Five-Minute College Education program, whereby the erstwhile *Saturday Night Live* comic taught his audience everything the average college-educated adult remembers five years after graduation. Call it "Professor Estleman's Five Steps to Writing the Queen's English."

1. **Spelling.** Almost everyone remembers the rule "*I* before *E*, except after *C*." The rest of it goes: "or when sounded as *A*, as in *neighbor* and *weigh*; not counting the exceptions." That last phrase transforms the rule into a meaningless series of syllables, exposing the entire language as the rattletrap jalopy it is. Let's bury it and erect a substitute atop the grave to discourage its resurrection: "If you're unsure where the *I* and the *E* go, look it up in a dictionary." Life is too short, and inspiration too fragile, to wrestle with bad doggerel when the answer is within easy reach.

   Pitfalls abound. When something *affects* you, it has had an *effect*. The first is a verb, connoting action, the second a noun, which is defined as a person or a thing. (On the other hand, you can *effect* a change; but that particular usage occurs so rarely, you're better off looking it up than overloading your memory. King Henry VIII *reigned* in 1509, but when his coachman wanted to stop, he *reined* in the horses. A tragic automobile accident makes for a *grisly* scene, but not much worse than that of a hiker being attacked by a *grizzly* bear. Words that sound the same but that are spelled differently are called homophones, but you needn't know that unless you want to write about them. Look up the one you need.

Remember that standardized American spelling differs from England's. We spell *gray* with an *a*, while our Anglo-Saxon cousins use *e*. *Canceled* has only one *l* this side of the ocean, and we *organize*, *jeopardize*, and *categorize* with *z*'s, as opposed to the English, who prefer not to jeopardise their organisation with such categorising.

We have Theodore Roosevelt to thank (or blame) for this parting of the ways. As President of the United States, he took the lead in persuading his fellow citizens to adopt a standardized and simplified phonetics system. Along the way, *honour*, *labour*, and *flavour* lost their Continental and unnecessary *u*'s. (It took Great Britain a grudging half-century to drop the *x* from *connexion* in favor of the American *ct*, and it's not too far-fetched to suppose that somewhere in Ireland or Scotland, people are still carting around an extra *g* in their *wagons*.)

Some people are born good spellers. Most are not, and many of the world's greatest writers belong to that majority. You can teach yourself the basics if you consult Webster's often and have a strong memory, but in any case, don't guess, and don't depend upon an editor to correct your mistakes. Nothing makes an educated person look ignorant more than a manuscript peppered with misspelled words. Look them up.

2. **Syntax.** This refers to the order of words in a phrase or a sentence, and the worst sin against syntax is the dangling participle. Don't be intimidated by the term. It applies to an error that's easily recognized when you read a sentence with an eye toward precision. "Crouched behind the car, my eyes went to Julie's." I actually have nothing against eyes that are capable of quitting their sockets and taking a walk, but I can't quite picture them crouching. The dependent clause—"Crouched behind the car"—doesn't match the subject—"my eyes"—and so the image is unintentionally funny. The sentence should read: "Crouched behind the car, I looked at Julie." This is the most common grammatical mistake

in our language, finding its way into political speeches, doctoral theses, and the news. It's sloppy, lazy, and easily avoided.

Split infinitives are also endemic today. "To be" and "to do" are infinitives, and one separates them at rhythm's peril. I like to think the original *Star Trek* wouldn't have been canceled if the crew of the Starship *Enterprise* were ordered "to go boldly where no man has gone before" rather than "to boldly go." Lately, even university professors have been heard exhorting their students "to not cheat," when they should be warning them "not to cheat." A split infinitive can set one's teeth on edge as badly as a split fingernail.

This is as good a place as any to slap a spade in the face of that hoary old rule about never ending a sentence with a preposition; or, as Sir Winston Churchill put it, "A preposition is something you should never end a sentence with." "With," "of," "for," and "to" are the most common prepositions. It's amazing—and disconcerting—to see the acrobatics some writers perform in order to satisfy this inexplicable dictum. Paraphrasing Sir Winston: "This is an affectation up with which I will not put." Some rules have a way of becoming holy commandments through constant repetition, never questioned. Whenever one of them gets in the way of the crystal flow of a good clear sentence, run right over it.

These are the main areas of syntax abuse. Mind them, and the good habits you acquire will protect you from embarrassing yourself.

3. **Usage.** I know we're all supposed to be *impacted* by great events, but the truth is we're *affected* by them. Only bowels and teeth become impacted. In the past, nouns have often been drafted to serve as verbs, but since the 1980s, the trend has turned into a full-scale assault on the language. The argument most often employed in defense of such tampering is that English is an evolving form that cannot be expected to remain static. However, evolution is a process of improvement, and hijacking one word to duplicate the efforts of another already in place is at best unnecessary, at worst a confession of a limited vocabulary.

Contact works as a verb because there is no one word equivalent ("get in touch with" rattles and clanks), but as long as we have *affect*, impact retains its greatest impact when used as a noun.

It's interesting—and perhaps understandable—how often well-educated people mix up *lie* and *lay*. A person lies down, an object lies on the floor. A person lays that object on that floor, and can be said to lay himself down. Where the confusion begins is in the past tense: "I lay there for a while, then decided to get up." Past tense is the only case in which a person or an object can be said to lay. And just to stir up some more dust, consider that in past tense, a person *laid* an object on the floor. This is prime material for a brain-teasing riddle, but people have managed to commit the usages to memory. If you don't, you'll alienate editors and miss sales.

A country that enforces compulsory education ought to blush whenever one of its citizens asks, "Where are you at?" The appendage at the end has no more business being there than a jar of leeches in a modern medical office. Equally redundant: "Five a.m. in the morning." A.M. never occurs at any other time of day. "Different than" is incorrect; "different from" is correct. It's a contrast, not a comparison.

"Most always" is just plain backwoods grammar, but it's taken on a sinister tone of late. It had nearly passed from our ken when Orville Redenbacher began touting his brand of popcorn with the boast, "Most every kernel popped." If he had said, "almost every kernel," his prospective customers might have realized the truth: Every kernel did not pop. Stripped of its first syllable, this adjective undermines the absolute ("always;" "every") that it's supposed to modify. It's an intentional attempt to mislead consumers without actually violating the truth-in-advertising laws, and any writer who wishes to appear objective should be ashamed to stoop to it.

Politics overstep their bounds when they monkey around with the basic rules of grammar. Women's-rights advocates may argue that the predominance of the masculine pronoun threatens gender equality, but the politically endorsed "everyone must do their duty" certainly threatens reason. If you're committed to equal rights, or squeamish about offending those who are, you may elect to use "her" and "his" intermittently when writing generally, but if you do, don't count me among your readers. It's mealy-mouthed and too distracting. Whatever your choice, remember that "everyone" is singular. (I treasure the comment made by a prison official: "Half of everyone who leaves prison goes back.")

Forget what your ancient high school textbook told you about never beginning a sentence with "and" or "but." People do it all the time in conversation, and written English has always tended to follow the lead of popular discourse. To swim against this current is to appear stilted and old-fashioned, which is fine, if you're writing an epistolary novel set in seventeenth-century London. But otherwise you'll come off as a prig. And no one has ever explained to anyone's satisfaction why the rule was drafted in the first place.

If the above seems overwhelming, it needn't be. Always look for the internal logic in a phrase and you will never go wrong.

4. **Punctuation.** We're in the middle of a revolution here. A century ago, writers used far more commas than they do today, and there's little risk in predicting that a hundred years from now, the minimal number I'm using in this book will appear excessive. Notwithstanding the lesson taught by your elementary school teacher, a comma is only necessary to establish the rhythm of a sentence and to ensure comprehension. If you can get along without one, do. Gore Vidal uses semicolons the way most writers use commas, creating a seductive style that will influence your writing unless you don't want it to and resist its allure. This handy tool provides a pause slightly longer than a comma's, but shorter than a period's and less abrupt than a dash's. It's useful in stringing together sentences that might otherwise appear short and choppy, and there's nothing like it for separating items in a long list:

> Inside the room, I found an unmade bed; four freshly shucked snakeskins lying side by side; a tractor-trailer rig; eight chande-

liers in various stages of dismantlement; a dwarf; an indeterminate number of hypodermic syringes; three mountain bikes; a half-eaten peanut-butter-and-jelly sandwich, decomposing on a pillow; and the man himself, standing with arms crossed, daring me with his expression to figure out how he managed to assemble all these items in one room without alerting the local homeowners association.

The semicolon is the wispy relation of the virile colon, which is a bold finger directing one's attention to what follows, as it did at the end of the paragraph preceding the above example. Use it sparingly, because it calls attention to itself with the same rough diplomacy.

Use dashes the same way. They can insert action into a piece of dialogue ("'I'm waiting for Raul'—he glanced at the spavined mule in the corner—'and so is Rosarita'"), or a snatch of relevant information into a line of narrative ("Oliver was particular—some said snobbish—and yet he'd been known on occasion to wear a striped shirt with a plaid necktie"). In our day, they seem to have gained ground against parentheses, which make almost any passage by Henry James excruciating for many modern readers. When too many of either appear on a page, it looks like Morse code, inviting only to a telegrapher aboard the *Titanic*.

If you use ellipses only once in your career, you may have overdone it. They're … distracting. Writers often use them when recording one side of a telephone conversation, to leave room for the unheard remarks on the other end, but if you do without them, the reader will supply the necessary pauses.

For the love of Mike, get your apostrophes straight. They're there to indicate possession (Hilda's dad) and dropped or missing letters (didn't, swimmin'), If you're using them to turn singulars into plurals (Employee's Only, the Henderson's, Trespasser's Will Be Shot), you shouldn't be allowed to paint signs, let alone write fiction.

Quotation marks enclose quotations. You'll be using them most often for dialogue. Some writers use dashes instead, to separate dialogue from narrative, or nothing at all, to appear arty; but if you choose either of these paths, you'd better be German or Cormac McCarthy.

Periods tell the reader when sentences come to an end. Like these.

5. **Vocabulary.** This isn't designed to compete with either *Reader's Digest* or the Word-a-Day Calendar; how you assemble your lexicon is your business, but you should be aware of the quicksand that awaits.

Be sure of the definition of a word before you use it. The wrong word in the wrong place is a *malapropism*, after Mrs. Malaprop, a character in Richard Sheridan's 1775 play *The Rivals*, known for her hilarious misapplication of words. The comic Norm Crosby and "Slip" Mahoney of the Bowery Boys split the sides of audiences with their mangled vocabulary, and I knew an editor who, years after the fact, still chuckled over the romance heroine whose lover "brought her to the very pentacle of desire." In this case, a little knowledge of a nearly infinite subject is not so much dangerous as it is humiliating.

Don't use *definitive* when you mean *definite*. The first means that an issue that has been debated has been settled once and for all; the second means that the issue was never open to question. Pundits and politicians use definitive across the board because they think it makes them sound worldly, when in fact it's exposed them as jackasses.

You can't *convince* a cat to eat tuna, or *persuade* a Christian that Jesus lived. You convince people of a fact, and you can persuade them to act. Persuade is always followed by "to"; convince never is. Since the second word is more common, those who misuse it are usually making an honest mistake, but those who replace it with "persuade" are almost always showing off. A common word used accurately is more noble than a fancy one used incorrectly.

Presently and *currently* head the list of unrelated words most often used as if they were interchangeable. Currently means "now," while presently means "in a little while." Heed: "Mr.

Dalrymple is currently in a meeting, but he'll be available presently." *At present* is an acceptable substitute when you've tired of "currently;" but if you find that too formal, the misapplication of "presently" occurs so often that few will sneer if you jump aboard the bandwagon. However, if your story takes place anytime before the turn of the twentieth century, mind the difference. The mistake was never made from Lord Bacon's time to Stephen Crane's.

Many of the other words frequently wronged in our slapdash time can be discussed with bullet points:

* You *refer* to something, and having done so, have made a *reference*. You don't "reference" anything.
* *Farther* is a measure of distance. *Further* is a measure of time as it applies to thoroughness. One travels farther down the road to investigate further. The English mix these up constantly, which is one of the reasons we took the language away from them.
* *Led* is the past tense of *lead*. *Lead*, when it rhymes with led, is a base metal.
* *Nauseous* refers to that which causes nausea. It's okay to be nauseated, but if you call me nauseous, I'll deck you.
* The speaker *implies*. The listener *infers*.
* A convict whose good behavior has earned him a position of trust is a *trusty*. A *trustee* is the beneficiary of a trust fund.
* *Sewage* flows through pipes and fills septic tanks. *Sewerage* is what a London cockney calls sewage.
* *Irregardless* is not a word.
* *Inflammable* means "that which may flame." *Noninflammable* means "that which will not flame." However, so many people became confused by the *in* that forty or so years ago the people who paint warning signs on the sides of tankers coined the word *flammable* to warn of combustible material and save the lives of semiliterates so that they could marry and breed more semiliterates.
* *Equal justice* is a redundancy.
* *Normalcy* is not a word.

* *Preventative* is a noun, not an adjective. A preventive measure is a *preventative*.
* *Alright* is not a word. Once you understand that *already* and *all ready* have different definitions, you'll know why this is so.

The right word in the wrong place can be as wrong as the wrongest. Here are some things you may not know about regional definitions:

* *Soda.* In the Midwestern United States, *soda* is a carbonated ice cream drink. If you offer someone from Michigan or Wisconsin a soda and give him a Coke, he won't thank you for it. To be safe, say *soda pop.* (Midwesterners say *pop.)*
* *Squint.* In America, *squint* means to screw up one's eyes. In Great Britain, it means to wink.
* *Bloody.* You probably know this one. When visiting England, don't use it in polite society.
* *On line.* New Yorkers use this phrase when they mean *in line,* as in standing in line. Everywhere else, it has something to do with the Internet.
* *Out of pocket.* Southwestern dialect for *out of the loop.* Most other places, it means short on money.
* *Sweater.* Brits wear *pullovers*—even, apparently, when they don't pull over. Until World Cup Soccer came along, the English didn't like to admit they sweat. And while we're on that subject …
* *Football.* Over there, this is what they call *soccer.* If you challenge an Englishman to a game of football, one of you is going to be dressed inappropriately.

Warning! Using the word you know to be right can backfire if your reader isn't as well-versed as you are. Misapprehensions are numerous and pervasive. *MAD Magazine* once published a satirical all-purpose, nonslanderous campaign speech in which the opposing candidate was said to have been seen "performing a piscatorial activity on a boat flying the American flag," and that his sister "once worked as a proselyte outside a church." If any word requires explanation that will break the storytelling spell, replace it with one more familiar.

You get the idea. When you don't, turn to Webster's. But *which* Webster's? Read on.

* * *

Fiction Fact

Determined to prevent opportunists from exploiting her two most famous characters after her death, Agatha Christie killed off the characters in separate books and arranged to publish them posthumously. Since the appearance of Sleeping Murder *(1975) and* Curtain *(1976), neither Jane Marple nor Hercule Poirot has appeared in new mysteries.*

* * *

5

Sources in Conflict

* * *

THIS IS A CHAPTER ABOUT REFERENCE GUIDES; which to consult, which to avoid. By now it should come as no surprise that I include Web sites and computer programs among the latter. No one's in charge, and here's proof. In 2002, *Michigan Studies Weekly*, a publication for students in elementary school, solemnly told its subscribers:

> *Every spring, the freshwater whales and freshwater dolphins begin their 1,300-mile migration from Hudson Bay to the warmer waters of Lake Michigan. There are several locks along the route, but the whales forge a water path each year.*

Now, there are no whales or dolphins in any of the Great Lakes, and the image of Moby Dick calmly waiting for the attendants at Sault Ste. Marie to raise the gates to flood the locks to allow him passage from one lake to the next is enough to make any Michiganian convulse with laughter. Yet when a fourth-grade teacher in Muskegon called the editor to request a correction, the editor insisted the story was accurate. Eventually the error was confirmed, with an explanation that the information had come from an Internet site. The retraction read:

> We at Studies Weekly *want this to be a lesson to you. Not all web sites are true, and you cannot always believe them. When researching, you should always look for a reliable site that has credentials (proof of truthfulness).*

The problem with this pompous advice is that any credentials posted on a Web site are liable to come from the same bozo who posted the misinformation in the first place. Cyberspace is too vast, and too easily accessible, to be considered a reliable source without corroboration of the old-fashioned, nondigital kind. Books err as well, but the number of hands and minds through which information passes before it reaches print reduces its chances of contaminating your research. Meanwhile any lout with a modem can upload an urban myth in Utah and watch it streak to Taiwan and Catalina in minutes—much faster than it takes those redoubtable whales and dolphins to migrate from Baffin Island to the Milwaukee docks.

Web sites are advertising. They're not to be trusted any more than a beer commercial or a campaign for public office. Yet it's easy to become addicted to any development that promises bigger, newer, and faster results, and for its humdrum competition to try to regain lost ground by claiming to be updated; "updated" in this case meaning gutted to make room for pointless ephemera and watered down to avoid giving offense. This chapter will stand as a guide toward truth and away from false prophets.

Webster's is more than a household name. It's recognized throughout the English-speaking world, in societies as yet unfamiliar with McDonald's, Coca-Cola, and O.J. Simpson. "Look it up in Webster's" carries all the somber weight of "I am the resurrection and the life," settling most arguments and giving parents and teachers temporary relief from relentless juvenile interrogation. However, Noah Webster has been dead for 160 years and his name has been in public domain for decades. Many pirates sail under its honest colors.

The last reliable American dictionary was Webster's Second International Edition. It was a *prescriptive* source, which like a physician prescribed the precise and accurate use of the material recommended. It was in print for a century before it was replaced by the Third edition, and the first *descriptive* dictionary, taking popular usage as its lead. In short, Webster's Third reshaped its definitions to conform to the meanings the public had come to associate with them. It was a case of the defendants taking over the courtroom, without benefit of appeal to a higher source.

Purists need only hear the words "Webster's Third" to fly into a fine rage; none finer, perhaps, than that of Nero Wolfe, the detective creation of Rex Stout. In *Gambit*, Wolfe's loyal-but-irreverent leg man, Archie Goodwin, told a visitor, "Mr. Wolfe is in the middle of a fit."

> *"... There's a fireplace in the front room, but it's never lit because he hates open fires. ... But it's lit now because he's using it. He's seated in front of it, on a chair too small for him, tearing sheets out of a book and burning them. The book is the new edition, the third edition, of Webster's New International Dictionary. He considers it subversive because it threatens the integrity of the English language."*

Wolfe's own explanation was more succinct:

> *"Do you use 'infer' and 'imply' interchangeably, Miss Blount?"*
>
> *She did fine. She said simply, "No."*
>
> *"This book says you may. Pfui."*

A journey that turns in the wrong direction and will not reverse its steps can only wind up more and more hopelessly lost. Forty years after that fictional book-burning, not one but *eight* more editions have appeared, surely an excessive slaughter of trees. Two were enough in Noah Webster's own lifetime. The tenth is the one most often used by today's copy editors, but it's simple to assume their publishing houses have the spanking-new Eleventh on order. The compilers of the Tenth saw fit to include the 1980s phrase *politically correct*—an unnecessary addition presupposing that the reader is incapable of looking up *politically* and *correct* and drawing the intended conclusion. The Eleventh compounds that malfeasance by adding (along with several hundred more New Age terms) *heart healthy*. These people must take us for dolts.

Suspiciously, the unabridged Eleventh is roughly the same size as the late lamented Second. Even we dolts must assume that a host of words and their definitions has been omitted to make room for the new. True, some may be obsolete, but pity the historical novelist who would season his or her narrative with quaint old language to match the coaches and chimney-pots. In any case, the excisions were made arbitrarily. The editors have circumvented the natural and social evolution of language in order to impose their own narrow-minded views of what's acceptable. It's a fact that the electronic revolution has given us hundreds of words that didn't exist before the 1970s, yet one wonders how many of them will still be in use come Webster's Twelfth, while those they supplanted witnessed the Norman invasion in 1066 and the first moon landing in 1969.

Webster's Second is still available in many public libraries, where it may be consulted at no charge, and in used bookstores, where copies may be obtained for as little as ten or twelve dollars; although a hundred would be a cheap enough price to pay to have this huge, stately, and endlessly fascinating guide at your fingertips.

While you're looking, go ahead and buy a reasonably priced dictionary and use it to check spellings and avoid writing *fulsome* when you mean *full*. Steer clear of useless vest pocket editions that fit handily on your person. All the words an educated human might want to look up in a pinch have been deleted in the interest of portability. Any bound unabridged dictionary is better than none at all; and none at all is better than a computer program, about which more anon. (Or has that word been flung upon the scrapheap with the rest?)

* Webster's Second is a stout workhorse, dependable whenever you encounter a rock in the road. The thoroughbred, ideal for trotting about Hyde Park on Sunday or hurdling the Queen's hedges, is the Oxford English Dictionary (OED). This massive source not only incises the language with the skill of the Royal

College of Surgeons, but provides an in-depth history of each word from its obscure origins through its passage into current usage. It also fills multiple volumes and strains the budget of a university to place on its shelves. Even the popular two-volume set, sold in a slipcase with a drawer containing a magnifying glass for reading its Liliputian type, runs several hundred dollars. If you have a rich indulgent aunt and are strapped for an idea for a birthday present to hint to her about, this is it; but check it against Webster's for the standardized American spellings.

I get along quite well with the one-volume abridged *Oxford Dictionary of English Etymology*, and glory in my recent discovery of the 1955 edition of *The Oxford Universal Dictionary*, which compares in size and weight with Webster's Second. The OED used to be a staple in most publishing offices, but corporate raiding and budget crunches have taken care of that. If you can acquire it, consider the advantage of being able to one-up any editing suggestion based on anemic common sources.

* Roget's Thesaurus will hoist you over many a block when it comes to sweetening your vocabulary and avoiding repeating a high-profile word you've already used in a preceding line. It's a book of lists, offering scores of synonyms—and, immediately following, antonyms—that will enliven your prose so long as you don't get carried away and end up sounding as comically pompous as a W.C. Fields lecture on the evils of strong drink. The standard version is most easily recognizable as the retro mass-market paperback found in just about any used bookstore for a couple of dollars, and was reissued in 1988 in a trade paper edition by P.S.I. & Associates, Inc., of Miami, Florida. You'll know it by the words listed alphabetically at the back, alongside numerals that will guide you to their synonyms in the body of the book.

Stay away from *Roget's II*, the so-called "expanded edition" issued by the editors of the American Heritage Dictionary and published in 1988 by Houghton Mifflin. It promises a larger selection, but makes room for it by supplying a bare fraction of the alternate words that appear in the classic Roget's. Like

Webster's, Peter Mark Roget's name is in public domain, so look for those numerals at the back.

* English usage has its Bible: *The Elements of Style*, universally known as Strunk & White, compiled by William Strunk Jr., an English professor at Cornell University, and revised in a second edition by E.B. White, the great essayist and children's book author (*Charlotte's Web, Stuart Little*, et al). This slim paperback, about the size of a passport, answers all of the most commonly asked questions about English grammar, in layman's terms and with examples that manage to make an opaque language brilliantly translucent. The chapter headings alone essentially sell the book: *Elementary Rules of Usage*; *Ele-mentary Principles of Composition*; *A Few Matters of Form*; *Words and Expressions Commonly Misused*; *An Approach to Style (With a List of Reminders)*. It's the last word in any debate relating to form, and will make your life simpler throughout the writing and editing processes. Every modern writer you've ever admired has owned a copy, and the customized style manuals employed by all the major publishers are based upon it. It runs a mere seventy-eight pages and is available everywhere.

A good one-volume encyclopedia—Merriam-Webster's Collegiate is recommended—should stand within arm's reach for those times when you need to spot-check a historical or geographical fact. There should be a multiple-volume set in your writing room as well, for when you need to go into greater depth. Choose a brand name—Rand-McNally, Funk & Wagnall, etc.— and be wary of those sets that superstores dole out a volume at a time with every purchase exceeding fifty dollars. Most of them are children's picture books and the text is unhelpful. I collect older sources going back a century and more, because some entries that ran several columns during the McKinley Administration have vanished from modern editions. (*The Annual Cyclopedia* of 1900 gave me everything I needed on the practice of harvesting ice in the era before refrigerators for *The Rocky Mountain Moving Picture Association*, a novel about Hollywood in 1913; later sources hadn't a clue.) I grew up with *The Book of Knowledge* (Grolier, Inc.), a twenty-volume encyclopedia aimed at children, and still consult it. Unlike today's dumbed-down versions, it includes step-by-step photographs of such things as automobile assembly lines and clear, detailed descriptions.

Twenty or more thick volumes take up a lot of room, but the obvious alternative—computer programs—ignore many of the classic sources, repeating the inadequacies of the remodeled Webster's and Roget's. They're no better than a desk reference, and you can thumb through the alphabet in the same time it takes to enter a keyword and wait for the response. And I'll race an experienced Web-surfer anytime when it comes to combing through a full set.

* Computer dictionary programs all have limitations, and grammatical programs are an annoying nag. Recently, after dictating answers to an online interview and making a cultural reference to the actress Salma Hayek, I was asked by the obliging program if I didn't mean *slam haiku;* which is an intriguing combination, but failed to make my point. Grammatik and its competitors similarly offer to help writers trim run-on sentences, flip-flop dependent clauses, and contort their syntax to embed prepositions that would otherwise appear (horrors!) at the ends of sentences. The goal of these style-Nazis is to make every writer sound like every other writer. William Faulkner, James Joyce, and Gabriel García-Márquez would cause these programs to burst into flame. The existing software is hidebound. If you met someone whose brain worked the same way, you would consider him autistic.

* I like those "what to name the baby" books when I need a name for a character. Page Murdock, my most enduring series hero—twenty-five years, as of *Port Hazard*—got his christening there, both names. The Bible is good for that as well, particularly when you're writing about early America, whose pioneers plundered the Old Testament to tag their progeny. Random House's *Word*

Menu, edited by Stephen Glazier, is priceless when you're casting about for a term related to a specific vocation or avocation. And stock up on English-to-foreign language dictionaries. You never know when a French character will erupt in a "Mon dieu!"

These are basic tools, a beginner's set around which to build your literary workshop. During your career, you will acquire and discard many more, but when fire breaks out, these are the ones you'll rescue. At bottom, they'll help keep the whales in the ocean where they belong.

* * *

Fiction Fact

The three greatest horror novels ever written, Frankenstein *(Mary Shelley),* Dracula *(Bram Stoker), and* The Strange Case of Dr. Jekyll and Mr. Hyde *(Robert Louis Stevenson), were all inspired by nightmares.*

* * *

6

Past Perfect

* * *

ALL FICTION IS HISTORICAL. Whether you're basing it on what's happening outside your window at the moment of creation or on events that took place a thousand years ago during the reign of Ethelred the Unready, you're chained to the demands of a time that has had its day. Even futuristic science fiction contains elements recognizable from yesterday at the latest.

When Edith Wharton began to chronicle the New York society of her middle-class youth, it was still very much in existence. By the time she returned to the theme, after World War I, she found that the world she knew so intimately had ceased to be. When she published *The Age of Innocence*—set, as were all of her best novels, in Gilded Age Manhattan—she was keenly aware that she was writing historical fiction. It's ironic to consider that when the Pulitzer committee voted to award her its prize for literature, it was for this period piece rather than for her impassioned earlier work, which cried out for the very reforms that time had provided.

I'm no Edith Wharton, but I experienced a similar epiphany when *Something Borrowed, Something Black* was in editing at Forge Books. I wrote it during the winter of 2000–2001, intending it as a realistically raw narrative of contemporary crime, with a retired professional killer as the protagonist and his former underworld cronies as the enemies that had to be destroyed if he were ever to lead a conventional life. A key scene called for the primary antagonist to smuggle a weapon through security at the Los Angeles airport. It worked, because I had discovered a loophole in the procedure involving metal detectors.

Then September 11 happened. In the crackdown that followed the attacks on the Pentagon and the World Trade Center, my loophole had closed up. A sharp copy editor asked if in light of recent events I shouldn't rethink the scene. I tried, but there was no way to achieve the same effect if I'd set it on the other side of the check-through, and since the scene was crucial to the structure of the book, to weaken it would be to collapse the whole. I told the copy editor that the readers would just have to understand that these events took place before that bleak September. At that point, *Something Borrowed, Something Black* became a historical novel.

In a social context, the book was more anachronistic than that one scene. Compared to the spectacle of a fanatical fundamentalist who would sacrifice his own life to massacre thousands of innocents, your garden-variety hit man—even a serial killer—seemed almost warm and fuzzy. The joyous *frisson* of "it couldn't happen here" had vanished, replaced by the grim awareness of an uncertain world. Written on the cutting edge of crime, my book must forever be regarded as a nostalgic glimpse at—well, an age of innocence.

All fiction dates; it's the author's responsibility to take steps to ensure that his or her fiction ages like good wine, improving in body and flavor with each experience instead of languishing on the shelves past its expiration date. A reference to a hot-button political topic or ubiquitous TV commercial may strike chords with a readership for whom the memory is still fresh, but in five years, intervening issues and campaigns will have rendered them vague and stale, and for the next generation of reader they'll be incomprehensible. Meanwhile,

Charles Dickens' horse-drawn hansoms and Cockney grave robbers resonate more deeply with each day that carries us further from his time, in ways that could not have been known by those who gathered on street corners awaiting delivery of each new installment of *David Copperfield*.

The trick is to choose details that will assure your contemporaries that you live in the same world, but that will continue to have impact long after you and they have passed on to the next world. How could Rex Stout know that comparing Archie Goodwin to Clark Gable would still have meaning forty years after the movie star's death, and how could Ian Fleming avoid confusing readers familiar with Pierce Brosnan's portrayal of James Bond onscreen by describing the spy in his books as "a young Hoagy Carmichael?" They could not. It was a crapshoot whether a matinee idol would still be remembered or a celebrated songwriter would long be forgotten. One gamble paid off, the other didn't. But it's a tribute to Fleming's storytelling skill that the force of his characters and the pace of his plots manage to propel readers past that head-scratching moment in their eagerness to learn the hero's fate. Conversely, the Stout story is anchored forever in time to the span of Clark Gable's life, but the reader pauses not at all.

There is no such thing as a sure thing, but no crystal ball is needed to guess that long-established popularity and the endurance of film should make the name Julia Roberts echo well into this century. Whether a more recent phenomenon like Britney Spears or Justin Timberlake will mean anything by the time you read this book is debatable. The durability of their appeal hasn't been tested, and music videos have the shelf life of yogurt. If you must make a topical reference, do it in such a way that it will still have meaning months and years from now. In *Gulliver's Travels,* Jonathan Swift presented a satirical observation on the nature of politics that's relevant after nearly four centuries. Compare that with the early Spenser detective novels written by Robert B. Parker in the 1980s, with their relentless emphasis on gender equality; when a few years later they were bought for television, the producers excised all the bromides on women's liberation. The movement had progressed so far so fast that Parker seemed to be stating the obvious.

Daytime dramas are even more ephemeral than dogma. In 1992, when it seemed everyone was watching a one-eyed soap opera character named Patch, I made some readers laugh when I had a working husband say, "Who's this idiot with the patch?" Now Patch is long gone, and if I don't edit him out of the next printing, readers will be just as clueless as the husband.

Writers of science fiction have always had to scramble to stay ahead of science fact. Recently, they've been joined by writers of contemporary mysteries and police procedurals. Not long ago, a private detective examining a murder scene might have expected to avoid joining the list of official suspects by smearing his fingerprints as he let himself out, but thanks to revolutionary strides in DNA identification, if he tried it today he'd be leaving behind more evidence than he removed. Each new weapon in the war on crime makes it that much harder to frame a murder mystery that will baffle the police for more than a few pages. Ideally, the perpetrator would have to wear an outfit similar to a radiation suit, to keep from shedding incriminating hairs and scales of skin at the scene and prevent being branded by trace elements of his victim's blood.

It's not surprising that some writers have chosen to suspend their mysteries in 1994, before the new scientific methods were available to most police departments. This formidable technology may also explain the widespread defection into the "historical mystery." Welcome back, Sherlock Holmes. Before he invented his own hemoglobin test, there was no procedure, in life or in fiction, to determine whether reddish stains found at a scene of suspicious activity were human blood or spilled paint. Since no effective machinery to investigate crime existed in ancient Rome, some envy Lindsey Davis' Falco his freedom to sleuth where and when he will without annoying a cop. Ellis Peters' medieval Brother Cadfael seems even better off; more worldly than most of his fellow monks, he's unimpeded by their superstitious belief in witches and demons.

This flight into the past is unnecessary, if it's to evade the infallibility of criminal science. Real-life crooks aren't so easily intimidated, or they'd have all gone straight by now. If they're smart enough to wear gloves to cover their fingerprints, they're smart enough to figure out how to keep track of their chromosomes. Okay, so it's a little harder to create a plausible murder mystery than it was ten years ago. Think how much easier it was before the first sharp reader dismantled the device of the least likely suspect.

In the happy event that crime continues to pay, it's still unlikely that the historical mystery will fall out of favor soon. This subgenre has filled a void left by the popular historical writers of the past. Those include Sir Walter Scott, Count Leo Tolstoy, Sir Arthur Conan Doyle, and, among the commoners, Willa Cather, Rafael Sabatini, Howard Pyle, Mary Renault, Booth Tarkington, and Edna Ferber. During the stark early days of the Cold War (and possibly as an antidote to it), they proliferated wonderously in the persons of Kenneth Roberts, Thomas B. Costain, F. Van Wyck Mason, C.S. Forester, Taylor Caldwell, Lloyd C. Douglas, and Pearl S. Buck, and they were joined from Olympus by Thornton Wilder and W. Somerset Maugham.

Analysts may argue over whether 1960s cynicism soured readers on stories of heroism and chivalry or that the genre simply reached its saturation point. Whatever the cause, as writers whose titles had dominated the market for years retired from the field, publishers took no steps to replace them. But while the mainstream press turned toward contemporary thrillers, the romance came along and rescued history.

Call it the literary equivalent of musical chairs. When the Western lost its franchise, it struck camp and pitched its tent in General Fiction. The historical went in the opposite direction, away from the mainstream racks and into genre. In romance, the Regency period discovered a whole new audience, and rapacious Vikings broadened their conquests to include science fiction—and if the writer wanted them to wear horns on their helmets against all the findings of researchers, he could damn well put them there, because *his* Vikings were rowing their warships along the canals of Mars.

The mystery followed. In 1975, author Joe Gores resurrected Pinkerton agent-turned-hardboiled writer Dashiell Hammett to investigate a murder outside the pages of pulp fiction. *Hammett* was a runaway bestseller, and by the end of the decade, dozens of other writers had plundered graveyards to turn real-life figures into fictional detectives.

Throughout the next quarter-century, the mystery delved further and further into the past. Umberto Eco's *The Name of the Rose* went back to the Dark Ages to track a serial killer through a remote monastery. Lindsey Davis then lapped Eco by several centuries with her Roman private eye, after which all tunics were off. The body count in the Egypt of the pharaohs took a sudden spike upward, as did those in Renaissance Italy, Germany under Hitler, England during the Crusades, Al Capone's Chicago, and Old New York (no doubt displeasing the ghost of Edith Wharton, whom W. Somerset Maugham once scandalized by asking if she read the mysteries of Edgar Wallace). Although it's difficult to imagine anyone trumping the team of Michael and Kathleen O'Neal Gear, whose Anasazi Mysteries take place in Stone Age America, Eric Garcia merits special mention for dressing a dinosaur in a trenchcoat and fedora in *Anonymous Rex*, in which the great carnivores and sauropods survive extinction to populate Los Angeles in our own day. Killers have stalked the decks of the *Titanic* and the *Hindenburg*. The "history mystery" is here for the long run.

There is no category where a solid grounding in historical research doesn't come in handy. All the drama, romance, and suspense you would ever want is in the pages of the past, and despite all this ransacking, there are plenty of stories that have never been told in the context of fiction. This is treasure trove if you're stuck for an idea, and heaven on earth if you're a buff. But whether your literary landscape contains the pyramids of Giza or McDonald's golden arches, you'll want to visit chapter seven first, and learn how homework almost got me arrested.

* * *

Fiction Fact

George Orwell didn't waste much time coming up with the title 1984. *He wrote his famous novel about a dystopic future in 1948 and simply transposed the last two digits.*

* * *

7

The Rapture of Research

* * *

ONCE UPON A TIME, I schemed to smuggle a bomb aboard a pleasure boat.

I was laying the groundwork for *Kill Zone,* in which a hit man is hired by the FBI to free a hundred hostages from a gang of domestic terrorists who had seized control of a historic riverboat on its way to the Bob-Lo Island amusement park in the middle of the Detroit River. Since I couldn't very well rescue the passengers without first putting them in jeopardy, I called the number listed for the Bob-Lo front office to ask if the security guards aboard the boat were armed and if it would be possible for someone posing as a musician to bring gelatin explosives hidden in a fiddle case up the gangplank.

There was a long pause. Then the woman on the other end asked, "Who did you say you were?"

Apparently I hadn't explained my mission as well as I'd thought. I had the distinct impression that someone in authority was now listening in on the conversation and no doubt preparing to call 911. But

I managed to establish my credentials, and within minutes my contact in the front office was gleefully conspiring with me to turn the Bob-Lo boat into a floating bomb.

At the time, terrorism was an alien concept to most Americans, who knew about it mainly through news reports from Europe and the Middle East. Today, I would probably be obliged to visit the office in person to confirm my identity and benign intentions. Having done that, I'd expect the experience to be no less rewarding.

It's amusing, and very encouraging, to learn that people in various occupations are fascinated with the writing life, particularly when it involves their job, which daily routine has robbed of whatever glamor it once held for them. This attitude extends to employees whose work many of us would consider mundane, but also to such seemingly exciting trades as police work, firefighting, and the military. People in these professions enjoy telling stories and are constantly on the prowl for a new audience, and like the rest of us are flattered to find themselves the center of attention. Direct questions yield reams of information that might otherwise consume a week in a library. All you need is a telephone or e-mail and contact information. And if you use what you learn responsibly and acknowledge the source (unless anonymity is requested), chances are you'll gain a new reader when the book comes out, along with several of his or her family and friends. It pays to send an autographed copy. It's the polite thing to do, and will provide you with a source for life.

We're fortunate to live in a time when information on everything is easier to acquire than ever before. In addition to personal sources, there are racks and stacks jammed with the published work of good researchers who also happen to be fine writers. The biographies of early Americans written by David McCulloch, Edmund Morris, Nancy Mitford, and others contain facts that were sealed to their predecessors and read like good novels. And condemn Baby Boomers as much as you like for their narcissism, their endless infatuation with themselves and their time has given us libraries of minutia about the years between the Korean Police Action and Operation Iraqi Freedom. In the past, recent history was inaccessible outside the pages of the newspaper you threw away last month. Now, if you need to know the earliest date your barfly could have heard "I Want to Hold Your Hand" on the jukebox, you don't have to rummage through the 45s in the basement: It's in Joel Whitburn's *The Billboard Book of Top 40 Hits*. If it's Eminem's latest, it's online.

On television, cable, satellite, and broadcast networks provide hundreds of hours of documentary programming. On almost any given night, you can watch Hitler dance his jig over the Fall of France, visit the ruins of Mesopotamia, and watch Madonna change costumes during an appearance on her *Blonde Ambition* tour. Before *COPS* and *America's Most Wanted,* you had to get permission from your local police department to ride in the back seat of a patrol car if you wanted to know what it's like to participate in a tour of duty. (Beware, however, of yet another facile medium sometimes given to emphasizing sensational graphics at the expense of hard facts. Check it against other sources. In fact, your best defense against outside skeptics is to obtain a second opinion on everything before you publish. Two attributive sources has always been the rule. Some writers aren't satisfied until they have five or six.)

The going can be treacherous. It's easy enough to weed the ballpoint pens and nylon hose out of a nineteenth-century setting, but difficult to establish whether the computer program you're using was available to the characters in a story about the presidential election of 2000. Our memories can't always be trusted when it comes to firsthand experience. And intangible things like common turns of phrase can be elusive when you try to put them in the mouth of someone who might not be familiar with them. Say he could be, and you've confirmed it. Now you have to convince the reader. If he thinks he's found an error, you've lost him, even if he's wrong and you're right. If something sounds out of place, you're better off substituting something most readers will accept, because stopping the action to explain your choice is as jarring as making the wrong one. A case in point: In London's East End under Queen Victoria, the molls and dips called police officers "pigs." All the documentation in the world won't erase the anachronistic image of 1960s war protesters on the Berkeley campus taunting cops in riot gear.

For the Detroit Series, I spent many hours in the microfilm reading room of the Detroit Public Library, scrolling through the back numbers of local newspapers. Journalism in the 1920s and 1940s was no more accurate than it is today, lacking the distance of time and the opportunity to collate and evaluate facts (and nonfacts) at leisure and arrive at an objective conclusion. But the period reportorial style, and the advertising that subsidized it, compose a time capsule that draws you deep into the atmosphere of the time. They tell you how people dressed and spoke, what products they used, the values they respected or rejected, where they ate, and how they entertained themselves. Brand names work like wizards' spells. If your villain brushes his teeth with Ipana, he and his world will seem more real than if he merely uses toothpaste. Even readers who know nothing of the era will react to the authenticity of a detail supplied with confidence. To spend two hours immersed in such heady ephemera is to stagger out afterward blinking into the twenty-first century—a Rip Van Winkle for the new millennium, perhaps, but an authority on the old.

When do you have enough to cast off? It's impossible to say. The more you know, the less inclined you'll be to show off what you've learned by forcing unchewed lumps of raw material down your reader's throat. If you're writing about Tibetan monks struggling for survival in the Himalayas and have read two good books on Asian monastic life, you may proceed to write with confidence right up until the brothers sit down to supper and you realize you have no idea what kind of utensils they use to eat. To avoid stopping the momentum to search frantically for that snippet, you'll have to have read half a dozen or more texts, discovered two lines on the subject, and made note of them for later use. You sure won't find it in the encyclopedia, digital or otherwise. The CD-ROM hasn't been invented that can contain such fine points.

Since you will probably use one-fifth of the information you take in, a ratio of five parts research to one part writing sounds like a good rule of thumb, except you won't know when you've achieved it. Find out as much as you can and make notes before you crank in that first page. Assign the material to categories boldly labeled *Household Items, Transportation,* etc. (I typed ten pages of notes breaking down each move in the gunfight at the O.K. Corral for *Bloody Season*; the actual fight lasted less than sixty seconds.) If the material is on loan, photocopy pertinent passages before you return it. If it will remain in your possession throughout the project, use bookmarks—colored tabs are good mnemonic devices—and make notes of what material is in which volume. The time you spend organizing now will save you from backtracking later, just when the writing catches fire.

You'll find the truth is both frustrating and accommodating. I nearly gave up on *Bloody Season* when I learned that Wyatt Earp and his brothers wore homely Mackinaws to the gunfight, and not the black frock coats of romantic myth. (This didn't stop the illustrators from dressing them in black on the covers of three editions.) Conversely, when I read about the death of Jesse James in St. Joseph, Missouri, for a key scene in *Billy Gashade*, I was delighted to discover that Oscar Wilde was in town that day, on the western leg of his North American lecture tour. His flamboyant wardrobe and snarky *bons mots* went a long way to lift the subject out of the traditional Western ghetto.

An old joke features two hikers being pursued by an angry grizzly. The first hiker says, "You know we'll never outrun that bear." The second hiker says, "All I have to do is outrun you." There will always be scholars who know more than you; your goal is to know more than most of your readers. Doing your homework increases your confidence and frees your brain to concentrate on story and character, which are more important than the background. You're an entertainer, not an instructor.

A lot of writers hate research because they can't wait to get to the writing. A lot of other writers prefer the preparation to what comes after. Some use it as an excuse to avoid putting it into practice, either out of laziness or fear of failure. (Fear of success is just plain stupid.) Some others get caught up in the hunting and gathering, and spend their lives stuffing their heads with arcane facts that will never benefit anyone. These last are called university professors.

All kidding aside, the allure of gleaning intelligence from musty folios and personal interviews can seduce you away from the sweaty business of creating, convincing yourself that you need to know more and yet more, when what you're really doing is stalling. The condition is closely related to Rapture of the Deep, in which insufficient oxygen impairs judgment, preventing scuba divers from surfacing until their tanks run out and they suffocate. Oxygen is the cure, for that and the Rapture of Research. At some point you must come up for air, and whether you have enough information stored away to carry you through the book or not, begin writing. Any experienced writer can tell you there is always another question to ask and another fact to check. It isn't an issue. Remember, no one will see what you've written until you're ready to show it.

But you needn't entomb yourself in paper and ink, or ruin your eyes staring at a flickering screen. Why not call your local police department and ask to ride along some night on patrol? It's a lot more exhilarating than watching some cracker trying to talk himself out of a domestic beef on the tube. Fly in a balloon, pilot a motorcycle, sit in a cheap hotel lobby and breathe in every seamy detail. Spend your vacation on the site of your book, not in front of its Web site. The late George Plimpton made a career out of pretending to be a pro football player, an actor, and a circus acrobat. Hemingway and Jack London built their legends on the strenuous life and mined the material for years. Dashiell Hammett and Joe Gores were private detectives. Herman Melville worked on a whaling ship. Who cares, when the opportunity comes up, if it has anything to do with what you're working on, or if it relates to anything you write from then on? It will look great in the author bio at the back of the book. And it's all tax deductible, every cent, once your work starts paying.

Actually, life experience is more useful than that. The method actor playing a killer doesn't have to go out and slay a fellow human being to explore the character. As a child, he may once have shot a bird with a B-B gun or pushed his sister off a swing, and he draws on that guilt to flesh out the role. Actors and writers are alike when it comes to spinning a web of imagination out of the raw silk of reality. Marcel Proust got a quarter of a million words out of turning over in bed, but for all its virtues *Remembrance of Things Past* is not popular fiction. Live, and write.

Fiction Fact

Kenneth Millar borrowed the surname of detective Lew Archer from the murdered partner of Dashiell Hammett's Sam Spade in The Maltese Falcon. *Hammett didn't kick, but fellow mystery writer John D. MacDonald demanded that Millar stop publishing under the pseudonym John Macdonald. Eventually, Millar settled on Ross Macdonald. (He'd come up with the original pseudonym to avoid being confused with his wife, author Margaret Millar.)*

* * *

8

Perspectives
on Point of View

* * *

ARISTOTLE SAID, "GIVE ME A LEVER and a fulcrum and I shall move the world." The only problem was finding a place to stand.

Why he should have wanted to move our planet out of a perfectly sound orbit is Greek to me, but ever since his time, writers have struggled with the problem of where to stand when they're telling their stories.

Who is observing the details, an all-seeing god or a flawed mortal? If the latter, is he telling the story himself or is someone speaking for him, inserting *he* (or *she*) in place of I? Finally, is he allowed the occasional break while another mortal takes up the slack? Does it matter?

The last question is the simplest to answer: Yes. And that reply opens the way toward answering the others. An understanding of the strengths and shortcomings of the various points of view plays a crucial role in determining where you'll stand while the story unfolds.

1. **First person.** This is the natural way to tell a story; which may explain why Puritans in the woodpile of literature have ever been quick to counsel against it. In their view, nothing so easy can be good. Fortunately, among those who didn't listen are Daniel Defoe, Dick Francis, Amy Tan, William Styron, Emily Brontë, Edgar Allan Poe, Daphne du Maurier, Ralph Ellison, Mary Shelley, E.L. Doctorow, Mark Twain, and Joyce Carol Oates, to name a dozen among the thousand. It's the choice made by the first communicating Stone Age man to relate the details of a momentous hunt to his listeners. It's the way your parents presented object lessons from their own pasts to prevent you from duplicating their mistakes. It's the method you used to report to them what happened to you on your first day in kindergarten.

> *"I take up my pen in the year of grace 17—, and go back to the time when my father kept the 'Admiral Benbow' inn, and the brown old seaman, with the sabre cut, first took up his lodging under our roof."*

So begins *Treasure Island*, and from the moment the profane ancient mariner enters young Jim Hawkins' life, Jim's story is ours, and has been from age seven to seventy for 120 years. It's impossible to imagine the scene in which the boy clings to a crosstree high above the deck of the *Hispaniola*, fumbling to reload a flintlock pistol, while wicked Israel Hands scrambles nimbly up the mast with dagger in teeth and murder in his eye, told from any perspective other than Jim's. Certainly the cool distance of even third-person subjective wouldn't answer. ("*He* felt a blow and then a sharp pang, and there *he* was pinned by the shoulder to the mast"? Please!) Magically, first-person hurls a dagger through the shoulder of the spoilsport who says, "Why should I hang around to find out if you survived? You're telling your own story!'

The disadvantage is a matter of confinement. Similarly harrowing experiences when the narrator cannot be present must be related to the reader at second hand; or, as Stevenson chose, by putting aside Jim's recollections during the "Narrative

Continued by the Doctor" chapters in Part Four, wherein Dr. Livesey tells us what happened to Jim's fellow adventurers while the boy was absent. At this point, for me, the story loses steam, and doesn't regain it until Jim returns to take up the throttle three chapters later.

Insofar as I may make suggestions to a departed master, I propose that this break in momentum is unnecessary. Stevenson could have jettisoned Dr. Livesey's narration in favor of a brief dialogue, Jim asking questions and the doctor providing answers. We care more what happens to Jim; we've lived with him longer and resent the separation.

Ironically, first-person's very confinement is often one of its great strengths. In expert hands, an account reported to the protagonist can heighten the drama, obliging the reader to supply details from his or her imagination. Consider Sherlock Holmes' remarks upon the death of Sir Charles Baskerville to Dr. Watson, Holmes' first-person biographer, in *The Hound of the Baskervilles*: "He was running, Watson—running desperately, running for his life, running until he burst his heart and fell dead upon his face." Three pages of on-the-spot description would read no more chillingly than those three brief lines.

I chose to write *Whiskey River*, the first book in the Detroit Series, from the first-person point of view of Connie Minor, a tabloid journalist of the Prohibition era. The hands-on, I'm-the-hero reportage of the days of armor-plated Cadillacs and bootleg hootch was tailormade for this highly personal story of violence, romance, and betrayal.

2. **Omniscient.** This one has passed nearly beyond the pale. George Eliot and other writers of the Victorian epoch wrote like God, gazing down upon and into entire casts of characters, so that every line carried total insight into the motive and behavior of each player. It's a difficult technique, requiring an even hand and absolute balance, like a teamster driving a twelve-horse rig. I used it in my first novel, and have never gone back to it. I was twenty-three and ignorant of my limitations.

What's often called omniscience today—alternating perspectives between scenes, chapters, or designated parts of the book—is a considerably diminished version of the original definition, and will be dealt with later in this chapter. True omniscience forces the reader to skip about among the innermost thoughts of several characters in a scene, and sometimes within a single paragraph. Mystery is a casualty, since the reader is privy to everything. This, more than just the enormity of the challenge, may explain why true omniscience is almost extinct from literature. Few are willing to risk writing anything as arid as *Silas Marner*.

Larry McMurtry is an exception. Consider this passage from *Lonesome Dove*:

> *"Call, if you want better food you have to start by shooting Bolivar," Augustus said, reminded of his own grievance against the cook. ...*
>
> *Bolivar stirred his sugary coffee and held his peace. He whacked the dinner bell because he liked the sound, not because he wanted anybody to come and eat. ...*
>
> *Newt laughed. Bol never had been able to get the war straight, but he had been genuinely sorry when it ended. ...*
>
> *Pea Eye got interested for a minute. The beans and sowbelly had revived him. ...*

There you have four separate points of view on one page selected at random, without a single break to warn us a shift is coming. (The ellipses are mine.) As a result, the transitions are invisible. I'd lay odds that among the hundreds of thousands of readers who made the book an international bestseller, not one in ten could have told you that the story was told by all of its characters.

Omniscience enables McMurtry to distill thousands of pages of frontier culture and history into *Lonesome Dove*'s brisk 843. At one point he shelves his entire cast and replaces it with another, cutting in and out of consciousnesses as easily as a veteran trucker changing gears on a downgrade. Through this device he manages to encompass a theme as vast as the Great American Desert.

3. **Third-Person Objective.** This most restricting perspective of all calls for the novelist to surrender his greatest advantage: the ability to get inside characters' heads. Deprived of his mind-reading tools, he can define character only through action. Screenwriters who prefer to avoid the hackneyed gimmick of voiceover narration are compelled by the limitations of their visual medium to work inside a straitjacket. When Christopher Walken enters and kicks a dog, audiences know he's a villain. When Mel Gibson clambers up a tree to rescue a kitten, they know he's the good guy. Nothing that either actor does from then on can conflict with that first impression, because there's no mechanism to explain it. The technique hasn't changed since the days of the silent cinema, and it's why there are no complex characters on the screen.

Compare this one-trick pony with the string that awaits the novelist: interior monologue, stream-of-consciousness, back-telling; *plus* dialogue and action. Why anyone would willingly sacrifice the first three is a mystery, and yet a depressing number of writers, with their sights fixed on a quick Hollywood sale, approach the narrative art as if they're writing a movie script. Their characters jerk across the page like stick figures in a flip-book, pulling smiley-faces when they're happy and frowny-faces when they're sad. If the neighborhood multiplex is your only goal, stop pestering editors and engineer an introduction to Steven Spielberg. Otherwise, let whoever adapts your story to the screen be the one who carves the guts out of it. It's his job.

Dashiell Hammett threw a nasty punch when he told *The Maltese Falcon* completely from outside the skull of Sam Spade. His readers were kept guessing as to Spade's motives and character until the final scene. But it only worked once. Spade appeared in three more stories, but once we knew what made him tick, he was just another mug in a hat.

4. **Third-Person Subjective.** This is the most frequently used point of view in fiction. It invites us to conspire with the protagonist while denying us the intimacy of the personal pronoun. "This far you may go," he seems to say, "and no further." Not for him the navel-

gazing egocentricity of first-person; its confessional quality repels him. By these lights, before knowing anything of his past or present, we form an unconscious first impression based solely on the method his creator has chosen to present him. It offers the opportunity to comment from outside the character's immediate experience. Seemingly less self-involved than first-person, third subjective paints the world in his colors, but with the brush of a disinterested observer. Edith Wharton, writing in *The Age of Innocence*, introduced both old New York and her flesh-and-blood protagonist in one jaded paragraph:

> When Newland Archer opened the door at the back of the club box the curtain had just gone up on the garden scene. There was no reason why the young man should not have come earlier, for he had dined at seven, alone with his mother and sister, and had lingered afterward over a cigar in the Gothic library with glazed black-walnut bookcases and filial-topped chairs which was the only room in the house where Mrs. Archer allowed smoking. But, in the first place, New York was a metropolis, and perfectly aware that in metropolises it was "not the thing" to arrive early at the opera; and what was or was not "the thing" played a part as important in Newland Archer's New York as the inscrutable totem terrors that had ruled the destinies of his forefathers thousands of years ago.

Substitute "I" for "Newland Archer," and you will see why this passage is appropriate only in third-person.

For Doc Miller, the ex-convict baseball pitcher in *King of the Corner*, the third book in the Detroit Series, I used third subjective for reasons similar to Wharton's. I wanted to create a character who could pass judgment upon his city without sermonizing. This approach was as right for Detroit in grim 1990 as Connie Minors first-person cant was for the Jazz Age Detroit of sixty years earlier.

5. **Shotgun.** A term I coined, symbolizing the scattershot pattern of a story told by several characters, each in his own assigned section. It's as close as most modern writing ever comes to classic

omniscient, yet it preserves mystery through the limited perceptions of the narrator *pro tem*. Anyone can play, including subjective and objective third-person, and the writer has the giddy privilege of being able to drop one perspective the minute it begins to pall and take up another. Had enough of Fred and his sweaty apartment? Cut to Ginger at the regatta. It's like having your own teleportation device.

The effect can be stately, with each character stepping up to the podium at measured intervals, or frantic, with many voices clamoring for scenes and fragments, some long and rambling, others short and explosive; change-up pitches, Doc Miller might call them. Stephen King, who has dismissed his horror novels as "fast food for the mind," often maintains his shock level by serving up a family fun meal of terrified viewpoints.

Shotgun—or semiomniscient, if you prefer—offers the best opportunity for suspense. The reader is witness to one character's nefarious plan, while the other character has no clue that he's about to be the victim.

When it came time for the Detroit Series to visit the 1960s—the years of race riots, drug happenings, and political unrest—I never considered any point of view but shotgun. The psychedelic effect of a story told through the observations of a black numbers boss, an Italian-American mobster, a white busted cop obsessed with muscle cars and speed, and a couple of dozen satellites captured the balloonlike dream quality of a Peter Max poster, the Beatles' *Yellow Submarine*, and an acid trip.

This perspective can support multiple first-person (one narrator per section) and mixing first with third. Make sure you identify each point of view clearly, to avoid confusion. It's a kind of controlled anarchy, and you may be surprised by how quickly it piles up pages without taking on fat.

As with most other aspects of genre fiction, rules and expectations regarding points of view have become greatly relaxed in recent years. The first-person detective story became so closely associated with the hardboiled mystery that the technique has been parodied in comic strips and television commercials ("She walked into my office on the longest legs this side of the home stretch at Santa Anita"). When it bordered on cliché, writers such as Joseph Wambaugh and Lawrence Sanders fled to shotgun and third-person subjective just to avoid being lumped in with Raymond Chandler's many imitators.

Conversely, when I published my first Page Murdock Western, employing Murdock's first-person narration, I got quite a bit of attention from reviewers more accustomed to the third-person perspective common to Louis L'Amour, Luke Short, Frank O'Rourke, and many other highly visible contributors to that genre. Neither Wambaugh nor Sanders nor I were the first to depart from the tried-and-true, but whenever a writer swims against the prevailing current, he or she is bound to draw attention.

Horror and science fiction have always been open to experimentation, and perspective has never been a consideration at the publishing level. The enduring classics, *Frankenstein* (first person), *Dracula* (multiple first- and third-person), and *The Strange Case of Dr. Jekyll and Mr. Hyde* (third, with a foray into first at the end) established the spread more than a century ago.

My own departures from the norms haven't stopped me from writing the Amos Walker detective novels in first-person, or using all the other perspectives for other Westerns. That's the point. The shackles are shattered, and point-of-view is no longer the publisher's decision. Although category romances are an exception, bound to the restrictions of the various lines (see chapter two), there are so many that a study of the market will tell you which is best suited to the choice you've made.

There is no formula for calculating what perspective is best for a particular book. However, it's useful to bear point-of-view in mind when the story you're writing doesn't seem to be working. Many years ago, having failed to place a first-person Western, I decided to rewrite it from scratch, only to learn that what I knew to be a good story no longer excited me. Rather than accept the suspicion that I'd burned out on it, I threw away the first fifty pages of the new version and tried rewriting them from third-person subjective. I flamed through those first fifty pages in a fraction of my earlier time and went straight through to the end, making changes and improvements in characters and plot that had never occurred to me the first time through. The book sold to the next publisher I sent it to, and has been reprinted many times since. When in doubt, try standing in another place. Then pick up your lever and fulcrum and move the world.

* * *

Fiction Fact

Mickey Spillane—author, at one time, of seven of the ten best-selling novels in history—said: "Your first line sells the book. Your last line sells the next book."

* * *

9

How to Ignore an Outline

* * *

BACK IN THE BEGINNING of recorded history, when I was trying to sell my first book, I followed some good advice explained
poorly.

It directed me to submit three chapters and an outline to publishers. Not knowing I was expected to send chapters one through
three, I selected my three best; nine, seventeen, and twenty-two.
Then I drafted an outline the way I'd been taught in school, with
headings set off by Roman numerals, alphabetized subheadings, and
bullet points subdivided under Arabic numerals.

None of the articles I'd read in writers' magazines had bothered
to point out that the outline was merely a plot summary, running no
longer than three or four pages and unencumbered by devices either
alphabetical or numerical. I won't embarrass myself further by saying
just how many sales that omission may have cost me. You can tell I'm
still testy.

But incomplete as it was, the outline advice was sound, and not just as an assist to editors struggling to sort through the slushpile. It's important to know the purpose of an outline so you can decide when to dispense with it.

Regardless of their age or wisdom, beginning writers are like kindergartners. They need to be taught structure and discipline, or they'll fidget and lose interest in class. Book production is a serious investment of time—months or years. Depend upon it, the time will come when all those sparkling ideas you started out with will sputter and die. They'll catch fire again, but until they do, it's a comfort and your salvation to know where you're going so you can trudge through the ashes. Trust me on this; you'll thank me later.

An outline keeps you on course. A novel is an odyssey, and peripheral characters and their stories are the sirens waiting to lure you into the backwater. Some lingering is acceptable, even recommended; it enriches your tale and adds flesh to its bones. But if fast-paced suspense is your aim, the outline is your compass, your chart, and your ship's bell. Heed it and move on. Otherwise you're marooned.

Unlike the outline you submit to publishers, the one you use for your writing can be long or short, elaborate or simple. It's your call. Some writers prefer a detailed outline, with complete biographies of all the major characters arid a step-by-step plot guide from beginning to end, including subplots and secondary climaxes. Some others are notoriously cavalier about preliminary work, and plunge right in with nothing but a basic concept and a few scribbled notes. In between these extremes are those short-order chefs who whip up satisfying literary meals out of one-line recipes jotted on envelopes or matchbooks, with characters designated A, B, C, and D.

Harry Whittington, a popular suspense novelist of the 1950s, went on record in 1986 in defense of thorough outlining:

> *… Several stellar performer-writers have averred on TV and other public dais that they start to write with no idea where they're going, or how their tale will resolve itself. …*
>
> *Despite the protestations of these best-selling writers, I personally find this lack of planning wasteful, unprofessional, and worst,*

even amateurish. Sometimes, I realize it's said to sound artistic. Still, it's much like setting out in a billion-dollar shuttle for outer space with no flight plan.

By Whittington's standards, Elmore Leonard is a bush pilot. In *Elmore Leonard*, biographer David Geherin reports:

Leonard likes unpredictable characters; an unplotted story affords him a greater opportunity to take advantage of such characters. Also, not plotting his books in advance ensures that the action will be natural and unforced. In many instances, Leonard doesn't know what will happen more than a scene or two ahead. Usually he doesn't even know how his novel will end until he is almost finished writing it. ... He figures that if he's curious about what will happen next, the reader will be too. What is surprising to him will then likely also be surprising to the reader.

But even Whittington might look askance—and Leonard with curiosity—at James Ellroy, author of *L.A. Confidential*, who's been known to write outlines as long as 150 pages before writing chapter one. They help him keep track of his huge casts and multitrack storytelling.

I've heard of one writer who won't commit to a book until he's written three hundred pages of preliminary material. I find this excessive, and borderline obsessive-compulsive; in his place I'd be tempted to submit the outline and call it a book.

I should point out that Leonard's anarchic working method belongs to a professional who's been writing more than fifty years. The memory of long experience assures him that when he encounters a slack spot, he'll find a way to pull it taut. The contractor who's built a hundred houses may be excused for building the hundred-and-first without a blueprint. (Building inspectors may disagree.)

A good working outline should contain the names of the main characters, with enough background on each to keep the cast straight, and a linear synopsis of the plot from the situation to the resolution. Ten pages should see you through the doldrums and prevent wanderlust. You may be more comfortable with twice that many, or content with half. Just make sure you have enough so you know your story, and avoid making a career of getting the outline Just Right; at some point, that becomes just an excuse to avoid writing the book, and you've got plenty of those without looking for more.

I was an inveterate outliner in my early days, and although in recent years my *modus operandi* has come to resemble Elmore Leonard's more than Harry Whittington's, I find the outlining process a godsend when approaching a complicated project.

When preparing to write *Sherlock Holmes vs. Dracula*, I read Bram Stoker's *Dracula*, outlined that book's major events, and wrote ten pages of my own in which I threaded my plotline through the gaps in Stoker's narrative. Since there were long lapses during which his intrepid vampire hunters were unaware of what the undead Count was up to, I supplied the details from my imagination, attributing them to the detective work of Holmes and Dr. Watson, his biographer and boon companion. Doing the first outline enabled me to write the second, and kept me from straying too far from Stoker's original vision while preventing me from simply retelling the story he'd already told. I used the same method when—with full credit to Robert Louis Stevenson—I incorporated the basic elements of *Treasure Island* into *Sudden County*, a tale of fortune-seeking in the Old West. The aim of both these books was to pay tribute to these two great writers (three, including Sir Arthur Conan Doyle, creator of Holmes and Watson) while exploring new themes. But my groundwork was never so painstaking as when I got ready to write *Bloody Season*; about which more in the next chapter.

The danger of becoming too deeply enmeshed in detail at this early stage is you may spend all your imagination on something no one but you will see. Inspiration and improvisation are conjoined twins, each dependent upon the other. By the time you've finished an exhaustive outline, you may feel as if your work is done, and find you have nothing left to bring to the book. You must, as Hemingway said, "leave something in the well," or find it bone-dry when you most need to draw from it. Some great actors have reputations for delivering listless readings during rehearsal, and brilliant, exquisitely nuanced performances when the cameras turn or the curtain goes up on opening night. They're called "money players"—an inspirational phrase if ever there was one. Save something for the audience.

Bear in mind that an outline is a useful tool, not a sacred text. No matter how much thought you put into them before you begin writing, you will never know your characters so well as when they take shape on the narrative page. Once a character touches down, he assumes a life of his own and won't always behave as his creator originally intended. When this happens, trust his instincts. Let him dictate his own actions, even if they run counter to your grand plan. Your people aren't marionettes. When you try to jerk them into line, they'll either sit down and refuse to budge or turn into bloodless zombies, going through motions that will become increasingly grotesque. As a reader, I lose interest in books written by "plot-driven" authors when, as a writer, I realize that some not-so-unseen hand has been busy separating star-crossed lovers, and resuscitating inconvenient corpses. When that happens, I lay the book aside and turn to one written by someone whom Harry Whittington would no doubt dismiss as "wasteful" and "unprofessional"; in short, a writer whose characters, like Elmore Leonard's, convince me they're real, even at the expense of an untidy plot. Some of the world's greatest literature has holes in its reasoning big enough for a Loch Ness Monster to swim through without brushing the sides. Meanwhile, some of the most clever, clockwork-action stories are long forgotten because the characters don't ring true.

So. Has your outline become a waste of time? Only if you put too much into it, without allowing for the occasional digression. Has your job become a little harder? Probably. But if you place your faith in your people, chances are they'll return the favor by doing something unexpected and wonderful. Once, during a firefight in *Gun Man*, the wrong sheriff's deputy died, leaving me with the idiot who swept out the jail cells, just when my city marshal needed someone intelligent and dependable. Yet the idiot came through, hoisting his own self-esteem and providing a pleasant surprise for both the author and his readers. Fortunately, I'd learned from experience that when a character meets an untimely end, no amount of work on the part of his creator will revive him.

When the book is finished, more or less according to the outline you drew up for your own guidance, the time has come to draw up another to show publishers. Don't groan; this is the easy part, especially if you get to it while your memory is still fresh. Editors are busy people, and have neither the time nor the patience to read through a synopsis as long as the one you wrote for yourself. (Anyone would rather watch a long, boring movie than sit still for a scene-by-scene replay of an exciting one furnished by a friend fresh from the theater.) Keep it short—three or four pages are ideal—and sketch out the story from start to finish, to show you can plot. Spare the details for the manuscript. The editor will see those intricacies in the three sample chapters you provide with the outline. Include a very brief cover letter, for no other reason than that it's more polite than sending the material cold. In it, list any publishing or writing contest credits you've earned, if any. If not, introduce yourself briefly, include the title of the book and one or two lines about what it's about (your outline will fill in the blanks), mention that you've finished the book, and close.

Finishing the book first is important. Once you've established yourself, you'll be able to arrange new contracts on the basis of outlines alone, but as an unknown and untried writer, you'll face an obstacle in trying to convince the editor you're capable of writing a publishable book, regardless of the promise showed by the early chapters. Remember, it's his neck if he sticks it out and you don't come through. If he's intrigued by what you've sent, he'll ask to see the rest. The first three chapters, an outline, and a professional cover letter are now the industry standard for all submissions. Do I need to add that neatness counts? Thought not.

Mastering the art of the outline will teach you discipline and give you confidence. Learning to ignore it will teach you humility. Maturity—in art as in life—occurs somewhere in between.

* * *

Fiction Fact

Fans of recycling must appreciate John Creasey, who wrote his first published novel on the back of 743 rejection letters.

* * *

Wyatt Earp and Me

* * *

HISTORY IS A SLIPPERY SLOPE. If you think historical figures automatically make believable fictional characters, you're deluded. If you can't conceive of any circumstances under which you'd ever use a real person in your fiction, stick around anyway. There's something in this chapter for the insecure artist in everyone.

Using real people in fiction exposes the basic conflict between literature and life. In fiction, characters must be consistent. In life, people rarely are.

Mark Twain said it best: "Of *course* truth is stranger than fiction. Fiction has to make sense."

Back in chapter one, I said that fiction is an oasis of order and reason in a desert of chaos. We accept inconsistencies in our friends' personalities because we know they're imperfect creatures like us, making things up as we go along. One of the ways we cope with this situation is to escape into a world where everything happens for a purpose and everyone behaves according to plan. When you, the creator of that fictional paradise, transpose one of the contrary inhabitants of the real world into it, the collision can be heard in outer space.

If a campaign were launched to cure the *angst* of the historical novelist, Wyatt Earp would be its poster boy. Had I realized that when I began researching *Bloody Season*, I might have given the project a pass, and missed a painful but important growing experience.

For nearly a century, this legendary lawman and gunfighter was celebrated in print and on screen as a paragon of justice, single-handedly bringing civilization to Dodge City and Tombstone by virtue of his pure vision and fast draw. Then the revisionists came along, excavating evidence of Earp's less admirable qualities and casting him as the villain in the drama that was the Old West.

Both characterizations are true. But each is only half the truth. In order to draw a three-dimensional picture of the man, I had to find the link between his two disparate sides.

Consider the problems:

FACT: Earp's strength of character won him the lifelong friendship of such polar opposites as John Clum, the upstanding mayor of Tombstone, Arizona, and Doc Holliday, the disgraced dentist and homicidal gunfighter.

FACT: Earp was arrested as a horse thief in Kansas in 1871.

FACT: Knowing that more bloodshed in Tombstone in 1881 would get him kicked out of town, forfeiting all his business investments, Earp placed duty before personal interest and answered the challenge to disarm a group of rowdy cowboys near the O.K. Corral.

FACT: In 1882, Earp deserted his second wife for Josephine.

FACT: Earp remained faithful to Josephine, his third wife, for forty years until his death in 1929.

FACT: In 1911, at the age of sixty-three, Earp was arrested in Los Angeles for vagrancy and trying to fleece a tourist out of $25,000 in a confidence game.

Three of the above facts establish Wyatt Earp as a man of loyalty, courage, and integrity. The other three make him out to be a scoundrel. None of the memoirs written by his friends or enemies explained the connection, nor did any of his many biographers, pro or con, serious historian or shameless maker of myths.

Finally, it was Wyatt Earp himself who gave me what I needed to make him live on the page.

But before I explain, come back with me to the fall and winter of 1985–86, and share the experience of writing *Bloody Season*. Following are excerpts from the journal I kept at that time:

October 31: *Bloody Season* started. Three pages. I'd hoped for five, but my First Day Ritual after 22 books is getting nearly as elaborate as a Zulu wedding and there were a few interruptions. Mainly, however, it was the writing itself. The description is as intensive as in the *This Old Bill* prologues. I hope I can sustain it. ...

November 5: Eighteen pages done, chapter one in and I've disposed of the gun battle. The details are frustrating. I move ahead a piece of a paragraph at a time and then have to stop and consult the books to see which calf Virgil took Billy Clanton's bullet in, etc. Finished the chapter yesterday but spent what little time I had to work on it today tightening the nuts and bolts. But I think it the best chapter I ever wrote—dramatic, sensual, as accurate as can be managed at this late date. ...

Tonight I hit the books again and lay some track. Funny how the more I research the more I want to know. My college instructors would be proud; the ones who haven't thrown themselves off the Golden Gate Bridge, anyhow.

November 10: Thirty-five pages. Long session, till past five-thirty, and I was back up at nine and then eleven, retyping pages to change a certain word to just the right one. Tinkering.

Research is a pain. I check one reference to fix a name or a date and then three pages and several hours later I consult another for something else and then the original name or date was wrong. Then I have to check a third reference to confirm it. Like asking directions of three different people and getting three entirely different answers.

November 23: Back at it after a short trip north. Shortly after stepping back into the traces, I learned that I'd screwed up and had the coroner's inquest and Clanton/McLaury funeral out of order. Which meant redoing the last thirty pages to realign my dramatic pauses. No great tragedy—something like this happens every book—but it's a day lost. …

November 25: Fifty-nine pages, four chapters, Part One finished. Hitting my stride now, and the balance is settling. It's going to be a good book.

December 3: Seventy-seven. Two steps forward, one back. Had to recast much of yesterday's eight pages in order to write Buckskin Frank Leslie out of the wrong part of the Benson stage hold-up posse. …

December 8: Eighty-five. I think I've discovered the key to Wyatt Earp's character, the common denominator linking all of his personalities—gunman, entrepreneur, politician, killer, lawman, and philanderer. He approached everything from the point of view of a gambler. He went with the odds, played the cards as dealt, and sometimes drew to an inside straight, with mixed results. Knowing that eliminates the need to explain him. It may be the most important find in the book.

(**To the Reader:** *The above was a step in the right direction, but on the wrong foot. Many pages and one whole draft later, I would have to return to that point and start again.*)

December 21: At 120, eight chapters in. Plenty of historical embroidering going on, but nothing that could not happen and a great deal that probably did but escaped recording.

Kate Fisher's character is coming along nicely and more sympathetically than expected. … Doc himself, woman-beater and largely amoral character that he was, may emerge as the book's one bona fide hero. He alone had nothing to gain from goading Ike Clanton and taking part in the corral fight. The acts represent a brand of loyalty that exists today only in crime and warfare. I hope I can show this without cleaning him up in other ways. The refusal of real people to remain consistent has to be the reason most writers avoid historical fiction.

February 6: At 242. Finished chapter sixteen, the first of Part Four. Another bleak spot, nearing the end of Part Three, behind me. Into Wyatt's revenge now, and the old spin is back on the ball.

In the final draft I may prune and consolidate some of the minor characters. Since there are no fictional characters in the book, this means monkeying with history; but I can't afford a confusing muddle of one-scene walk-ons. …

February 28: First draft finished. And miles to go.

Came to 303. The final will need the usual polish plus some more depth (background?) on such characters as Allie Earp and possibly a prologue flashing forward to Wyatt and Virgil's investigation of Warren's death in 1900.

But at this point I'm happy with what I was able to bring out this time through, particularly in the final three chapters.

Averaged 75 pages per month. That's of no importance to posterity, but steady work is a fetish. …

March 14: 80. Problem with Wyatt's character continues.

His brutal side comes through but no other, and there is not much use in a book about the O.K. Corral without a living, breathing Wyatt. Still, it's early. ...

April 3: 331—Finished.

Wyatt Earp came through stronger in the final draft. I got that with a few touches—a line of dialogue here, a lingering close-up there. One bit of business, describing his strong jowls being the last to fade into darkness during the freight-car ride from Tucson to Contention, was worth nearly as much as the whole long chapter about Big-Nose Kate. I didn't soften him or make him more of a bastard; I just made him breathe.

Morgan fared better too, and his death scene is more poignant for a couple of added lines of dialogue at the end. Such scenes are always trouble because I'm desperate to avoid maudlin clichés and tend to leave too much out first time through.

I think it's a hell of a book. I also think I'm capable of better. This ends the *Bloody Season* journal.

In addition to highlighting a few of the many patches of quicksand that await writers of historical fiction, these selected passages hint at the amount of self-flagellation that even a veteran writer undergoes in the course of hammering an entertaining narrative out of a scrap heap of cold inflexible facts. At that, it deals with only the writing. Since I didn't keep a journal during the many months of research, I must reconstruct them from memory.

Armed with pencils, notebooks, and a personal copier, I culled information from a twelve-foot shelf of memoirs, biographies, and general histories relating to my subject; fattened a file folder with maps of Cochise County and the City of Tombstone in 1881; jotted down character notes on the Earp brothers and Doc Holliday, their wives and sweethearts, and the rest of the central and satellite figures whose actions led to the notorious gunfight and whose lives were affected by it; typed ten pages in which I choreographed all the separate movements in the fight itself; and drew charts recording the locations of all the players before, during, and after the event. Then I flew to Tombstone, where I walked in all their footsteps, carefully ignoring the historical markers that my research had shown to be spurious, purchased additional reliable published material in the museums and gift shops, and interviewed respected historians residing in the area. Back home in my study, I commandeered every available workspace, including the floor, to spread out my information, moving the pieces around like parts of a jigsaw puzzle—all to bring order to the details and ramifications of a bloody gun battle that began and ended in less than a minute, more than one hundred years before; and all of it useless until I could figure out the enigma that was Wyatt Earp.

And then he went and told me himself.

I was close back on December 8, when I stopped thinking of him in the separate terms of the many faces he showed to the world—lawman, outlaw, staunch friend, swindler—and rolled them all into the definition of a gambler; which he was everywhere he went, dealing faro in saloons from Wichita to the Yukon during the Alaskan Gold Rush. But even that was unsatisfactory. Why would a gambler swear to enforce the law?

However, I was convinced I was making progress. I reread all the interviews that Earp granted to the press during his long life (he died at the age of seventy in 1929). I noticed the same phrase coming up again and again: "I'm a businessman."

At last it sank in. In the parlance of Gilded Age America, the term *successful businessman* applied to J. Pierpont Morgan, E.H. Harriman, James Fisk, and Jay Gould; robber barons who built financial empires on such sharp practices as annihilating the competition, cheating on their partners, and bribing elected officials. Wyatt Earp saw himself as one of them, went to the places where money was being made—cattle towns and mining camps—sewed up the local gambling interests, and invested his profits in mineral rights and real estate. But these were wild places, with brigands waiting around every corner to stick up the would-be entrepreneur and rob him of his capital. To curb this type of activity, the various town councils drafted ordinances prohibiting citizens from carrying firearms inside the city limits. Failure to comply meant a stiff fine, a jail sentence, or both.

The solution? Wyatt Earp became a lawman so he could wear a firearm so he could protect his business interests. He would curry favor with popular politicians (John Clum) and ruthless gunmen (Doc Holliday), and with their support would move swiftly to crush any threat to his authority (the Clanton and McLaury brothers at the O.K. Corral). To a robber-baron wannabe, such things as thievery and callous disregard for the sanctity of marriage were hardly obstacles to success. (Josephine, the wife to whom he would prove faithful, belonged to a wealthy family—a never-ending source of venture capital.) That he still managed to fail spectacularly and die in a rented bungalow in southern California is delicious irony for any writer.

If all this sounds like *The Sopranos*—which at the time of writing was not part of the American cultural scene—it says a great deal about recurring cycles in history. No matter how remote the period, the forces that shaped it still exist. But who'd have guessed Tony Soprano wore a cowboy hat?

I've included these pages from my journal to demonstrate that writing a book is always an uphill climb in the dark, whether you're making the journey for the first time or the twenty-fifth. A bit about some of the references:

On October 31, the first day of writing, I made self-deprecating mention of my "First Day Ritual," which ranges from perfunctory to elaborate in direct ratio to the size of the project and its challenge. Nothing about it is unique to me, or for that matter very interesting, except perhaps to other writers: sharpening pencils, shoveling clutter off the desk, cleaning my typewriter keys with lighter fluid and a toothbrush, threading in a crisp new ribbon, wiping inky fingerprints from the surface. It's like warming up for a workout; mindless, repetitive exercises selected to clear my head and loosen my joints. No matter where I am, the smell of lighter fluid and ground cedar sets my imagination aflame. The business awakens most of my senses and stokes my creative furnace.

However, there's always the danger of prolonging the five-finger exercise just to put off getting to work. In the beginning, when I was attending school and later working a job, I hadn't the time for this luxury; when I found myself with fifteen minutes or an hour free, I leapt right in, and hang the gloppy keys and tattered ribbon. If you're still vamping twenty minutes after you started, that's time you'll never get back.

On November 23, I complained about having to realign my dramatic pauses. I'm a great fan of white-space, which when used effectively can pack as much wallop as your strongest prose. In the interest of pace, I will often spread a scene over two or more chapters, with breaks nearer the middle than the end. I dislike books whose chapters always end with a jerk and start with a gasp; it's monotonous, and as unpleasant as riding with a driver who doesn't know how to work a clutch. My way lets me spring surprises where the reader may least expect them, and whisper my poignancies rather than scream them at the top of my lungs.

Here as an example from *Bloody Season*, ending the scene in which Wyatt Earp's brother Morgan is mortally wounded, and beginning the next, with loyal Doc Holliday's quest for vengeance:

> *"Put my legs straight."*
>
> *"They are straight, Morg," said Wyatt.*
>
> *"They're my legs, damn it."*
>
> *Wyatt adjusted them.*
>
> *"Is Bob here?" Hatch spoke up.*
>
> *Morgan smiled, "This is the last game of pool I'll ever play in here."*
>
> *"Damn it, Morg," said Wyatt.*
>
> *"Tell Ma and Pa. I don't want them getting it in the papers."*
>
> *"They won't."*
>
> *Matthews was unbuttoning Morgan's shirt. He motioned him away with a feeble gesture. "Wyatt."*
>
> *Wyatt bent over him.*
>
> *"You were right, Wyatt," he said. "I can't see a thing."*

The latch split on the second blow and the door whacked the wall on the other side, throwing crooked a framed Stephensgraph of the Blessed Mother and sucking dust balls out of corners in the current. The nickel-plated Colt's Lightning hurtled into the room towing Doc behind it. He towered there in his tall-crowned hat, the tails of his greatcoat spreading behind him like buzzard's wings.

"Where is he?"

Think of these breaks as a sudden pause in a lively conversation. Mark Twain, who understood the power of both blank spaces and silence, once opened a public appearance by standing stock-still on stage without opening his mouth for five minutes, a staggering example of self-control. The humorist drew the biggest laugh of his career for this stunt. Use it sparingly in your writing lest it become a tic; but the next time the rabbit jumps out of the hat before you're ready to drop the curtain, try standing still for the applause.

On December 21, I alluded to "historical embroidering." This is unavoidable in historical fiction, since a great deal of history is based on speculati rather than eyewitness testimonyny, and you want to fill out your tapestry rather than just document facts. Very little dialogue appears in biographies and books of history, because even those who were present remembered the gist of crucial conversations more than the actual words and phrases used. The historical novelist brings these events to life by reconstructing the conversations based on journals, letters, and interviews that demonstrate the participants' language and speech patterns. When Ike Clanton corners Wyatt Earp at the Alhambra saloon in *Bloody Season*, the dialogue proceeds as follows:

"Feeling lucky today?" Wyatt restacked the chips Ike had spilled and slid the card counters into position. He had his coat off and red silk garters on his sleeves.

"I looked for you in the Oriental."

"That place is commencing to take on a bad reputation."

"It has one less skunk in it today."

Wyatt went on straightening the stack. "You are drunker than you look to say that to me."

History records that Ike and Wyatt "had words" that day in the Alhambra, which helped lead to the infamous gunfight; it doesn't accommodate us with a verbatim account of their conversation. For that, I drew from snatches of Ike Clanton's trash-talk recounted on other occasions and Wyatt Earp's own measured, better-educated speech as it appeared in the many interviews he gave afterward on various subjects. I'm satisfied that if their encounter did not go precisely as I've written (it would be spooky if it had), it is not the way it could *not* have gone. This is an area closed to the historian, but it is the stuff and substance of historical fiction. No one knows, for instance, if Wyatt Earp was wearing red silk sleeve garters that day; but they were compatible with his sense of style as recalled by acquaintances and confirmed by photographs. To pull off this kind of embroidery, you need to borrow your thread from contemporary sources.

On February 6, I considered having to "prune and consolidate some of the minor characters." The events surrounding the O.K. Corral gunfight included a huge and varied cast, many of whom performed duplicate roles, and far too many of whom were named Billy, Bill, Frank, and John. (There were even two Stillwells: one a judge, the other a killer and stagecoach bandit.) In order to avoid complicating further an already complex story, I considered omitting some characters entirely and superimposing some others on top of one another to eliminate redundancy. However, as it happened, a number of these Billies and Franks did not share the same scenes, so I was able to make full use of most of them without confusing readers, although I jettisoned a few peripheral players and rolled Turkey Creek Jack Johnson and Texas Jack Vermillion, who played nearly identical roles in Wyatt's vendetta against Morgan's killers, into one character.

This is a fundamental difference between historical fiction and fiction in general. When you assemble a story from the imagination, you find the characters you need to tell the story. When you set out to write from history, you try to find functions for all the members of the original cast. One creates workers for jobs, the other jobs for workers. In the latter case, you can't always employ everyone without dragging down the plot. (Fortunately, historical figures don't belong to labor unions.)

The best place to make these decisions is in the outline, before the actual writing begins. But this particular episode in history posed so many complications, including multiple outlines (the actual story, my telling of it, individual scenes involving dozens of characters and their actions), I decided it served me better to get the entire story down on paper in the form of a rough draft and make the adjustments in the final.

On April 3, the last day of writing, I said, about Wyatt Earp, "I just made him breathe." I wasn't being overly modest. Once I'd solved his riddle, the rest of the evidence—his appearance, the way he spoke and handled himself in public, his likes and dislikes—was there waiting for me in the historical record. Those "strong jowls," visible in every photograph taken of him, spoke volumes about his steely self-confidence and ruthless determination. In the end, he was as consistent a character as you could hope to find in fiction, and a good deal more so than you're apt to come across in life.

The humane genome is intricate, and cannot be summed up in one sentence. But for the purpose of fiction, in order to understand the motives and behavior of a fascinating person, it's crucial to view him in the light of his own self-image. Had I known that going in, I might not have come quite so close to becoming another casualty of the gunfight at the O.K. Corral.

Fiction Fact

*"A Good Man Is Hard to Find,"
Flannery O'Connor's story ending in
the senseless slaughter of an entire
family, inspired a letter to the author
offering her the romantic services of
"a good man." O'Connor said she
doubted the man had read the story.*

* * *

Series and Standalones

* * *

TWO OF MY MOST ENDURING SERIES started out as one-shots. The hero of one of them wasn't even going to exist.

The other first.

More than twenty years ago, I put together a proposal for a novel to be called *.38/72* (later changed to *Kill Zone*), about a Mafia hit man, armed only with a .38-caliber revolver, who has just seventy-two hours to foil a plot by terrorists to commit mass murder. The book was intended to present a character study of the kind of man who kills people for a living; neither thrill-seeking sadist nor emotionless psychopath, he approaches his work as if it were any other job, at the end of which he goes home to his family and refuses to discuss his day at the office. Saddled with the same challenges and responsibilities as millions of other wage-earners, he begins and ends each day in a hell of his own making, and from which there is no escape. Nothing like it had ever been written, to my knowledge, and I had my agent send it around to publishers with keen anticipation.

A proposal differs from an outline in that it sets forth a premise, with some character details and major plot points, but does not necessarily include an ending. The intention is to pique an editor's curiosity—and at least in my case, prevent the writer from having to commit to a conclusion that may not suggest itself until the project is well under way. Generally speaking, proposals are taken seriously only when they're submitted by writers with a long list of publishing credits; guarantors they'll follow through.

An editor called. First of all, he didn't like the numerical title. I offered *Kill Zone* as a substitute. He liked that. Then he got to the crucial question: "Is your protagonist alive in the end?"

"I don't know yet," I said. "Why?"

"Well, if he's alive, we might want to turn it into a series."

"He is *so* alive," I replied.

That was the beginning of the Peter Macklin series. Because the character was only going to appear in one book, I'd burdened him with the kind of baggage writers seldom give action heroes: a wife, a child, a home in the suburbs. These features, normally considered enemies of fast pace, provided plots for the first three books in the series, as Macklin set out to complete his assignments, defend himself from his adversaries, *and* deal with such problems as a deteriorating marriage, a son who's begun to experiment with drugs, and the nosy neighbors next door. Once I'd resolved those situations, I shelved the series for fifteen years to prevent it from becoming just another "Executioner"-type bloodfest with body counts in double digits and numbers on the covers so readers can tell the books apart. After all that time, I asked myself, "What if Macklin takes a second wife who knows nothing of his past?" *Something Borrowed, Something Black* appeared in 2002, and 2005 will see *Little Black Dress*.

Page Murdock, the deputy U.S. marshal I've been writing about for twenty-five years, sprang up unexpectedly at the end of chapter one of *The High Rocks*, and has since appeared in seven books, most recently *Port Hazard* (2004). That first book was the story of a half-wild mountain man living in the Bitterroot Mountain Range of 1877 Montana Territory who's been waging a one-man war with the Flathead Indians for years. I'd written several pages of opening narration when it occurred to me that Bear Anderson was illiterate, and was therefore incapable of the vocabulary I was using to tell his story. However, the language seemed appropriate to the book, and in any case I couldn't see sustaining a shambling backwoodsy narration for three hundred pages. Annoying dialect had finally killed off the traditional Western, and would certainly destroy Anderson's legendary mystique. I continued on the course I'd started. At the end of the first fifteen pages, I found myself writing the following:

> ... By the fall of 1877 Thor Anderson's boy rivaled Wild Bill Hickok and Buffalo Bill Cody for reader interest in places where Indians were things unknown and a gun was something worn by a policeman.
>
> The interest was not confined to the East, however, and that's where I come in.

I don't expect you to believe me—I hardly credit it myself—but at the time I wrote that last sentence, I had no idea who *I* was.

Well, I had all the time in the world between the end of chapter one and the beginning of chapter two to answer the question, whereas if I'd hooked even a single reader, he had only a few seconds. I reasoned the speaker must be some sort of lawman, sent by an uneasy civilization to bring this vengeful primitive to justice; since a sprawling mountain range lies outside any city jurisdiction and crosses county lines, he would be neither a town marshal nor a county sheriff. U.S. marshals in those days were presidential appointees—desk jockeys, mostly—who appointed deputies to do their fieldwork. These deputies answered to both the marshal and the U.S. District Court, but since they could be dispatched anywhere within the territorial boundaries of the United States, they *were* the law in many places. I cranked in a new sheet and wrote:

> I had been sent out from the U.S. marshal's office in Helena to bring back a wife-murderer named Brainard who had been picked up on a drunk and disorderly charge in Staghorn, where the sheriff had identified him from his description on a wanted dodger. Now, it was a rule of Judge Harlan Blackthorne's court that each of his deputies check in

with the local peace officer immediately upon reaching his destination,
but it was a rule of my own not to let any rules hinder me. ...

Page Murdock was born, as iconoclastic at the starting gate as he still is more than half a million words later. His hard-won pragmatism, and his individual interpretation of justice, gave *The High Rocks* an edge that I was loath to abandon after that first outing.

In the interim, I've created two other series, including seventeen Amos Walker detective novels and the seven books in the Detroit series, and fifteen novels that stand alone, most of them in the field of the historical Western. As with most things, both kinds of books present challenges and advantages unique to them.

Publishers love series, for the same reason that Hollywood loves sequels. Once a character or a set of characters captures the appreciation of an audience, a brand name is established, with the promise of carrying the original audience to additional titles in the series while attracting new converts along the way. If the main character survives his or her first adventure, and the sales figures are encouraging, it's more than just a good bet he or she will have others. (Sometimes, even survival is unimportant: After my main character died at the end of a historical Western, an editor asked me if I'd consider turning it into a series. When I asked him if he'd read the ending, he said, "That's no problem. We can do prequels.")

The concept of brand-name identification is nothing new in publishing. In polls, more readers have said they recognize Sherlock Holmes than Sir Arthur Conan Doyle, his creator. Indeed, a cottage industry has been built around send-ups and pastiches involving the character of Holmes, written by others whose grandparents weren't born when Conan Doyle died in 1930. The same can be said of Raymond Chandler's Philip Marlowe, Clarence E. Mulford's Hopalong Cassidy, and the entire cast of Gene Roddenherry's *Star Trek*; and Mary Shelley and Bram Stoker would rise most appropriately from their graves if they suspected how many shelves groaned beneath the depredations of those one-shot characters Frankenstein and Dracula.

Publishers bought Nancy Drew and Tom Swift outright from their creators and have employed armies of writers to maintain their adolescent adventures into a second century. In fresh hands, Nick Carter traded his Edwardian bowler for the jet-pack of a Cold War secret agent; and have you seen what's become of Edgar Rice Burroughs' Tarzan? It's difficult to believe he was a hard sell in 1914. Businesspeople prefer to invest in products with a proven track record.

If you can agree to subvert your own ego and write under a company name, and your own name has not exactly opened doors, this is an opportunity to break into print. If this sounds like hackery, consider that Louis L'Amour supported himself early by writing Hopalong Cassidy novels under a house pseudonym, and Lawrence Block wrote some of the Nick Carters. Often, this has also been a venue for veteran writers whose careers have suffered because of the vicissitudes of the marketplace: A host of veterans whose paperback Westerns dominated drugstore racks throughout the 1930s as well as newcomers still searching for fame have contributed to the well-named Longarm series published since the early 1980s under the name Tabor Evans. Along with category romance, this market fills the void left by pulp magazines as a place to acquire on-the-job training.

Most house series come with a bible, containing important facts about the character you've inherited as well as about other regulars, recurring villains, etc., and dictating what is and is not considered acceptable behavior on their part. Don't be misled by the lower-case *b*: You should know it backward and forward, keep it handy at all times, and depart from it only at your risk. My closest brush with a bible came when I submitted a short story about Batman at the request of an editor who was assembling an anthology to be published in conjunction with the theatrical premiere of *Batman: The Movie* starring Michael Keaton and Jack Nicholson. I'd thought it might be fun to give Batman and Robin a bad case of the flu, forcing Alfred, their aged butler, to put on a cape, climb behind the wheel of the Batmobile, and answer the Bat-signal. The story, which I still think clever, was rejected by an official with the Batman franchise, who sniffed that nothing so inconsequential as a serious virus would prevent Batman from answering the call of duty. I learned then and there to respect the bible, and not to expect comic-book people to have a sense of humor.

Such things go with this territory, and if you're the kind of writer who bridles at being told what to do, contributing to a house series may not be for you; although God help the editor who suggests something that might improve a series of your creation.

Once you've established your own series, you'll find the process of starting a new book less frightening. As many novels as I've written, the prospect of writing a new one makes me as nervous as if I'd never done it before. It's like going to a party filled with strangers. But when the book is part of a series, it's as if one of the guests is an old friend, who will meet me at the door, put a drink in my hand, introduce me around, and spare me the embarrassment of breaking in on someone else's conversation. I need merely follow him around until I've found my bearings. When he's Amos Walker, whose sense of humor I share, along with his likes and dislikes, I take comfort in knowing we've both been here before.

One difficulty of series writing is having to introduce your character over and over. Most readers discover a series near the middle. They need salient facts—name, occupation, backstory, physical description—because each book must stand as an introduction to the series. The books should not have to be read in order just to make sense. *And* these things need to be told in such a way that readers who have been there from the beginning aren't bored by being fed the same information all over again.

Here are Amos Walker's vital statistics, as he presented them to his client in *Motor City Blue*, his first appearance:

> *"I'm thirty-two years old. I was raised in a little town you never heard of about forty miles west of here. I've a bachelor's degree in sociology; don't ask me why. I tried being a cop but that wasn't for me so I let myself get drafted. The army taught me how to kill things and sent me out to do it, but along the way someone found out what I'd done before and they made me an MP. I liked almost everything about it except the uniform, so when I got out I looked for a way to do the same thing without wearing one. I'm still looking."*

> "You dropped out of the twelve-week police training course after eleven weeks. Why?"

"Like I said, it wasn't for me."

"You can do better than that."

I shrugged. "Another trainee propositioned me in the shower room. I broke his jaw."

"That doesn't sound like something they'd bounce you for."

"The trainee was the nephew of a U.S. congressman."

This résumé appears in chapter three. As the series progressed, I found myself pushing the information farther and farther back—avoiding the issue, perhaps, but it seemed less and less important the better I got to know Walker. Establishing him as a private eye is a brief and painless process, and as most of the rest has to do with his personality, his comments and actions confirm that without having to spell it out. Since he's a first-person narrator, I was never greatly concerned with drawing a vivid physical picture of him, trusting the reader to assume he's tall, well-built, and reasonably good-looking, as a hero should be. He certainly isn't thirty-two any more; his background as a Vietnam vet is sure to cause problems in the physical-prowess department in a few years, so I only refer to it when it's germane to the story.

Without risking becoming lost in their world by checking, I tend to remember that the more often Dame Agatha Christie turned to Jane Marple to solve her mysteries, the less mention she made of her "china-blue eyes," and that Rex Stout's Nero Wolfe went from weighing "one-seventh of a ton" to just plain "fat." There comes a time (and I hope it does for you) when providing such details is as pointless as describing the Empire State Building or the Eiffel Tower; if people don't know what they look like by now, you're going to have to explain everything else as well. There aren't enough trees in Oregon for that.

All readers need to know about your character is what they need to know, and not before they need to know it. If your story is good, they'll be so caught up in wondering what will happen next they probably won't notice when you tell them something some of them already knew.

So how long do you stick with a series? As long as the paying public demands it, and as long as you want to; they go hand-in-hand. Conan Doyle and Nicolas Freeling got fed up with Sherlock Holmes and Inspector Van Der Valk, and killed them off. Conan Doyle relented and brought Holmes back from the dead, Freeling let Van Der Valk rest in peace. Eventually, readers grew weary of Holmes and his infernal infallibility, and his creator put him out to pasture. When you run out of alleys and asteroids to send your character, and the mere thought of suiting him or her up for yet another adventure thrills you as much as matching socks, you're doing no one a favor by going back to the hamper. Move on.

Series don't always revolve around a single character. In the Detroit series, I made the protagonist the City of Detroit, which passed through seven distinct incarnations in the course of the books: the turn of the twentieth century (*Thunder City*), the 1920s and '30s (*Whiskey River*), the '40s (*Jitterbug*), the '50s (*Edsel*), the '60s (*Motown*), the '70s (*Stress*), and the '90s (*King of the Corner*). Although some members of the human cast appeared in more than one book—as a child, say, in *Edsel*, and as an adult in *Stress*—and sharp-eyed readers might trace some family trees back to the beginning, no one character continued throughout the series. I drew my inspiration from Gore Vidal, whose series about American power politics (*Burr, Washington, D.C., Lincoln, Empire,* many others) began in the 1960s as a trilogy and forty years later shows no sign of ending, and from John Jakes, whose Kent Family Chronicles enjoyed enormous popularity at the time of the American bicentennial and brought new life to the faltering family saga. This approach weds the consistency of series fiction with the unpredictability of the stand-alone novel; readers embrace each new title as a reunion with an old friend, but they're never quite sure that the characters they're reading about won't die.

The family saga is currently out of favor, probably because it was overexposed during the 1960s and '70s. But it contains all the advantages mentioned above, and because one person cannot be expected to be in several places at once (or to happen to sit in the front row whenever the curtain goes up on history), its larger central cast allows the writer to bring great events front and center. There is no better example of this than Herman Wouk's massive two-volume chronicle of World War II, *The Winds of War* and *War and Remembrance*. Not since Tolstoy's *War and Peace* has another writer managed to encompass so grand a subject within the perceptions of a relatively small cast of regulars; the Henry family and Pug, its stalwart patriarch, have become part of American literary history. These books deliver the cardiac-threatening suspense of a Tom Clancy action novel with the depth of characterization one finds in Henry James. As long as these books remain in print—and they passed the million-sales mark long, long ago—the family saga will continue to reinvent itself every few years. (If you still need convincing, let me whisper one word in your ear: *Sackett.*

This is not to say that America's bookstores are walled floor-to-ceiling with blocks of volumes in matching format. The standalone book is alive and in roaring good health. It has served as a battering ram for talented writers to smash out of the ghetto of the four-figure advance into the vaulted lobby of the Millionaires' Club. Harlan Coben (*Tell No One*), Robert Crais (*Demolition Angel*), and Dennis Lehane (*Mystic River*) struggled for years writing good private-eye novels for a static readership with little promotion from their publishers until each tried his hand at a nonseries suspense novel. All three are now major players.

While a comfortable familiarity with the characters and situations is a prime factor in the popularity of series writing, uncertainty as to how the story will resolve itself is the foundation upon which stands the novel that stands alone. Any of the people the reader has come to know and care about during the first hundred pages may not make it through the third. Sue Grafton's Kinsey Milhone (*A is for Alibi, B is for Burglar, C is for Corpse*, etc.) will probably escape from that cement overcoat before her abductors toss her into the Pacific—there are several letters remaining in the alphabet, after all. We're not so sure about Joseph Wambaugh's messed-up cops. Fans who would resent killing off a beloved continuing character ("You brute!" one woman wrote Conan Doyle, after Holmes' apparent expiration) turn to a standalone with the thrill of risk. Many a career has been rescued from obscurity when a writer has left safe waters behind and sailed off the edge of the chart.

The benefits are spiritual as well as commercial. Many fans of Sara Paretsky's V.I. Warshawski did not read *Ghost Country*, in which that character did not appear (and missed a terrific read); its sales fell short of most of the books in her series. But when Warshawski returned in *Hard Time*, reviewers across the country called it the strongest entry yet, and sales went through the ceiling. It was clear that this brief break from routine had brought a fresh outlook and new energy to Paretsky's writing. (In chapter twenty-four, I'll discuss further the importance of climbing out of the rut.)

Whether you write series or standalones, the same rule applies about consistency of character; yet there must be growth. By the close of *Mystic River*, the relationship among three childhood friends is altered forever by the story's events, and each man has come away different. In a long-running series, the continuing characters should develop as well, although generally over a longer period of time. If the hero of Book Seven commits an act that would never have occurred to the hero of Book One, and they are one and the same, then he or she has been changed by experience. Much of the power of a standalone is that these experiences take place rapidly, and sear themselves into the senses. There must be change—growth is good, but so is diminishment, and just plain change is also revealing—but it must be seen to happen, because a sudden unexplained shift in personality is a cheat and a lie. And if there is no change, it makes for stale reading. The 1970s produced a number of multipart series involving spy heroes who kept blundering into traps and shooting their way out, only to blunder into other traps. They never seemed to learn, and the heroes themselves seemed to have been cut from the same piece of cardboard, with only the names changed so readers could tell one series from another, and numbered covers to prevent them from buying and reading the same book twice; as if that would make any difference. They burned out quickly, and none is in print today. And the ten-cents-a pound bin at your local used bookstore is rounded over with standalones whose characters were similarly unaffected by the twists and turns in plot.

It's flattering when an editor asks a writer to consider turning his or her book into a series, but that's the author's decision, and the author should be comfortable with it. Margaret Mitchell certainly never intended to follow the post-Reconstruction high jinks of Scarlett O'Hara and Rhett Butler into middle age (notwithstanding Alexandra Ripley's *Scarlett*, and its abominable advertising tagline: "He said he didn't give a damn; but he did!"), and nothing could dim the luster of J.D. Salinger' s *The Catcher in the Rye* more quickly than *The Return of Holden Caulfield*. Some stories need only be told once to resonate for generations. (I'm no Mitchell or Salinger, but I knew instinctively that a Peter Macklin series was a sound idea, and that that other editor's suggestion of writing "prequels" to one of my best Westerns was not.) On occasion, a publisher with your best interest at heart may urge you to "break out" with a "big book"—meaning, literally, a standalone measuring at least two inches across the spine—but although this is encouraging, don't rush into it unless you have an idea or two already in the hopper. Publishing is the only major industry in the country that rarely does market research (romances excepted); they have no idea what readers want, or even who buys the books they publish, and up until the rise of the chain bookstore with its banks of computers, they had only a vague idea of how many books they sold, after subtracting returns from the initial print runs. Don't look to them for career advice.

It's useless to assume there aren't snooty critics still lurking about who dismiss series out of hand as trashy. Undoubtedly there have been many series that fit that description, and we needn't offer them a measure of immortality they don't deserve by listing them here. But if the concept had never been invented, we would have no Waverly novels, no *Forsyte Saga*, no Harry Potters to introduce children to the wonders of reading. And even some that might be defined as trash are guilty pleasures I should hate to abandon: Give me a rainy evening any time, a comfortable chair, and a stack of Sax Rohmer's Fu Manchu thrillers on the floor next to it; that series has been in print continuously since 1913. On the other hand, I reread great stand-alones like *The Great Gatsby*, *The Age Innocence*, and *I Am Legend* every few years, and rediscover gems there I'd forgotten, and some are as new to me as the latest book in Richard Stark's (Donald Westlake) Parker series. If you manage to tilt any of those heights even once, you and your work will live forever.

* * *

Fiction Fact

Three American desperadoes have become nearly as famous for their contributions to literature as for armed robbery:

Stagecoach bandit Charles Boles, apprehended in California in 1883, left snatches of his own poetry in the freight boxes he emptied of their treasure, signed "Black Bart, the Po8."

Bonnie Parker, on the run from Texas Rangers and FBI agents in 1933, sent her poetry to newspapers, which published it.

Her partner, Clyde Barrow, preferred nonfiction. He wrote a letter to Henry Ford, praising the merits of the V-8 Ford as a getaway car. The letter is on display in the Henry Ford Museum in Dearborn, Michigan.

* * *

Talk Is Action

* * *

PICK UP ANY THREE NOVELS on this month's bestseller rack and you'll find they have one thing in common: The characters talk to each other.

A lot.

This wasn't the situation a hundred years ago, when reading was the only respectable form of home entertainment apart from the phonograph and the singalong in the parlor. When the Edwardians came home after twelve hours of work, they unwound by churning their way through dense columns of narrative description broken up by occasional exchanges of dialogue. Frequently, these exchanges resembled nothing so much as two-handed monologue, with each speaker rambling on uninterrupted until his point was made, whereupon he yielded the floor to another soliloquy delivered by someone else.

Some of the greatest fiction ever written took this form, and still makes absorbing reading, most appropriately in a Pullman parlor car or a first-class cabin aboard the *Queen Mary*. Unfortunately—despite the four-day work week—few modern readers can spare the time, and so content themselves with cramped seats in coach, reading breakneck thrillers with lots of pithy dialogue. At home, they're more likely to turn on the tube, listen to a CD, or surf the 'Net than slither through serpentine speeches and chip away at block after block of descriptive detail. If you were Dickens, they might make an exception; but, Guv'nor, you're not.

Many beginning writers freeze up when two or more characters are in a scene, all the furniture has been described, and there is no longer any excuse to put off oral discourse. They're afraid the momentum of the plot will grind to a halt for the sake talking heads. Obviously, they've never read the nail-biting exchanges in Tom Clancy's cockpits or white-knuckled their way through one of John Grisham's cross-examinations.

Clancy, Grisham, and company don't use conversation to mark time or fill pages, but to advance the action. When their characters talk, the spectacle is as exciting as a volley at Wimbledon, a red-hot jam session, or a pair of psychos playing catch with live hand grenades. This is because they recognize dialogue's five major points of strength:

1. **Dialogue presents information succinctly.** With this in mind, the writer can scrap paragraphs of exposition and establish essential information quickly and painlessly while making his or her characters live. Consider this exchange between the hero and a gun shop proprietor from one of my early Westerns, *Murdock's Law*:

   > "What's your business?"

   > "Page Murdock. I wired you last week from Helena looking for a Deane-Adams. You said you had one."

   > "Hell of a long ride just for a gun."

   > "I was coming anyway."

   > His eyes narrowed. "You some kind of law?"

   > "Does it show?"

   > "You could be on one side or the other, from the look of you. In this business I see my share of both."

> "Maybe you've seen Chris Shedwell lately," I said. "My boss got a report he's on his way here. He's wanted for a mail train robbery near Wichita ten years ago."

Here, in a dozen typewritten lines, I've explained who and what my hero is and why he's there, and set the scene for the book's central conflict. Without this passage, I might have clogged three pages with tedious background. Note how each line advances the action. Never lose sight of the reason for this kind of exchange in the first place, which is to bring certain information to light. Don't wander.

2. **Dialogue brings immediacy to the prose.** After more than fifty years of live, on-the-spot television broadcasting, and such recent innovations as "embedded" journalists armed with satellite equipment connected directly to your home, audiences are no longer content to be told what happened. They want to see it as it happens. I reached for that "You are there" effect in this scene from "The Used," a short story that appeared in *Alfred Hitchcock's Mystery Magazine*. Charlie Murch, on the run from the Mob, has gone to his friend Bart Morgan looking for a getaway stake.

> Murch said, "I need money, Bart."
>
> "I figured that," Morgan's gaze dropped to the table. "You caught me short, Charlie. I got bit hard on the last three at the Downs Saturday."
>
> "I don't need much, just enough to get out of the city."
>
> "I'm strapped. I wish to hell I wasn't but I am." He removed a quarter from one stack and placed it atop another. "You know I'd do it if I could but I can't."
>
> Murch seized his wrist. "You owe me, Bart. If I didn't lend you four big ones when the Dodgers took the Series, you'd be part of an off-ramp somewhere by now."

The "now" feeling is achieved by the characters' simple statements and by a minimal use of narrative. The actions that are described—moving a coin, seizing a wrist—meaningless in themselves, assume importance because of the conflict inherent in the dialogue. Murch's desperation and Morgan's uneasy reluctance are experienced firsthand. Everything else has been pared away.

3. **Dialogue is informal.** For better or worse, the average person hears far more than he reads, and what he hears in everyday conversation is rarely phrased as eloquently as an address to Parliament. Good dialogue pleases him because it's not above kicking off its shoes and getting familiar without being hindered by the rules of usage. It creates an illusion of real speech while turning its inadequacies into assets.

In *The Hours of the Virgin*, I capitalized on mangled English during an encounter between private eye Amos Walker and a lowlife acquaintance offering him a client:

"… You think I ain't got no culture? I gaped at a Van Gogh there once." He pronounced both g's.

"Forget it, Merl. Where would you fence it?"

He thought about getting mad, then let it blow. "This is about missing property. There's a ten percent finder's fee, might run ten grand."

"Stolen painting?"

"A book, if you can believe it. I mean, with the liberry right across the street, where you can borrow one free gratis and nobody chases you. Crime's gone to hell in this town."

If I'd committed half of Merl's crimes against the language back in high school, kindly old Mrs. Zemke would have boiled me in library paste. But the effect is authentic without sacrificing clarity. And in spite of his shady nature, you can't help but like Merl for the way he gets his point across without dressing it in a top hat and a monocle. As I've said before, shatter the rules if they get in the way, but above all make yourself understood.

4. **Dialogue provides a change of pace.** In most fiction, anyway. I once read a book that was *all* dialogue, without a line of narrative, and it gave me just as big a headache as if the situation were reversed. I don't know about you, but I'd hop a bus the wrong way across town to avoid someone who talks *all* the time. In person it's annoying; in fiction it's artificial, and just as hard to take as unbroken blocks of description and pointless action. Often, I will insert a scrap of dialogue between long descriptive or introspective passages just to kick the reader out of his apathy, as in this from *Something Borrowed, Something Black*:

    > The map was cheap and shoddy, garishly colored, and most of the points of interest were connected with actors and directors who were dead or in retirement elsewhere. The fabulous mansions, those still standing, would have been partitioned off for apartments long since, or used by Arab oil sheikhs and rap stars enjoying their three weeks in the spotlight. But it did provide a layout that helped her establish her bearings in the confusing sprawl of freeways, parks, suburbs. inside suburbs, and crooked streets and boulevards named for saints she'd never known existed.

    > "Miz Macklin?"

    Like an uppercut out of a clinch, the interjection shocks and alerts. Also, the use of "Miz" as a substitution for the more conventional and formal "Ms." hints at the speaker's character before he's even been introduced. Which brings me to:

5. **Dialogue creates character.** This is as noble a reason for existing as any device can claim. Examples of how a character's speech reveals his or her inner workings have appeared in each of the passages I've quoted. Here is another, from *Black Powder, White Smoke*, in which Ernest Torbert, a white writer from back East, interrogates a black chambermaid in 1886 Texas about her missing ear:

    > Torbert's stomach did a slow turn. "Who did that?"

    > "My husband, sir. Well, we never took no vows, but I kept his

house and done my wifely duties for two years. It was the third straight night of boiled chicken necks for supper that set him off. He said if I weren't going to listen when he said he was done sick of eating boiled chicken necks, there weren't no point in my having ears at all. He cut it off with a barlow knife and he was fixing to cut off the other as well, but he done passed out."

"From the blood?"

"No, sir. It was that bobtail he drunk. That man never could hold his liquor. Two shots and he was out like the cat."

"Was he colored?"

"Yes, sir, though he was high yeller and liked to pass. He picked the pockets of them that come in on the cotton boats, but he never give me none of it but what I could afford to buy chicken necks was all. That's why I ain't shamed I done what I done."

"You ran out on him?"

"No, sir. Well, I did, but before I done that I opened that man's trosers and cut off his phizzle with that barlow knife and threw 'em both in the bayou. He was dead to the world and never felt a thing."

"Lord Jesus."

"Yes, sir. The Lord Jesus done got me through six months in the women's workhouse. That's where I learned to make hospital corners." She jerked an elbow shyly in the direction of the bed she had just made.

This indomitable, and refreshingly (frighteningly?) candid woman shows enough interesting qualities to fill a book. As it was, she had one scene, which even its author finds impossible to forget.

Another reason many new writers are reluctant to use dialogue is they're afraid of it, fearing that the characters they've worked so hard to describe will come off sounding stilted and unnatural the moment they open their mouths. Yet these same writers, when telling friends and family

---

about an interesting experience they had with others, invariably quote what was said from memory, and always manage to make it sound natural. It's only when they commit a story to paper that they hesitate. What works for the ear strikes them as foreign to the eye. Consider taking these five steps to bridge the gap between the senses:

1. **Write plays.** Even if you never try to get them produced, the emphasis on verbal interaction forces you to exercise speech usage. Best of all, you'll learn to draft only lines that will advance the action. All else is dross, and your pace will pick up. All the great plays of the modern theater are available for study. You'll find them as entertaining to read as to watch; and should you ever grow tired of being a successful novelist, you'll have a head start on your conquest of Broadway.

2. **Listen to people.** Next time you're in an airport or a doctor's waiting room, put down that magazine and eavesdrop on your neighbors. Listen for favorite idioms—the manner in which, for example, someone born in Germany constructs sentences as opposed to a lifelong Philadelphian, the vast differences in expression that separate the elderly from the middle-aged and the middle-aged from the young, the professional jargon of a CEO and the shop talk of the operator of a forklift truck. Remember, it's not rude if it's for your work.

3. **Read a lot of dialogue.** Stage plays offer a variety of speech patterns, but novels and stories by writers known for their dialogue will teach you how to make it work with narrative. Choose a writer you like and pick apart the technique. Ray Bradbury and Kurt Vonnegut brought science fiction to millions of readers who thought it was all technospeak and Martian gobbledygook. Gregory McDonald's Fletch mysteries sparkle with realistic talk, and Elmore Leonard and the late George V. Higgins are widely celebrated for their perfect pitch.

4. **Read your dialogue aloud.** Pretentious language, long-windedness,

and awkward structure jump off the page when read aloud, and demand fixing. Reading to an audience—a writers' group, friends, or family—is even more effective, because you'll hear things when listeners are present that you might not if you were reading only to yourself. Their comments may or may not be useful; always consider the source, and trust your instincts if they disagree. Having someone read your work to you is tempting, but beware: Very good readers can make bad writing sound better than it is.

5. **Relax.** Good dialogue is delicate, and collapses when leaned on too heavily. If you're tired or concentrating too hard on the deft phrase, the snappy comeback, your results will sour. Unremittingly glib people are as hard to stomach in fiction as they are in life. Tackle the job fresh, and once the conversation starts flowing, don't tinker with it. You can do up the seams later.

Develop an ear for dialogue as a musician develops an ear for rhythm, timing, and tone. Once you've learned to make its five strengths work for you, your writing will live. And sell.

* * *

Fiction Fact

> *Elmer Kelton, asked to compare his novels of rural Texas to the Westerns of Louis L'Amour, said: "Louis' heroes are six-foot-two and fearless. Mine are five-foot-eight and nervous."*

* * *

A Sense of Reader

* * *

MANY YEARS AGO, advertisements for a major brand of disposable tissues featured a spokesman named Manners the butler. Manners was a natty little fellow dressed in a swallowtail coat and derby hat, who stood about six inches tall. Whenever someone sneezed, this bite-size manservant was literally at his elbow with a tissue the size of a bedsheet.

Manners is long gone, decamped to that commercial studio in the sky along with Mr. Whipple, Speedy Alka-Seltzer, and the Taco Bell Chihuahua. But every time I sit down to write, I picture him sitting on my shoulder, reading and whispering comments and questions in my ear.

He doesn't always look the way he did on television. Sometimes he wears jeans and a baseball cap or greasy coveralls or slacks and a bowling shirt. Sometimes he's a she. Frequently he's invisible, and the only evidence he's present is his slight weight on my shoulder. I'm always aware of him on the edge of consciousness, like the radiant warmth of a cat who's been curled up on my lap for an hour. He's my reader.

Manners is the one who reminds me I'm not writing just for myself. He keeps me from assuming too much and not assuming enough, chastising me when I go too far and challenging me when I fall short. He's a pain in the butt is what he is, but without him I'd be looking for a real job.

Every writer has a Manners, under one name or another. Hemingway subtracted the human element, referring to him bluntly as his "built-in, shock-proof shit detector." For Stephen King, it's a real-life, flesh-and-blood reader who critiques his work before it leaves his house. Most often, that person is his wife, author Tabitha King. In *On Writing*, he identifies her as his "Ideal Reader":

> *Do all opinions weigh the same? Not for me. In the end I listen most closely to Tabby, because she's the one I write for, the one I want to wow. If you're writing primarily for one person besides yourself, I'd advise you to pay very close attention to that person's opinion (I know one fellow who says he writes mostly for someone who's been dead fifteen years, but the majority of us aren't in that position). And if what you hear makes sense, then make the changes.*

The operative sentence is the last. Whether your Ideal Reader is a trusted intimate or a creature of fantasy, the feedback you get must be tempered by your own judgment. This is a partnership, not God dictating to Joan of Arc. If you belong to a writers' group and read your work to members for their opinions, chances are you will hear some very good suggestions (and some crackpot ones), but if you try to follow them all, or any one without understanding and agreeing with it, your story will end up a mess.

King's philosophy has paid off for him, artistically as well as materially. No writer enjoys a closer bond with his audience than King's. He has an almost telepathic knowledge of the monsters that lurk beneath all our beds and knows just when to unleash them for full effect.

When I was a teenager with aspirations of writing professionally, my Ideal Reader was my mother. She wasn't a writer, but she read widely, had broad experience of the world, and was quick to point out implausibilities. Yet she seldom read my work. Instead she listened attentively as I sketched out my plot and described scenes, and invariably jumped on the very things I'd had doubts about myself. With her support, I learned to trust my inner voice.

Today, my wife, author Deborah Morgan, serves as my sounding board. Most of the time I agree with her suggestions; sometimes I argue with them, only to see their merit later and put them into practice. On rare occasions, after weighing them thoughtfully, I reject them. Despite the opinion of certain literary critics, who are always telling you what the writer is *really* saying, no one knows a story as well as its author. Manners is, after all, my own common sense talking.

Mysteries are especially vulnerable to miscommunication. Their creators are continually playing chess with readers. If they fail to provide the information necessary to solve the murder, they're guilty of fraud. On the other hand, if they divulge too much, readers will arrive at the solution too early, and respect is forfeit. Proper balance depends upon the writer's having absolute knowledge of the reader's intelligence and ability to reason. Having achieved that balance, he or she is capable of working in any area of fiction.

Some writers who have mastered every other art never succeed in developing a sense of reader. James Joyce and William Faulkner wrote with genius, but at times their self-indulgence borders on contempt. The pages of Hemingway's own copy of Joyce's *Ulysses*, a book he praised to the skies, were cut only a third of the way through, suggesting his enthusiasm flagged early among the run-on sentences and carloads of stream-of-consciousness. Faulkner once dismissed an editorial query with the remark, "How do I know what it means? I was drunk when I wrote it," and fretted to his dying day that he'd sold out when he aimed *Sanctuary* at the mass market. Both writers are held in high regard for their contributions to letters; but they are not popular writers. They are admired, not loved. Try to picture a young reader crawling under the bedcovers with a flashlight to enjoy a few stolen moments with either *The Sound and the Fury* or *Finnegan's Wake*.

Understanding your target audience is the most important lesson you can learn. It's absolutely essential to writing popular fiction. Editors look for it. Readers take it for granted, and are ruthless about deserting when it fails to appear. It isn't an accident, like genius or talent. No writer is born with the ability. You have to go out and get it.

The best way to develop a sense of reader is to be one yourself. Of course, if you're not already an avid reader, you have no more business writing professionally than a confirmed bachelor has counseling married couples for a living. Read first of all for entertainment, then find out *why* you were entertained, and make note of how the writer went about satisfying your expectations. Apply the techniques to your own work. At this point, you have become your own Ideal Reader.

One thing you may notice is that, just about the time you feel a question coming on, the author comes forward with the answer, as if he were reading your mind. What he's really doing is listening to you, speaking through the elfin creature perched on his shoulder.

But your work won't end once he's perched on yours.

Manners is a sensitive fellow, who will hop right off the moment he suspects you're ignoring him. That moment comes when he finds you becoming intoxicated with the arcane beauty of your prose, hanging garlands on your story and characters and bogging them down in their tracks. In the end he bailed out on Hemingway, taking with him the discipline that kept the work spare and the style clear. (Perhaps that shit detector wasn't so shock-proof after all.) Read your own writing with the same gimlet eye you bring to your mentors'. It should be a lifelong practice.

Fiction Fact

Strapped for a solution to his first locked-room murder mystery, Fu Manchu creator Sax Rohmer accepted an invitation from his American publisher to travel from London to New York City and work out his writer's block en route. By the time several chapters of the serial novel were in print, Rohmer was still stumped, and pacing the floor of his Manhattan flat in a panic. Too late, he realized that if one of his characters had given a different answer to a question asked in chapter one, he'd have his solution. He turned to his friend, the great escape artist Harry Houdini, who broke him free from his dilemma: "Bring the fellow back and get him to tell you why he lied."

* * *

Having Fun

* * *

EARLY IN *BARTON FINK,* Joel and Ethan Coen's devastating cinematic black comedy about writers in 1940s Hollywood, the title character—a turgid young New York playwright based on Clifford Odets—discusses writing with William Mayhew, a thinly disguised William Faulkner:

> *Mayhew: I haven't known such peace since the grand productive days. What do you think, Barton? Ain't writin' peace?*

> *Fink: Actually, no, Bill. I've always found that writing comes from great inner pain. I don't think good work is possible without it.*

> *Mayhew: I just enjoy makin' things up.*

Mayhew's is the better philosophy. I've read and listened to many a writer, and whenever I hear a writer bemoaning the hard work and loneliness involved in producing a book, I feel like sending him or her a brochure for a course in learning meat-cutting at home. I can't stand to see a fellow human being suffer so just for the sake of art, and people need meat.

I love doing what I do. I'm getting paid for work I enjoy, maybe the only kind I'm good at, and the only serious worry I have is that the people who sign my checks will find out I'd do it for free, and stop payment. I watch a gainfully employed writer writhing in agony over the creative process the same way I stare at a strange animal in a zoo or the subject of an alien autopsy on video, with a mixture of incomprehension and pity. But then it doesn't seem so long ago I had a real job, with a boss and a schedule of hours drawn up by someone else, and resented every soul-destroying minute it took away from writing. Maybe these martyrs never had one of those and don't know how good they've got it.

Maxwell Perkins, the legendary Scribner's editor from whom we've heard previously in these pages, once broke up a bitter squabble on the editorial board by pointing out that if a maintenance man in uniform walked in just then, they'd all feel ashamed.

Maybe these are crocodile tears. Some pro baseball players put mustard on a play, turning a routine catch into a demonstration of acrobatic skill or sliding into homeplate a good ten minutes ahead of the ball, in order to sweeten the deal when their contracts come up for negotiation. Maybe there's a bigger advance involved, or even cover approval, if the work looks hard enough.

Then again, it could be that old puritan ethic rearing its buckle hat. "No pain, no gain" was our national mantra long before the exercise craze came along. Nothing that's as much fun as making up stories and writing them down and selling them for money strikes us as a good thing, and so some of us exaggerate the hardship in order to justify our existence.

Writing is certainly hard work most of the time, and when it's going badly, the depression is almost clinical. But when it's going well, when your fingers can scarcely move fast enough to record the stuff that's whooshing through your head—when you find yourself jumping out of bed in the middle of the night because you can't wait until sunup to write the entire scene that just came to you while you were falling asleep—the rush is orgasmic.

Yes, you say, but the words don't gush that often. Most of the time you have to wrench them out like nails from a plank; and how about when you're writing a difficult scene? That maintenance job doesn't look so bad then.

Complicated, challenging scenes are backbreaking. If your goal for the day is five pages and sunset finds you still struggling at the top of page two, writing is hard, physical labor. It makes your neck stiff, your muscles sore, and your mood ugly. Sometimes it's a matter of keeping several characters alive in a room without sounding like they're just taking turns talking; sometimes you fill the wastebasket trying to make an improbable situation fly. Or maybe your next scene is your favorite, the showpiece you've been looking forward to since you broke ground, and you feel as if you're wasting all your energy slogging through the problematic scene that precedes it.

That's the scene you need to have fun with.

I can always tell when a writer has rushed through a scene or written around it in order to get to the good stuff. The dialogue is hurried, like the wedding vows in a tired old comedy where the bride's in labor. Descriptions are sketchy or nonexistent. Too often, the scene isn't even there; the writer has lifted it out and thrown it away, or not written it at all. At best, this leaves an annoying gap. At worst, the "good" scene has not been set up and so it falls in like a cake because someone skimped on the eggs. In between is a lost opportunity, because sometimes the scene you dreaded most turns out to be the best in the book.

About fifteen years ago, I read a thriller about a detective investigating a murder that closely resembled a series of homicides for which a man had already been convicted. There was no question that the man who was in custody was guilty of the earlier murders, but the detective decided to visit him in prison in hopes of uncovering a lead. The concept of an investigator appealing to a notorious serial killer for help was unique, and I looked forward to this meeting of the minds, one analytical and earnest, the other dangerously insane. I turned the page with anticipation—and met the detective coming out of the prison, shaking his head over the futility of interrogating a nut. After pages of build-up, the writer had bailed out.

I don't remember if I even finished the book. I *do* remember that shortly afterward, Thomas Harris published *The Silence of the Lambs*, about a young FBI trainee who enlists the aid of a serial killer to solve a string of murders, and built a stellar career on the very premise another writer had avoided. Although it's impossible to say that the convict in the earlier book would have become as important a figure in popular culture as Harris' Hannibal Lecter, the fact remains that Harris tapped into the collective unconscious and founded a wildly successful new genre while his predecessor merely wrote a conventional and forgettable mystery.

I can't speculate about the other author's motives. Often, a writer will avoid writing a particular scene or rush through it because he or she is unfamiliar with the subject. Research is the cure for that. Sometimes the subject is repugnant, or doesn't seem interesting. Yet a lot of fascinating fiction has been written about things that many people regard as dull. Life in a military school never excited my emotions until, after some arm-twisting by a publicist, I read Pat Conroy's *The Lords of Discipline*. It's now one of my most treasured books, and Conroy is one of my all-time favorite writers.

I don't swim, for the very good reason that I almost drowned twice trying to learn how. No power on earth will persuade me to strap on an oxygen tank or a snorkel and explore the undersea world. Before I wrote *Kill Zone*, I always redirected the conversation whenever some ardent diver began talking about his hobby. But the plot called for my protagonist to board a boat that had been taken over by terrorists and free the hostages, and the only way to approach the craft without being observed was from under water. I'd constructed the plot around the tantalizing premise of a mob hit man taking on a boatload of fanatics armed with explosives and automatic weapons, and moaned about the prospect of having to learn a foreign and (to me) aesthetically unappealing discipline and use what I'd learned in a way that would hold my reader's attention long enough to get to the good part. However, there was nothing for it but to do the homework and apply it to the book or abandon a project I'd already sold to a publisher. My character, at least, was a novice, so I didn't have to become an expert. I picked up some literature on snorkeling and studied the rudiments. Then I combined what I'd learned with my visceral fear of drowning and wrote the following:

> Although the suit absorbed most of the shock of the cold water, he was completely immersed before his heart started up again. He tried a couple of side kicks to get his blood circulating, raised his head clear of the water to get a fix on the boat, then submerged again and flutter-kicked in that direction, stroking his arms close to his body in a streamlining movement that bartered minimum effort for maximum speed. Even so, in just a few hundred yards his chest was pumping fit to burst his damaged ribs. He came to the surface again and removed the snorkel to breathe air untainted by rubber, treading water.

> The droplets on his mask gave him a bee's-eye view of the triple-decked boat, fully visible now, its interior lights spilling out onto the water. He could make out figures moving within. The vessel was at anchor and reluctantly giving way to the motion of the more persistent waves; tall and curved and white and suggestive of mint juleps and magnolia blossoms, it seemed more at home than Macklin on this ancient lake. The danger would begin when he entered that circle of light. From that point on he would be square in the kill zone.

> He ducked his head and resumed swimming, slower now.

I'm proud of that passage. It isn't Shakespeare, and it may not be Thomas Harris, but it still gives me chills. It's at least as good as the scenes that follow—the money scenes, the scenes I wrote the book to showcase. And the book is better because of it.

Many writers, I suppose, conceive their stories based on What They Have to Say. I've never flattered myself that my philosophies have any more merit than my barber's simply because my audience is bigger, and since it's difficult not to let slip one's own cock-eyed worldview anyway (Yes, Mr. Poe, I agree that premature burial is a bummer; but what happens to Fortunado?), I'd rather amuse myself making things up. I often start with a title, then think up details to support it, which in turn lead to scenes I'd enjoy writing, i.e., the money scenes, those that will pay off in satisfaction, the coin of my realm. Sometimes, as in the case of *Kill Zone*, which I'd originally titled *.38/72*, the title gets tossed, but the scenes remain. Getting to them, a necessary chore, often winds up being half the fun. Those lead-ins only seem like a chore, because I don't know what they'll entail. But once I know, and have gathered enough information to write them with confidence, I take my time to wring all the drama from what I've learned, like a teenager waxing his first car to a mirror finish. If that doesn't pump up your adrenaline, you're beyond hope.

I was afraid of that snorkel scene, and not just because of my fear of swimming. I was afraid I wasn't good enough to tackle a thing I'd never tried before. Wasn't seasoned enough. But the only way to get experience is to have it. You still won't see me in a wetsuit, or even paddling water in the kiddie pool at the YMCA, but the next time a story takes me into foreign territory, I know I'll be equal to the challenge. And I had fun.

Fun is important. Fun is crucial. If you don't have a good time, neither will your reader, and if your fear of the untried keeps you from it, you'll never know what you missed out on. Don't just stare at the floor and run for the exit. Take your time, look around, and see what you can salvage. Just because you don't know anyone at the party doesn't mean you won't enjoy the company if you'll just walk up to someone and introduce yourself. You may end up with a new best friend. And you may have written the best scene of your career.

This is good advice for the veteran as well as for the cadet. The reason so many established writers disappoint their audience just about the time they should be dazzling it with the fruit of long practice is they've lost interest in their own work. It's more comfortable to go on writing the same scenes you've written so many times before than to leave them behind and try something new, but it's boring. There's an old saying: "If you ain't livin' on the edge, you're takin' up too much space." Safe territory is a graveyard.

* * *

Fiction Fact

Offered two hundred dollars to write two thousand words on the subject "Should the Writer Have a Social Conscience?" Lolita *author Vladimir Nabokov wired back: "No. You owe me ten cents."*

* * *

Jump Starts

* * *

IN *THE WAGES OF FEAR,* the French-Italian classic cinema thriller, a group of desperately out-of-work men agree to drive two truckloads of volatile nitroglycerine over a hundred or so miles of treacherous road to a burning oil field. As star Yves Montand climbs in beside his partner behind the wheel, he notices the driver is sweating.

> *Montand: What's wrong?*
>
> *Driver: My malaria is back.*
>
> *Montand: Good beginning.*

He's being ironic, of course; but for those of us watching, it's a great beginning, as witty as it is ominous. Here are some great beginnings from books, each followed by an analysis of why it works:

> *I awakened that morning to birdsong. It was only the little yellow bird who lives in the locust tree outside our bedroom window, and*

I could have wrung its neck for it was not yet six and I had a hang-over. That was in late summer, before Harvest Home, before the bird left its nest for the winter. Now it is spring again, alas, and as predicted the yellow bird has returned. The Eternal Return, they call it here. Thinking back from this day to that one nine months ago, I now imagine the bird to have been sounding a warning. But that is nonsense, of course, for who would have thought it was a bird of ill omen, that little creature?

—Thomas Tryon, *Harvest Home*

In another time, a writer such as Lord Bulwer Lytton—famous for the opening lines "It was a dark and stormy night" and "Merry was the month of May"—would have gone on from that first sentence to paint a bucolic picture of life in the country from start to finish, but somewhere in that passage, before even the chilling phrase "bird of ill omen," Tryon hints that this country is more serpent than paradise. "I could have wrung its neck" sticks out not so much for its wicked humor as for its threat of actual physical violence, underscoring the payoff at the end of the paragraph; and then there is that "alas" in the middle. The reader is rare who can resist reading further to learn what horrors and loss lie behind that heartbreaking word.

This use of foreshadowing, often referred to as the "had I but known school," is sometimes disparaged, usually by writers who are themselves incapable of employing it without telegraphing all their punches. Tryon manages to sustain this brooding level throughout the book, which would inspire many imitations, including Stephen King's story, "Children of the Corn," most of which lack the subtlety of the original.

I turned the Chrysler onto the Florida Turnpike with Rollo Kramer's headless body in the trunk, and all the time I'm thinking I should've put some plastic down. I knew the heap was a rental, but I didn't like leaving anything behind for the inevitable forensics safari. That meant I'd have to strip all the carpeting in the trunk, douche out the blood with Clorox, and hope Avis took a long time to notice. I should've just taken a second and put some plastic down. Shit.

—Victor Gischler, *Gun Monkeys*

This, in addition to being an effective use of the hook—hard to stop reading after that headless body makes its appearance—is a marvel of character compression. Nearly everything we need to know about Gischler's narrator—his recklessness, quick temper, tendency to second-guess himself after the fact, and some definite shortcomings in the wisdom department—is introduced in this first paragraph. With these character flaws in place, the implication that he's no stranger to homicide promises one wild ride.

I like the way Gischler switches back and forth between past and present tense. This is the way most people tell stories when among friends and family. It creates an informality that prevents the reader from realizing he's being manipulated by a professional writer.

An opening hook presents the challenge of maintaining that same level of excitement throughout all the pages that follow. I once read a crime novel that begin similarly, with a decapitated body in the protagonist's trunk, that never quite managed to return to that high point. *Gun Monkeys* delivers all the way through. And it's the author's first novel!

> *No live organism can continue for long to exist sanely under conditions of absolute reality; even larks and katydids are supposed, by some, to dream. Hill House, not sane, stood by itself against its hills, holding darkness within; it had stood so for eighty years and might stand for eighty more. Within, walls continued upright, bricks met neatly, floors were firm, and doors were sensibly shut; silence lay steadily against the wood and stone of Hill House, and whatever walked there, walked alone.*

—Shirley Jackson, *The Haunting of Hill House*

Stephen King, in *Danse Macabre*, his masterful booklength essay on the history of horror fiction, singled out this same passage, and he chose wisely. If Shirley Jackson had stopped writing after publishing "The Lottery," she still would command an exalted place in American literature. Fortunately, she went on to write other classics, of which *The Haunting of Hill House* is the most famous, for reasons which are obvious in this beautifully written, ineffably chilling opening. There are no pyrotechnics of vocabulary or style, just a measured, confident rhythm sustained by perfect word choice and the finest use of commas anywhere. The pure reason of the language—note what she does with "sanely" and "sane"—prepares us for a story that will defy all reason. Most writers of Gothic horror rely on electrical storms and fog to create the brooding effect Jackson accomplishes simply by describing an otherworldly house in determinedly worldly terms.

The mood is relentless, and the author doesn't spare us even at the end, where she repeats this paragraph; by which time all its awful implications are fulfilled. The next time some know-it-all in your writers' group blathers on about the importance of always beginning with a hook, sit him down, read him this passage, and show him how a writer in full command of the language can draw the reader in without resorting to a flashy artificial device.

> *He rode into our valley in the summer of '89. I was a kid then, barely topping the backboard of father's old chuck-wagon. I was on the upper rail of our small corral, soaking in the late afternoon sun, when I saw him far down the road where it swung into the valley from the open plain beyond.*

> —Jack Schaefer, *Shane*

For setting a scene immediately but without haste, making full use of the senses of sight and touch, and asking a question central to all fiction, you can't beat those three sentences. Who is this stranger?

We don't know, of course. But we know he is bringing change.

Win Blevins, himself an excellent writer of historical Westerns and an editor with Forge Books, has said that every story begins with this premise: "Things started to go wrong when ..." *Shane* is no exception. In terms of the Western, it's the quintessential tale of the man on horseback riding in from no one knows where, delivering the innocent from evil, then riding off into the sunset, and it was by no means new when Schaefer wrote it. But his decision to tell it from a child's perspective (borrowed from *Treasure Island* and borrowed later by Harper Lee for *To Kill a Mockingbird*; not exactly shabby company) elevated the story to the level of ancient mythology, a tone set at the very start. "Who is this stranger?" indeed. We must read on to learn the answer, and we've been doing so for fifty-five years.

I was fifteen when I first met Sherlock Holmes, fifteen years old with my nose in a book as I walked the Sussex Downs, and nearly stepped on him. In my defence I must say it was an engrossing book, and it was very rare to come across another person in that particular part of the world in that war year of 1915. In my seven weeks of peripatetic reading amongst the sheep (which tended to move out of my way) and the gorse bushes (to which I had painfully developed an instinctive awareness) I had never before stepped on a person.

—Laurie R. King, *The Beekeeper's Apprentice*

Here again, senses and setting come square up front; and of course, one must acknowledge the device of easily dropping the legendary name Sherlock Holmes. But new Sherlock Holmes stories comprise a genre unto themselves these days, and if that were the strongest thing this opening had going, I might have moved on to any of the others. However—well, she *steps* on the man, or nearly does. One reads all the time about characters stumbling over clues, etc., but this is one of the few cases on record where the stumbling is literal, and we stumble right along with her, out of our lives and into the story. Short of Alice falling down that rabbit hole and us with her, I can't think of a more precipitous start in fiction. King maintains that spontaneous serendipity through the book, and through five sequels (and counting).

It was a pleasure to burn.

It was a special pleasure to see things eaten, to see things blackened and changed. With the brass nozzle in his fists, with this great python spitting its venomous kerosene upon the world, the blood pounded in his head, and his hands were the hands of some amazing conductor playing all the symphonies of blazing and burning to bring down the tatters and charcoal ruins of history. With his symbolic helmet numbered 451 on his stolid head, and his eyes all orange flame with the thought of what came next, he flicked the igniter and the house jumped up in a gorging fire that burned the evening sky red and yellow and black. He strode in a swarm of fireflies. He wanted above all, like the old joke, to shove a marshmallow on a stick in the furnace, while the flapping pigeon-winged books died on the porch and lawn

of the house, while the books went up in sparkling whirls and blew
away on a wind turned dark with burning.

—Ray Bradbury, *Fahrenheit 451*

This terribly beautiful, frankly phallic passage freezes my marrow and makes me sweat at the same time—and it's a houseful of books he's burning, not people. Bradbury's reverse-fireman (he starts flames rather than puts them out) is as frightening a maniac as Hannibal Lecter, and his conflagratory use of words—*burn, blackened, blazing, burning, orange flame, gorging fire, red, yellow, black, fireflies, furnace*—raises our body temperature, parches our throats, and scorches our skin. The pages seem to be combusting in our hands. It can't be healthy to put the book aside with our pulses racing so fast.

I've grown weary of the post-*Blade Runner* school of gloomy apocalyptic science fiction, with its buzzing neon in an eternal night and characters plodding through it like somnambulists with lobotomies. Bradbury's cautionary tales of a dystopic future and grotesque planets work because his characters are all as alive as that demented, sexually frustrated functionary who gets such a charge out of destroying the written word.

I am the vampire Lestat. I'm immortal. More or less. The light of the
sun, the sustained heat of an intense fire—these things might
destroy me. But then again, they might not.

—Anne Rice, *The Vampire Lestat*

Rice is well known for her voluptuous style, more familiar to nineteenth-century readers of Mary Shelley and Bram Stoker than to fans of the stripped-down, high-powered prose of Michael Crichton and Robin Cook, but very much in keeping with her gothic subjects. But here, she delivers a trim, straightforward, and candid introduction to a charming fiend. Once again, everything about the character that will be supported by his actions throughout the book is spelled out at the start. How can you not like a bloodsucking undead thing who knows so little about his own situation, and is willing to admit it? He seems to be saying, "Let's wheel me out into the sun, and find out." Which is, literally and symbolically, what the succeeding pages do.

When I finally caught up with Abraham Trahearne, he was drinking beer with an alcoholic bulldog named Fireball Roberts in a ram-shackle joint just outside of Sonoma, California, drinking the heart right out of a fine spring afternoon.

—James Crumley, *The Last Good Kiss*

I don't know what I like about this more, that alcoholic bulldog named after a famous gonzo race-car driver (a dog with a first and a last name!) or that last bit about drinking the heart out of an afternoon. The whole thing sings, and if we don't know as much about the storyteller as we learn about the characters in most of the openings I've quoted, the implied promise is we will. Meanwhile, it raises the question why he's chasing this Trahearne fellow, while forecasting a potentially interesting acquaintance. There are hardboiled-mystery fans who can recite this passage by heart, and do.

My favorite struggling writer is the Billy Crystal character in *Throw Momma From the Train*, who spends much of the movie trying to write the first line of the book that will free him from his crippling writer's block. "The night was," he writes, over and over, never getting beyond those three words. In the end, recent comic and harrowing events in his life cause him to throw away the line and just start writing. The lesson is, there is no magic opening line. The magic is what creates the line in the first place.

Hemingway said he began every project by just writing, then going back to read what he'd written until he came to "the first true sentence," after which he crossed out everything that came before and resumed from that point. He didn't say what makes a true sentence, but we can assume that we'll recognize it when we see it. Following are the opening lines to twenty great books. Some are funny, some shocking, some compelling, some just are, and the reader must make what he or she can of them. The next time you're stuck for a place to start, try writing one of these on a fresh page and following it up with *what you think* should come next. See where it takes you. Then go back and read what you wrote, and see if you can find your own first true sentence. Perhaps nothing will come of it; perhaps everything will. In any case, it beats staring at white paper or a blank screen, and should get "The night was" out of your system.

When the phone rang, Parker was in the garage, killing a man.

    —Richard Stark (Donald E. Westlake), *Firebreak*

Last summer, in a season of intense heat, Jim Burden and I happened to be crossing Iowa on the same train.

    —Willa Cather, *My Ántonia*

They threw me off the hay truck about noon.

    —James M. Cane, *The Postman Always Rings Twice*

Happy families are all alike; every unhappy family is unhappy in its own way.

    —Leo Tolstoy, *Anna Karenina*

It is a truth universally acknowledged, that a single man in possession of a good fortune must be in want of a wife.

    —Jane Austen, *Pride and Prejudice*

A green hunting cap squeezed the top of the fleshy balloon of a head.

    —John Kennedy Toole, *A Confederacy of Dunces*

Mary had loved the family axe as a glittering extension of her own arm.

    —Deborah Larsen, *The White*

Robert Cohn was once middleweight boxing champion of Princeton.

    —Ernest Hemingway, *The Sun Also Rises*

Evelyn Couch had come to Rose Terrace with her husband, Ed, who as visiting his mother, Big Momma, a recent but reluctant arrival.

    —Fannie Flagg, *Fried Green Tomatoes at the Whistle Stop Cafe*

"The war ended last night, Caroline. Help me with these flowers."

—Gore Vidal, *Empire*

It is difficult to know quite where to begin this story, but I have fixed my choice on a certain Wednesday at luncheon at the vicarage.

—Agatha Christie, *The Murder at the Vicarage*

Trust me for a while.

—William Goldman, *Magic*

It was not until several weeks after he had decided to murder his wife that Dr. Bickleigh took any active steps in the matter.

—Francis Iles, *Malice Aforethought*

The stranger came early in February, one wintry day, through a biting wind and a driving snow, the last snowfall of the year, over the down, walking as it seemed from Bramblehurst railway station, and carried a little black portmanteau in his thickly gloved hand.

—H.G. Wells, *The Invisible Man*

In our family, there was no clear line between religion and fly fishing.

—Norman Maclean, *A River Runs Through It*

Maybe I shouldn't have given the guy who pumped my stomach my phone number, but who cares?

—Carrie Fisher, *Postcards From the Edge*

Around quitting time, Tod Hackett heard a great din on the road outside his office.

—Nathanael West, *The Day of the Locust*

I scarcely know where to begin, though I sometimes facetiously place the cause of it all to Chancy Furuseth's credit.

—Jack London, *The Sea-Wolf*

He thought: When I get there nobody will believe I could have managed a ride like this and neither by God will I.

—Glendon Swarthout, *The Shootist*

"Who is John Galt?"

—Ayn Rand, *Atlas Shrugged*

Now all you have to come up with is a second line. Good luck.

* * *

Fiction Fact

Crime novelist Eugene Izzi's death remains his most famous mystery. He was found hanging outside the window of his office in a Chicago high-rise in 1994, armed with brass knuckles and wearing a bulletproof vest. A decade later, no one has been able to determine whether he was murdered or committed suicide or became a victim of his own research.

* * *

The Eleventh Hour

* * *

HAVING DEALT WITH THE BEGINNING, let's now cut to the end.

While your opening will often make the difference between a pass-by and a sale, it's the ending your readers will take away with them. The amount of satisfaction you deliver will determine whether they come back next time.

Of all types of popular fiction, the one that depends entirely on the success of the conclusion is the mystery. If the central question of the story isn't answered, plausibly and entertainingly, in the final chapter, all the work you've put into all those that came before is wasted. If you can write a good ending to a mystery, you can end anything—possibly even war and famine.

Okay, so the missing heiress is locked in a soundproof cell on the top floor of the abandoned sanitarium, the stolen sapphires are in a black velvet pouch on the examining table in the old shock-therapy room, and a bookend set of hired thugs is holding your detective at bay with big automatics while a disembodied voice boasts over the intercom of having committed every successful crime since the sinking of the *U.S.S. Maine.*

Whose voice is it? And how do you fuse together all the loose fragments you've been scattering helter-skelter throughout the previous three hundred pages without making your climactic scene read like the autobiography of a former mayor of Cleveland?

The overwhelming majority of mysteries that go wrong do so at the point where the solution is revealed. This is fatal, as it is precisely for this scene that the patient reader has kept dozens of seamy neon-lit liaisons, sat through pages of tight-jawed dialogue, gnawed his nails through a couple of car chases, and withstood untold numbers of brutal beatings. Once there, flushed and breathless, he finds himself being *talked to* by the suddenly long-winded detective—or worse, the murderer.

His eyes glaze. His attention wanders. He counts the number of pages remaining. Oh, he goes ahead and finishes; at twenty-five bucks and up for the average hardcover novel and three-fifty at rock bottom for paperback—not counting his time invested thus far—he's not about to give it up in the eleventh hour. But he won't buy another book by the same author. Bored he can get for free watching *Survivor XIII: Lost in Buffalo.*

But he needn't fret, because the book won't even get that far. No editorial board worth its collective salary will accept it for publication.

Suspension of disbelief is a high-wire act, requiring plausibility on one end of the balance pole to counter the pull of audacious invention on the other. The detective's gun fell through a sewer grate? Okay. His cell-phone battery went dead so he couldn't call for backup? Cool. Failed to recognize the blackmailer's handwriting as that of his best friend? No problem. Just don't expect me to sit through paragraph after paragraph of jaw-breaking monologue about timetables, motives, backstory, and microscopic clues without another character interrupting. I don't get to make speeches on informal occasions, so why should I accept one on the part of a character in a story? It's unrealistic and a snooze besides.

It's bad enough when the detective starts talking and won't stop, but still worse when it's the murderer. We're all familiar with this scene: The criminal mastermind gets the drop on the hero, then says: "I'm going to kill you, but before I do, let me tell you why I did what I did and how I did it."

Now, I'm no mastermind, criminal or otherwise, but all this seems like a waste of breath (not to add paper), if I'm going to kill him anyway. As a reader, I see the writer at work at this point, throwing switches right and left to unsnarl the mess he's made and incidentally give the detective time to wriggle free from his bonds, dive for the nearest weapon, and turn the tired old table. This device creaked when Agatha Christie cranked it in *Murder Is Easy* in 1939, and had a real renaissance ten years ago in Mary Higgins Clark's otherwise-suspenseful *Remember Me* and Caleb Carr's unintentionally hilarious *The Alienist*—complete with one of those stop-and-start climaxes Carol Burnett used to spoof so well, with one bad guy after the other trooping in with gun in hand, to be dispatched by the next. All it lacked was Tim Conway and Harvey Korman.

Oh, but weren't those best-selling books? Without a doubt. In the case of Christie and Clark, they were written by proven performers who had established themselves years earlier, and who might expect their loyal readership to forgive a bit of carelessness in the face of an imminent deadline. Carr published one more book to close out his contract and at this writing has been silent ever since.

Babble has less excuse now than ever. In the 60,000-word format that ruled the detective novel from the 1940s through the 1970s, a lot of talk near the end was merely irritating. The 100,000-plus-word blockbuster of today, with its longer suspect list, compound crimes, and labyrinth of plots, subplots, counterplots, and burial plots, demands so much explaining that to attempt to do it all in one scene would put a caffeine junkie to sleep on a bed of bottlecaps.

The ideal, for me, would be to craft a mystery in which everything is explained by the events themselves, with no wheezy exposition at the end, the way Ethan and Joel Coen do in their quirky suspense movies (*Blood Simple, Miller's Crossing, Fargo*, etc.). But theirs is a visual medium, and the technique is next to impossible in print. The next best plan is to explain away the mystery a piece at a time, painlessly, like taking arsenic by the drop and building up an immunity to the poison—or in this case, boredom. But it requires cooperation from readers.

Suspense writer John Lutz says he misses the 160-page detective novel of the 1950s. It could be read in two or three sittings, he points out, and no prompting was required for the reader to remember the essential clues. In those days, too, the average adult had much less to remember in general than he or she does now. Forced to commit to memory eleven-digit telephone numbers, nine-numeral zip codes, a pocketful of PINS, computer passwords, and constantly shifting time slots for favorite television programs on cable, satellite, and the proliferating broadcast networks, the reader can hardly be expected to keep straight even the names of characters in a long mystery. Reminders are mandatory.

A little past the halfway point in *Never Street*, an Amos Walker novel, I let Walker pause in the midst of his deepening investigation into the disappearance of his client's husband to take stock of what he has learned and what he still needs to find out:

> ... I sat back and thought about the Pakistani psychiatrist, brown and pleasant-looking, sitting in his green office and not discussing the nervous breakdown that had placed Neil Catalin in his care eighteen months ago. I thought about Tom Balfour, the island brat and all-around dogsbody, and his suspicions that Naheen videotaped his sessions with his patients for purposes of shaking them down ...

> ... I supposed I was indirectly responsible for Fat Phil's beating death. ... On the other hand, if the Iroquois Heights detective hadn't tried to cash in on Webb's homicide, I wouldn't have had any reason to feel guilty. So that was one more thing to stuff into my little internal box of angst and sit on the lid until it locked.

Feeling out of it? Yet this represented a lifeline for readers who'd stuck with me for two hundred pages and found themselves treading water. Such introspection, which comes naturally to a character of average intelligence—there is only one Sherlock Holmes, after all—maintains the illusion of reality while quietly bringing the reader up to speed. It also allows insight into the character's personality, enabling him to express self-doubts he would never reveal in dialogue. Since no one else in the cast has this access, the reader is let in on secrets exclusive to the detective. It's an expression of trust, instantly sympathetic.

Just as the expanded form requires the protagonist to take these little information breaks from time to time, so the long succession of mysteries within mysteries must be disposed of one by one as the story progresses, to avoid dumping them all at the end. Think of the plot as a string, into which knots have been tied at intervals. The detective unties each knot as it presents itself, saving the biggest and most difficult for last.

In tying these knots, it's useful to think backwards.

Say an important official in the U.S. State Department has been killed in order to conceal a crime of international proportions. Her faithless husband has been paid off and relocated to a tropical paradise to ensure his silence, taking along his mistress, who leaves her cat in a friend's care. When the cat disappears, the friend engages the detective to find it—at which point the story begins. Suspecting that the cat has returned to its owner's apartment, he breaks in and finds a recent bill for hundreds of dollars' worth of tropical resort clothing; a mystery, since the woman had told her friend she was going to Anchorage. Curious, he checks the airport, where a ticket clerk identifies the woman from a photograph as a passenger on a flight to Marseilles. Before long the detective is on his way to the French Riviera, up to his trenchcoat collar in murder and international intrigue.

Along the way he will encounter his fair share of red herrings, dead-end leads, false assumptions, and cases of mistaken identity, and it will be in the best interest of the story if he follows each one out in its turn, tidying up as he goes, so that he is faced at the climax with naught but the Awful Secret that the State Department official was slain to cover up. He will also find the cat.

That's important; the cat must not be forgotten. Not because mystery readers seem to harbor an odd affinity for the species (ask Lillian Jackson Braun and Carole Nelson Douglas), but because whatever device the writer uses to involve an investigator in an unfolding case must be dealt with on its own merits. The solution to this simplest mystery can be a throwaway; the cat waltzes in through an open window while the detective is examining the sinister clothing bill. The first knot thus comes undone while he is looking for a place to start on the next. Officially, the case is closed; but the detective has become hooked by another mystery, and so has the reader, who now knows the writer can be trusted to answer all the other questions.

Mind, the story should be more than just a series of problems to be solved. That approach was appropriate for the Labors of Hercules, and no one working a crossword puzzle would thank the person who designed it for going off on tangents. But the novel of detection aspires to be something more than just an exercise in logic. Interesting, realistic characters, a compelling plot, natural-sounding dialogue, and believable settings are what brings readers back to find out what they may have missed the first time. The cat of our generic plot is more than just a handle for the detective to take hold of, but a living, breathing, furball-hacking feline, suitable for stroking or kicking off the couch. The murdered public servant is not just a corpse, but a fellow human being cut down before her time, and whose spirit cries out for justice. For all its skimpy bikinis and foaming surf, the Riviera of the story is a dazzling trap, seductive and fatal. To reduce all this in the penultimate scene to figures on a clicking calculator is a crime worse than the one under investigation.

For the climax to work, only one serious question should remain to be answered. This eliminates distraction and allows the reader to concentrate on the issue. Whether that issue is the identity of the murderer or the reason for the murder (the Awful Secret) depends upon the point the detective keeps returning to during his personal briefing sessions. Since clearing it up may involve a fair amount of talk—preferably in dialogue between two or more characters, but in any case with a lot of information being exchanged—something must be happening in the scene to draw attention away from those talking heads. And since the story is suspense, it should be something dangerous.

Guns are good, as Raymond Chandler knew. A gun is a marvelous prop, so insidious a symbol of death in our mechanized society as to transcend cliché, and in the hand of a villain, where it's liable to go off at any second, it's always useful. A bomb is just a bigger version of a gun, but the ticking or the burning fuse rachets up the tension; remember that digital nuclear countdown at the end of *Goldfinger*, the movie. Someone inching toward the plug of a lamp, poised to plunge the room into darkness, is a reliable standby. In *Angel Eyes*, I used a gun and a lamp:

> ... I looked at the floor, pretending to be choosing my words. After a moment I located the cord to the lamp where it plugged into the wall. It was good to know for future reference.
>
> "... you kept a cool head, not forgetting to collect your father's derringer afterwards, so that your mother could carry out the plans she had for it. But you should have taken time to search his office and grab the account book he used to record DeLancey's blackmail payments."
>
> "Who'd have thought he was stupid enough to bank them?" Clendenan brought out the little Forehand & Wadsworth.
>
> I fired the .38 through my jacket pocket. He fired at the same time, but his shot went wild and shattered the front window behind me. Then he folded his knees and pitched forward, still holding the now-useless single-shot. His mother screamed.
>
> I didn't bother to look and see what the bodyguards were up to. Instead I twirled the lamp cord around my ankle and jerked the china-base lamp off the end table beside Janet Whiting's chair. We both hit the floor at the same time ...

Amos Walker does most of the talking. It was unavoidable, and at least it spared the villain's having to explain himself to his intended victim. The early introduction of the lamp cord sets up the ending and breaks up the monologue. The scene is a three-ring circus: Walker, the villain and his accomplices, and Judge DeLancey, bleeding copiously from a critical head wound into the lap of Janet Whiting, Walker's client. It's a powered-up version of the old mystery staple of a gathering of suspects for the murderer's unmasking.

Researchers at the University of California at Berkeley concluded recently that there is twice as much new information in the world as there was three years ago, and that most of it isn't interesting. That's all the more reason for writers of fiction to dole out data judiciously—what's needed only, and only when it's needed. Your books should not read as if they were dictated by a machine. They should keep the reader tied up until the last knot is unraveled, then make him or her want to be tied up all over again next time.

* * *

Fiction Fact

Nora Roberts, who compounded her stellar credits as a best-selling romance writer by writing equally successful mysteries under the name J.D. Robb, wrote her first novel in 1979, to avoid becoming stir-crazy while snowed in with her two toddler sons in rural Maryland. "I macraméd two hammocks," she says. "I needed help."

* * *

Dressing Up

* * *

WHEN OG THE HUNTER'S CAVE-NEIGHBORS asked him over a leg of woolly mammoth how he managed to bring the beast down, he wiped his fingers off on his lion skin and told his story. He started with his first sight of his prey and finished with it cold and still at his feet. It would never have occurred to him to describe the carcass first, or start with himself astraddle the mammoth looking for a place to stick his spear and then go back to tell his listeners how he came to that pass. If it did, they'd have beaten him to death with the entree.

These days, it seems, Og's tribe is thinning. Many writers flee from a tidy narrative as if it were that same charging mammoth. They throw prologues, flashbacks, and dream sequences in its path; any device that will slow it down. Nature may abhor a vacuum, but these writers are terrified of a straight line.

I've gotten very suspicious of prologues. When I lift a book off the rack and the first page doesn't say chapter one, I'm tempted to put it back. The petulant child in me asks, "You mean I have to read all this stuff just to get to the story?" The mature reader in me has seen the prologue's purpose subverted too many times not to have developed a prejudice against its use. Finally, the cynical writer in me knows that you can disguise a ludicrous plot and thin characters under a lot of embroidery.

I've used prologues myself, and will use them again when I consider them appropriate. But they've been abused so often that I refuse to use the word prologue at all. Instead, I'll time- or date-stamp the passage or slug something else at the top, a title or a character's name or the name of a place, to separate it from the body of the story. And if there's no good excuse for not just going ahead and telling the thing from start to finish, I drop the device like the dead mammoth it is.

To know when to use a prologue, it's necessary to understand its purpose. It's a tease, like a promo for Must-See TV or a trailer for a theatrical motion picture; a snare laid in cold blood to capture interest. Whether it's a flash-forward to a compelling point in the plot or a frame in which the end is foretold (*this is now*), its point is to make the reader curious enough about how that situation came about to read the book (*that was then*). Flash-forwards and frames are handy when the story would otherwise begin too pragmatically or when the scene thus set off is so riveting few could resist its call.

No one ever wrote a flash-forward with more wicked punch than Max Shulman's on page one of *Sleep Till Noon*:

> Bang! Bang! Bang! Bang!
>
> Four shots ripped into my groin, and I was off on the biggest adventure of my life. ...
>
> But first let me tell you a little about myself.

The ellipsis is Shulman's. Many pages stretch between that three-line prologue and the details of those shots to the groin, but they read *fast*.

The opening of Daphne du Maurier's *Rebecca* is arguably the most noble frame any writer ever built. Beginning with the now-classic line, "Last night I dreamt I went to Manderley again," du Maurier's nameless narrator provides pages of lush description of an abandoned estate, its long driveway winding between feral overgrown rhododendrons and neglected shrubbery, ending before the grand house with the narrator's handkerchief still lying on the table in the library where she'd left it, and finally the heart-rending declaration: "Manderley was no more."

Manipulative? Definitely. The prologue capitalizes without flinching on the insatiable curiosity of the reading public. Yet it's risen many times to the level of great art. Far too often, it stoops to the tawdry depths of flung tinsel. Writers have used it to pad a manuscript to salable length, lifting passages verbatim from the middle to tack onto the beginning, or scratched out *Chapter One* and scribbled in *Prologue* because it happened to run short. This is Hamburger Helper. In clumsy hands, it serves no better purpose than to dress up a dull book. Saddest of all, works of potentially stunning simplicity have been ruined because the authors second-guessed themselves and painted up a fresh young thing until it resembled a harridan of the streets. Give a fourth-grader a Magic Marker and he'll doodle all over the margins of a perfectly good geography report.

Whatever your thoughts about Shulman and du Maurier based on these fragments, you can't help but admire their restraint when I mention that both examples appear not as prologues by name, but as the openings of the first chapters. They're models of the form, yet neither author felt the need to dress his or hers up by isolating it from the rest of the book. One is a blast from the brass section, the other a symphonic overture, but between them there isn't a bell or a whistle to be found.

Call me a cockeyed optimist, but I don't put back that book with its brazen prologue until after I turn to the back and learn if the author has been responsible enough to balance it out with an epilogue at the end. I hold that where the one appears, so must the other, like *u* with *q*, "nor" with "neither," and Paul Simon with Art Garfunkel. It completes the frame—"bookend" is an appropriate alternative term—and keeps the edge of the story from fraying.

The Master Executioner was a complex psychoanalytical profile of an Old World personality who applied the techniques of master craftsmanship to the grisly business of hanging prisoners convicted of capital crimes. I opened with a day-in-the-life vignette of hangman Oscar Stone at fifty, approaching yet another execution with all the attention to detail heed acquired over the course of thirty years. Then I went back to his upbringing in Pennsylvania Dutch country, his apprenticeship as a carpenter, and the twisted path that led him to his specialty. The epilogue brought the story full circle back to his jaded middle age. So completely self-contained was the prologue that I sold it as a short story to an anthology before the novel appeared. I'd done the same thing earlier with the prologue to *Journey of the Dead* with some alteration, and won two Golden Spur Awards from the Western Writers of America, for Best Short Story and Best Novel, for what was essentially the same material. Before you recycle, you'll need to gain permission from your publisher to avoid infringement of copyright.

The flashback is a very old device. I've traced it as far back as 1818, when Mary Shelley used it to present the synthetic man's story in *Frankenstein*. Probably a better scholar than I can find it in Aristophanes. These days flashbacks are all over the place, partly because of the influence of those "How to write a Bestseller" books that tell writers to begin a scene in the middle of the exciting action and then go back to tell what came before. It's gotten so I can tell which book the author has studied and predict where the story will go from there based on how well he learned its lessons. A typical chapter opens at warp speed, slows down in the middle while we take stock, and closes on a cliffhanger, to propel us into the next chapter.

It's pretty dreary stuff, once you recognize the pattern, and all those subjunctives in the middle ("*He'd risen* that morning," "It *had taken* a moment to realize," etc.) bog you down like wet clay. Then all those climaxes at measured intervals make you think you're watching an old-time Saturday afternoon serial, without the week's rest in between chapters. And those *in medias res* starts aren't flashbacks in their purest form.

A flashback is a scene from the past, set prior to the events of the principal narrative, but told as if it were happening before the reader's eyes. It can take the form of a dream sequence or an insertion made by the godlike hand of the writer. If it's an account related by a peripheral character, or if as in the above example the writer stops the action to bring the reader up to speed, it's backtelling. It's the difference between reading about the Battle of the Bulge and dodging bullets among the bomb craters.

Old as it is, the flashback is cinematic, using visual imagery to trigger a memory. Movie audiences are conditioned to know that when Humphrey Bogart dumps over his glass and the screen starts to swim, they're leaving Casablanca for another place and time. The action is repeated when Ingrid Bergman's glass falls over during a poignant moment in long-ago Paris. If we accept the opening of *Rebecca* as chapter one and not a prologue, then all the events that follow comprise one long flashback, bracketed fore and aft by du Maurier's abandoned handkerchief. (In such cases, the device *is* the story.) But books are capable of invoking senses other than visual. Dennis Lehane uses the smell of rotten apples in *Mystic River* to catapult one of his three protagonists back to the nightmare of his abduction as a child, which finds its legacy in the tragedy at the end. None of these stories could be told as effectively without the use of flashback.

In *The Hours of the Virgin*, Amos Walker is hired to find an ancient manuscript that's been stolen from the Detroit Institute of Arts. When the suspect turns out to be the man who murdered Walker's mentor and partner twenty years before, repressed memories return to haunt the detective in the form of conversations with the dead man, forgotten for years, including their last:

—What's the job, Dale?

Just another Dagwood Bumstead with a snake in his pants, kid. Don't worry your pretty little head about it. It's a one-man job.

—You're always telling me a P.I. who takes on a tail job solo is keeping company with an idiot. I'm not doing anything tonight.

Like hell you're not. You're being a husband. New wives got a thing about their men checking in once or twice a week for some reason. They grow out of it, and it's just too bad. Enjoy it while it's here. Go home. Make a kid. Where are all the new dicks going to come from otherwise?

—If you're sure.

Who said anything about sure? Your mother didn't send in the guarantee when she took you home. The only sure is dead sure.

—Okay, see you tomorrow.

Sure, kid.

Since in this case it's a dialogue, I set off Walker's speech with dashes instead of quotation marks, to signal the reader I've switched gears. Here and in other places, when the flashbacks take the form of monologues on the craft of detection and his philosophy of life, the partner's speech appears in italics. As a visual device, it's just as effective as using a prop within the scene, but because the flashbacks recur throughout the book, it's less obtrusive and redundant. Rounded out further with more conventional reminiscences by Walker and others, this character who's been gone for two decades comes through as the most memorable in the cast, with a poignancy unavailable to the living.

These examples notwithstanding, I consider starting at the start, proceeding to the middle, and ending at the end the most useful way of telling a story. Og the hunter certainly knew his audience. The linear or structure requires less explaining, since the events occur in natural order. For me, the ideal read avoids paragraphs of gassy exposition, and a narrative that is constantly charging back and forth like a switch engine needs to flash its signals frequently to keep from running over the reader. It's hard enough for an experienced writer to do this without reminding his audience it's being written at; the tyro, less confident, is tempted to change fonts and empty out his cartons of parentheses, dashes, and ellipses to separate past from present. When you hold the page at arm's length and squint your eyes, it looks like a distress message from Planet Paintshop.

The same goes for stream-of-consciousness, which has fallen on evil times since its birth in the little literary magazines of the 1920s. These string-cheese constructions of dependent clauses stuck together with spit and no punctuation may have seemed representative of the human thought process back when Molly Bloom enchanted

Prohibition readers with the wondrous variety of her bodily fluids, but in the real world, random thoughts are by and large wordless, more like bad MTV than a runaway tickertape. Tell us what your character has on his mind and for God's sake move on.

If your story needs an elaborate device, pick one and use it consistently throughout. If it can be told without one, it should be. Such tricks are dandy for filling pages; but filling pages is easy. My dog did it all the time.

* * *

Fiction Fact

Writers are their own harshest critics.

Robert Louis Stevenson burned stories based on listeners' informal responses, and Leo Tolstoy tossed the manuscript of War and Peace *into a ditch, where it was rescued by his son.*

* * *

Ten Things You Can Do
to Avoid Success

* * *

THIS SHOULD BE FUN. There are many more self-ordained experts out there than there are credentials to go around, and they need to be taken down at least ten pegs.

It's been said that advice is offered in bushels and taken in teaspoons, but a single drop of the following can be a fatal overdose:

1. **Write what you know.** It took a lot of nerve for your junior high Creative Writing teacher to turn her back long enough to write this on the blackboard. At the tender age when most of us encounter this morsel of Bizarro wisdom, we were still waiting for the bones in our skulls to grow together, let alone any sort of experience that anyone else would care to read about. Even in adulthood, few of us have dug for gold in the Yukon or survived ten rounds with Mike Tyson, and if we choose to make writing a career, eventually even the richest store of personal anecdote will go empty. For every Linda Fairstein, shaping her firsthand knowledge of life in a public prose-

cutor's office into gripping fiction, there are ten Stephen Cranes, writing vivid accounts of battles without ever having seen one. Imagination is an excellent substitute for memory, and it can be augmented through research. Know what you write.

2. **Always make your main character sympathetic.** Okay, we've just lost Count Dracula, Madame Bovary, Heathcliff and Cathy, Don Vito Corleone, Richard Stark's Parker, half of Shakespeare, and all of Guy de Maupassant. The reasoning is that readers have to care enough about the protagonist to want to find out what happens to him or her. It's nice when people are nice, and happy endings make everyone happy; but Little Nell dies anyway and Long John absconds with the swag. Undoubtedly there was a time when most readers wanted to hug Eleanor Porter's Pollyanna to death, but more recent polls run 80 percent in favor of strangulation. All your characters have to be to hold your reader's interest is interesting.

3. **Begin with a hook.** I opened *Port Hazard* with a doozy: "I was killing a conductor on the Northern Pacific between Butte and Garrison when my orders changed." But I'm just as proud of this first sentence, from *The High Rocks*: "For three years running, the north central section of Montana's Bitterroot Mountain range was struck by a series of harsh winters that paralyzed transportation and left the old-timers with nothing to talk about in the way of worse winters gone by."

   Both narrations are provided by the same character, a deputy U.S. marshal I've been using for many years. The first example (and the latest) is intended to snag the reader straight away. The second (and the earliest) is designed to draw him in gradually. The chief drawback of a sharp instrument is it gets dull fast. If you develop a reputation for opening with hooks, the novelty will wear off soon. When it comes to capturing the reader, quicksand is just as effective.

4. **End each chapter with a cliffhanger.** The same philosophy applies here. It's supposed to keep the reader from putting the

book down because he can't wait to see what happens in the next chapter. And so on. Readers expect to be manipulated, but relentless pushing will only get you a bust in the snoot. Also, the pattern becomes redundant and jerky, like an airplane pilot practicing his stalls. Try bringing a chapter into a gentle landing now and then.

5. **Keep a journal.** I'm glad I did it when I was writing *Bloody Season*, if only to remind myself I've overcome obstacles in the past, but at that point I was already a self-employed full-time writer, and I had the time for it. I never kept one before and haven't since. If it's practice you want, practice on your book. Save your creative energy for paying work.

6. **Join a writer's group.** I never attended one until my career was already established, and I still find reading my work aloud before an audience valuable because I hear things I might not if I read it only to myself. Many of the comments afterward make sense; others run along the lines of the stuff I'm picking apart in this chapter. Between the thrice-warmed-over advice of writers who know everything except how to get their own manuscripts past an editor's reader, and the party-pooping cynicism of jaded old failures, you're better off keeping your own counsel.

7. **Copyright your work.** The reasoning here is you need to protect yourself from unscrupulous editors who reject your manuscript, then give or sell the idea to another writer. If you deal with reputable publishers (and how desperate do you have to be to deal with *dis*reputable ones?), the odds of this happening are extremely slim; but if it does happen, you're protected by common-law copyright, and need only prove your book was written first to win any legal action.

   The simplest way to establish proof is to seal and mail the manuscript to yourself. When it's delivered, store it unopened, with the dated postmark intact. (I've never bothered, but do it if it makes you feel better.) Applying for formal copyright takes time away from writing, and makes editors nervous; some would rather return a submission unread than risk being sued for unconsciously sharing something in it with someone else. And if you're that paranoid, ask yourself what's to prevent a flunky in the U.S. Copyright Office from pinching your idea?

8. **Rent an office away from home.** Sure, working at home can be distracting, and certain family members can't be trained to consider you unavailable during working hours. But the benefits of the twenty-foot commute outweigh all the disadvantages. Fighting your way through traffic and the snowstorm of the century, only to encounter a slow writing day when you get where you're going, is exasperation you don't need; and then there's the pressure of rent being wasted. And are you likely to make the trip all over again that night, when the ideas are jumping around like fleas and you might get in five pages before bedtime.

    Let the machine answer the phone, stuff cotton in your ears if you have to, and work in your tattered old bathrobe if you like. People who have no choice but to go to an office would nail your hide to a barn wall if they found out you volunteered for it. Doesn't your paper carry *Dilbert*?

9. **Write screenplays, not novels.** Some people can't get enough rejection. If you think publishing is a tough room, you've never tried to crack the Hollywood closed shop. Big-time screenwriters make fabulous money, but unless you live in Beverly Hills, share a carpool with George Lucas, and your last screen credit was *The Cat in the Hat*, your chances of getting a seat on the next space shuttle are better than they are of smuggling your script past the slushpile. Meanwhile you've wasted months you might have spent writing a novel that knocks Patricia Cornwell off her pedestal and sells to a studio that pays you millions to let someone *else* write the screenplay.

10. **Give up your day job.** I saved my favorite for last. This one falls under the category of Hand Grenades for the Other Guy to Throw

Himself On. The theory is that if you sever all your connections to financial security, you'll be more motivated to write, if only to avoid starvation. Whoever came up with it should be shoved off the roof of the Chrysler Building and encouraged to fly.

Unless and until you've established yourself as a writer, maintaining another source of income will prevent you from knuckling under to your editor's every whim. When you're working with your first publisher, it's normal to make certain concessions, including some you don't agree with; but if you don't want your firefighter hero to be changed into a plucky Dalmatian or your tragic romance to end with a pie in the face, it's much easier to say no when you have a regular paycheck and a healthy balance in savings. You need that last inch of steel.

And one piece of good advice: *Beware of lists of ten.* Very little in writing ever comes to an even number.

* * *

Fiction Fact

Thomas Wolfe preferred to write standing up using the top of his refrigerator for a desk. (Did I mention he was six-foot-six?)

* * *

Editing

* * *

I DON'T HAVE TO READ SELF-PUBLISHED BOOKS, so I don't. If I never had to submit to a root canal, I wouldn't do that either.

I don't look down on self-published writers. It took me eight years and one hundred sixty rejections to break into print, and many times I was convinced there was some zombie on the publishing end, mindlessly transferring the fruit of my flesh and spirit from one envelope to the other and sending it back without explanation. (To add theft to indifference, nine times out of ten Dead Ned stole my paper-clip.) Had desktop publishing existed back then, I might have given it a try. I'm grateful it didn't.

In theatrical terms, publishers are a tough room. But as a member of the entertainment-consuming public, I'd rather go to a legitimate theater where the players have passed auditions and listened to the advice of an experienced director than trust my spare time to a self-proclaimed actor who hired the auditorium.

Put bluntly: Most undirected actors are awful, and so are most self-published books. The biggest result of desktop publishing has been a flood of bad literature printed and bound on the cheap.

There has never been a writer so good that he or she couldn't be made better through the efforts of a veteran editor with vision. As Dirty Harry said, "A man has to know his limitations." In the most talented among us, the temptation is strong to revert to childhood and find out just how much one can get away with. Without the occasional waggle of the editorial finger, the work will grow self-indulgent and flabby. The writer who turns his back on the system and performs as his own publisher, editor, and distributor has deprived himself of the one consistent force that has shaped every great literary artist since Plato. (Given the right software, he might have bypassed Socrates.)

Editing is far from a pleasant experience. In the early days, my manuscripts passed through so many hands, each armed with a different-colored pencil, that by the time they were returned to me, I was left with no color of my own to make the revisions. Even now, when my idiosyncrasies have become notorious and often pass without remark, I snort and sputter, "How dare they?" whenever some cooler head in New York suggests a change. But I take it seriously, because those are the first professional eyes apart from mine to see the book, and because I'm a better writer for the comments and queries directed to me in the past. When I disagree and let the passage stand as written, it's because I've learned the difference between what I can get away with and what's good for the book.

At one time, most writers dealt with one editor, who read manuscripts, acquired those he or she liked, and suggested whatever revisions were needed down to the smallest detail. Today, each book is assigned at least two editors, and may be read and evaluated by as many as three. Many publishing houses employ acquisition editors, whose job it is to persuade the publisher to buy a particular manuscript. Once the purchase has been made, the book is then handed to a line editor, to read it for style and content and communicate directly with the author over corrections and improvements in character and plot. When that editor is satisfied with the author's response, a copy editor goes over each page to correct spelling and grammar, check facts, and make sure that details remain consistent (i.e., that the blue eyes in chapter one haven't turned green by chapter sixteen). Throughout this process, the author will have read his or her book a minimum of three times: (1) when it comes back with the line editor's queries; (2) when it's been scribbled over and appended with Post-It notes by the copy editor; (3) when it's been typeset and sent to the author for one last look before going to the binders. Not counting how many times the author read it before submitting, the manuscript is read straight through no fewer than five times. Double that for those sections marked for closer attention, and the figure is still conservative. Quite a filtering process, yet impurities routinely wind up in the finished product. Usually, these are minor typographical errors. On occasion they're not so minor. Consider the probability, then, of a herd of howlers stampeding past just one pair of eyes and into the reader's hands. That's self-publishing.

After the author's, the copy editor's job is the hardest. It requires a solid grounding in basic English, a trained eye for detail, some knowledge of the ways of the world, and the patience to track the most arcane assertion to its source. It's also one of the lowest-paying, which explains why good copy editors are scarce. The best I ever had called me to task on the matter of railway movements between London and Whitby, England, in 1890. The worst, split infinitives and dangled participles in her own queries. But the lessons I'd learned working with the first gave me the confidence to overcome the inadequacies of the second.

Most editors are conscientious, but overworked, and are not so different from that zombie I once blamed for my chronic rejection. Faced with an ever-growing slushpile of manuscripts, they read them looking for a reason to reject rather than accept, in the desperate hope of clearing their desks before their children graduate college. The writer's job is to deny them that excuse. This means capturing their attention on the first page.

I'm not talking about an opening hook. The hook is not the miracle tool it's often made out to be, as I've already pointed out. What follows is almost always a letdown, and when you try too hard to live up to a jackrabbit start, you've written a cartoon. And don't forget that most editors have seen all the hooks. Impressing them with yet another is as hard as getting applause from a magician's booking-agent for sawing a woman in half. What they want to know is if you can write. Having proven that, you must then transport them from their cluttered offices to somewhere else, even if it's another cluttered office; to make them forget for a moment they're working rather than reading for pleasure. If they turn over that first page to read any part of the second, you've made a sale. (If, as one editor once remarked, you've given him or her a reason to call colleagues in from their offices to read them a passage, your book will lead the season's list.)

Congratulations. Now the book has become the editors' property, to toss back and forth like a medicine ball and see how much sawdust they can knock out.

Editing is humbling. Even before the glow of arrival fades, the writer finds what seems to be his every idea and method of expressing it questioned, criticized, and (in rare cases of editorial arrogance) ridiculed, and wonders why the manuscript was accepted at all, and whether there's any future for him in publishing. His responses swing between two extremes. If it's meek acquiescence, the work will suffer because of the restraints placed upon imagination and experimentation. If it's stubborn resistance, he may acquire a reputation as an uncooperative writer, and jeopardize future sales.

If the choices terrify you, they needn't. It helps to know that copy editors have no authority. Every change they make is subject to the approval of the line editor, and ultimately the author. And the line editor's suggestions are just that, usually ending with question marks. The thinking is that since the author's is the only name that goes on the book, he or she is responsible or everything that appears in it. However persistent the editor may be about the proposed emendations, the writer's preferences are sacred. If his instincts clash with his editor's, the author's own intimacy with the book outweighs all the years of experience the editor has brought to it. (This power increases with time, if you don't abuse it at the beginning, and if you choose your battles carefully.)

Before you swing that formidable club, remember you're dealing with a professional, who knows something of books and has as much to gain or lose from the way yours turns out as you. By the time it's reached the editing stage, you should have been away from it long enough to be able to read it objectively, and to apply that disinterest to the editors suggestions. If in your opinion they improve the book, follow them; it's no less your creation for the amount of constructive criticism you accept, and understanding the reason for the change will make you a better writer. It's one correction that won't have to be made again.

Occasionally, you'll encounter a piece of editorial advice that neither improves nor harms the original. I call this sideways editing; the change made for the sake of change alone, that serves only to fulfill the editor's need to edit. (Maybe his boss just came in and he wanted to look busy.) I'm no fan of it, because it's stupid, but since complying with it makes no difference anyway, save your energy for the battles that count. As I've said, you'll make most of your compromises early in your career, and this is a good place to earn some good will and gain leverage to stand firm where it matters. You'll have your revenge later, when a genteel expletive scribbled in the margin satisfies your urge to box someone's ears.

If, on the other hand, the suggestion strikes you as just plain wrong, you won't be doing anyone a favor by submitting to it. This is where all that turning the other cheek pays off and you get to go on the offensive. Consider this rhyme, which I just now made up:

Stet's the friend I call,
who's never out to lunch.
In size he's kind of small,
but he packs a mighty punch.

Okay, so now you know why this book isn't called *How to Write Poetry*. The message is more important than the meter. Stet is Latin for "let it stand," and it's been a printing staple since Gutenberg. It's also the writer's best friend. Pretend your editor's a vampire; stet is your crucifix. He may bridle against it, try to persuade you to remove it, but in the end he's powerless against it. When it appears next to a suggested change, the typesetter is bound to set the line as originally written. Matt Braun, the Western writer, once became so incensed by a copy editor's attempts to translate his authentic frontier terminology into grating modern "easternisms" that he wrote on the title page of the manuscript: "Stet the whole damn thing." The book was published as submitted, and Braun became even more of a legend among his fellow writers. With luck, you'll never need to take so drastic a step, but use this tool wisely and it won't let you down.

During editing, your stock will be higher if you can show a basic knowledge of the signs and symbols involved in responding to alterations and queries. The best source I've found is *Encyclopedic Dictionary of English Usage*, by N.H. Mager and S.K. Mager, which displays all the commonly used proofreader's marks with an explanation beside each and a sample page of text showing how they're used. The references appear on the last two pages of this 342-page book, but they alone are worth the cover price. (The rest echo the wisdom of *The Elements of Style*, arranged alphabetically.) Every now and then I still pull it down to refresh my memory. Editors are less likely to give you an argument if they see you're hip to the lingo, and you'll avoid embarrassing yourself by asking why someone drew a pig's tail through one of your commas.

Don't lose your cool. Matt Braun's experience was an extreme case, involving a copy editor's incompetence, and at the time it took place, he was already an established writer with an international readership. Had he been a relative unknown, he probably would have been more circumspect in his response. There's a reason professionalism and politeness begin with the same letter. However strongly you feel about the way your work has been edited, the process will go more smoothly if you argue your point with courtesy. The time will come when you've assembled enough credentials to let loose the dogs, but don't make a habit of it. I know a magazine editor who routinely rejects stories submitted by a well-known best-selling writer because he's too unpleasant to work with. No one listens to someone who shouts all the time, and there are too many writers out there waiting for an opening to go around alienating editors by the long ton.

There's no getting around it; you will be corrected, emended, questioned, badgered, and second-guessed. But you can avoid the worst by editing yourself before giving anyone else a crack at you. If what you're submitting isn't the best you're capable of, you might as well stick it in the basement and feed the crickets. Double-check your research, and make notes of all your sources so if your editor questions a detail, you'll have your answer ready. If you depart from reality in the name of drama, convince yourself it's justified, and be prepared to defend it; literary license is a privilege, not a right, and you can have it revoked if you are too lazy to do your homework. Check your spelling; you know my feelings on that, and on grammar. You wouldn't go to a job interview with your shirttail hanging out (I hope), and you shouldn't send a manuscript to an editor with participles dangling all over the place. This stuff is elementary.

Are your sentences too long? Too short and choppy? Did a metaphor you were especially proud of slip the surly bonds of earth and soar so far out of the atmosphere that not even Carl Sagan could follow it, much less understand it? Did a secondary character with a wife and six children in chapter two show up again in chapter twenty-seven a lifelong bachelor? These kinds of things have happened to me, and I'd have been mortified if anyone else had discovered them.

Minor demons shouldn't get past your radar, either. If you spot something just as you're about to seal the envelope, shrug your shoulders, and figure it's not worth taking time to fix, remember that flaws are like rats. For every one you see, there may be ten you don't. Jump on the ones you see, and look hard for others.

I clean as I go, go back and clean, then go back again. When the fever is on and I'm in a rage to pile up pages, I slap the words down, fast as my fingers will move, and go back over them later at my leisure. I wrote all my early books in two separate drafts, leaving the first draft unread for a month before reading it start to finish. The time away gave me distance and objectivity, and the ability to see seams in need of straightening I might not have seen when I was still close to the writing. I learned this in art class, when I stepped back to look at what I'd painted without being distracted by the individual brush strokes. I recommend it. You don't have to let go of the book until you're ready, so take advantage of this cooling-off period. You may be surprised how good an editor you can be of your own work when you're less personally involved. Just as no one has a tougher boss than the man who works for himself, you should be the most pitiless editor you'll ever have.

Many new writers seek out freelance editors. Most of these writers are looking for praise, not criticism, but those hoping for an honest assessment are often disappointed. This is an excellent way to get rid of money you don't need; too many editing services will tell you you're the biggest thing since Isabel Allende, then empty your savings account doing things to your manuscript you could just as well do yourself, or worse, junking it up with useless sideways editing just to hike the fee. Some of them are crooks. When you're ready to show your book to an outsider, send it to an agent or publisher (see chapter twenty-one: Fifteen Percent of Your Life). Agents work for a percentage of the advance and royalties *after it sells*, and the editor who buys it will do the rest at no charge to you.

* * *

Fiction Fact

Ernest Hemingway's fondness for four-letter words worried his editor, Maxwell Perkins, who once wrote a list of them on a Things to Do Today pad, intending to discuss them with the editorial board at Charles Scribner's Sons. Scribner stopped by his desk to chat, glanced at the pad, and said, "Max, I'm putting you in for a vacation. When you have to remind yourself to do those things, it's clear you need a rest."

* * *

Legal Limits

* * *

NOT MY FAVORITE SUBJECT. Worse, applying it to the craft of writing fiction is as much a downer as filling out an income tax form on Christmas Eve.

I suspect it's not so much the legal part that depresses me as the concept of enforcing limits on the imagination. But new writers are curious about such things as libel and invasion of privacy, so the subject needs addressing. It might surprise you to learn that I go months and months at a time without thinking about legal matters.

With one exception.

Plagiarism is the cardinal sin, as far as I am and everyone else in this business ought to be concerned. The theft of imagination and months of creative toil is cold-blooded and callous, and nearly as heinous as child abduction. It's also lazy. A forger who sets out to pass off his own painting as the work of a great master needs the skill to produce a good copy, as well as the time and expensive materials to invest in the project, but all a plagiarist has to do is scan someone else's work into a computer and substitute his own byline. In recent years, desktop publishing has even eliminated most of the cash lay-out involved in printing and binding the evidence of the crime.

I was plagiarized a number of years ago, along with several other writers, when a young twerp in Maine excavated a half-dozen or so short stories from mystery magazines several years old, computer-generated a collection under his own name, and even duped the Associated Press into giving him free advertising by writing a feature story about him and wiring it to newspapers across the country. I found out about it when a friend in Maine obtained a copy of the book and sent it to me. The little pissant had taken one of my Detroit-based Amos Walker stories, changed *Amos* to *John*, lifted all the references to local architecture, and replaced them with Bangor land-marks. (He even traced the illustration that ran with the story in *Alfred Hitchcock's Mystery Magazine* and reproduced it on the cover, pla-giarizing the artist; there wasn't an original thought in the entire mess.) He did the same with the other authors' stories, including one of Bret Halliday's Michael Shayne mysteries set in Miami, renaming the world-famous detective *Michael Fayne,* and incidentally treating his readers to the spectacle of a character sporting a Panama hat in frosty New England.

I called my lawyer, who got in touch with the other writers and threatened the creep with a class-action lawsuit. The cash settlement he eventually ponied up was piddling, but an angry Associated Press gave us the satisfaction of reporting his crime from coast to coast. I used my part of the settlement to pay my lawyer's costs, and occa-sionally I manage to forget all about the feelings of violation for two or three days at a time. Chiefly I remember the little crook's response when my lawyer explained to him that being the victim of plagiary is very much like having ones child stolen: "Children are our greatest resource; it's a sin to make that comparison." (My wife's assessment: "Oh; a *politically correct* plagiarist.")

But his ploy was more sinister than just a bout for immediate sales and the chance to pose as an author. The book carried an adver-tisement for a writing contest, inviting readers to submit original sto-ries for a shot at a cash prize and publication. It's safe to assume the prize would never be paid, and that the contestants would merely be furnishing fodder for more plagiarism, tantamount to giving a counterfeiter a full set of treasury plates. That little addition opened the door to a charge of intent to commit fraud, and why his Carpal Tunnel Syndrome isn't being treated in a prison infirmary is a matter between him and the state and federal authorities.

If neither the legal nor the moral implications make you hesitate to follow his example, I don't want to know you. But consider this: Whether your aim is money or fame or both, the more successful your crime, the greater grow your chances of being caught. The crime itself is evidence that a crime has been committed, and sooner or later it will fall into the hands of someone who recognizes it and decides to take action. Even if you avoid litigation and official punishment, your chances of ever publishing your own work are nearly nonexistent; publishers are paranoid about lawsuits, as witness the length of the Warranty and Indemnity clause in every publishing contract. Should you somehow squeak through anyway, someday your past will come back to haunt and humiliate you. Buddy, you're screwed.

The law regards plagiarism as the lifting of written material copyrighted by someone else, or the use of characters created by someone else, without obtaining the prior consent of the copyright holder, or in the case of brief material quoted from other sources, without giving credit to those sources. (As with the examples cited in this book.) It doesn't cover the use of plots or ideas, for the simple reason that criminal intent is difficult to prove without such *prima facie* evidence as a line-by-line comparison. Also, the world is filled with unlikely coincidences; it's more than conceivable that two or more writers will come up with the same concept at the same time, or that a previous idea will find a home with another writer without his or her being aware that it was used before. Less excusable, but understandable, is the chance of unconsciously borrowing someone else's plot and situation, having been exposed to it and forgotten the circumstances of that exposure. (This is a strong argument in favor of not discussing unfinished work in public, particularly when other writers are present.)

Titles can't be copyrighted, again because it's possible for a number of writers to dream up the same short combination of words or syllables without consultation or prior exposure. That's why there are so many mysteries called *Sudden Death*, and why a TV movie that aired in 1972 and a novel published twenty years later by Tom Clancy are both called *Clear and Present Danger*. (The odds of this happening with one-word titles are astronomical.) Personally, I consider a writer who knowingly uses another writer's title guilty of plagiarism, even if it's not actionable in court, and hold that in most cases a little research will avoid unwittingly stepping on someone else's toes. I don't know whether a romance novel published fifteen years ago under the title *This Side of Paradise* was a case of deliberate theft or howling ignorance of the work of F. Scott Fitzgerald, but in either case I'm just as ticked off. It's a question of respect.

Just don't steal, okay? It's a rich language, capable of infinite combinations, and ideas are free and all around. I have more each day than I have lifespan to put them to use. So will you.

Libel is the other word that spooks publishers. It means telling a malicious lie about a person or an institution in print. (Spoken aloud, it's slander.) If you do it, that person or institution will sue you. Even if you do it without malice—say, for entertainment purposes only—you'll be called upon to prove before a judge that you bore the offended party no ill will. (Libel and slander are exceptions to the rule of law, which places the burden of proof upon the accuser.) If your allegations are sound, you haven't committed libel if you can offer evidence that your senator is indeed corrupt or your physician a drug addict, but you will still have to testify, and spend money on a good attorney if you're smart. It's smarter still, and much cheaper, not to accuse anyone of anything in the course of your narrative; in which case you're guilty of nothing but having written a dull book.

Let's make that our last resort. If you have a specific person or institution in mind, and you cast that party in an unfavorable light, you may dodge the judicial bullet by using a fictitious name, but the U.S. Supreme Court has ruled that insufficient defense. You need to take further steps to disguise the party's identity. Making your skinny congressman a fat county supervisor and changing his name from

Thingummy to Glarg renders the character no less useful artistically, and provides some security, so long as there's no actual fat county supervisor named Glarg waddling about. Picture yourself in the docket, pointing out discrepancies between the complainant and your character; the more, and the sharper the contrast, the better for your case. If you do want to use a real figure, make sure he's dead—and I'm not advising you to go out and hit him with a shovel. The dead can't sue, and no one can sue on their behalf. You hear a lot of noise to the contrary from the families of the famous dead, but they never get beyond threatening to go to court.

Public figures are similarly restricted in their ability to seek reparations for how they're portrayed in print. Because of their exposure, their right to privacy is diminished; but this is a gray area. U.S. presidents are nearly powerless in anti-defamation suits, but depending upon the judge and the details, that movie star you raked over the coals may take you for everything you've got. I'd choose Tyrone Power and let Alec Baldwin alone.

If, on the other hand, you want all your readers to know exactly whom you're writing about, and are prepared to prove all your assertions, go ahead and use real names and publish the book as nonfiction. I've never understood the reason for the *roman a clef*. If it's about real, living people, what makes it fiction? If raking muck is your aim, Current Events is the place for you. A novelist without a social conscience is like a frog without a vacuum cleaner.

Some writers go to great lengths to avoid offending someone who might see himself in their books. Once they've chosen their setting and put together a list of characters, they'll call Information and ask if anyone by any of those names is listed in that region, and if anyone is, they change it. At the opposite end of the spectrum are writers like Guy Owen, who throughout the first draft of *The Ballad of the Flim-Flam Man* used the real names of the inspirations for his characters, then methodically changed the names in the final draft—overlooking one, which he happened to have assigned to a notorious bootlegger. The name made it into print, and when last heard from, Owen was still waiting for the other boot to drop. The point of these two examples is that they both stand the same risk of lawsuit.

We live in a litigious society, and the system is so arranged—or disarranged—that anyone can sue anyone for anything. Burglars have broken limbs while robbing people's houses and brought suit against the homeowners for negligence. A woman dumped coffee in her lap at a drive-through, burning herself, and collected from the restaurant chain for serving hot coffee. It's possible to attend a party where the champagne is flat and the conversation boring, and to file a case against the host for pain and suffering. Sometimes the suit is so frivolous an indignant judge throws it out before too much damage is done. More often, the defendant wins his case only after he or she has paid huge sums to cover attorney fees and court costs. Anyone can sue anyone, and no one is safe from being sued, regardless of the steps taken to prevent it.

Many years after Ernest Hemingway published *The Sun Also Rises*, a British noblewoman sued him and his publisher for defamation of character in the case of Lady Ashley, the novel's promiscuous female lead. As it turned out, the real-life Lady Ashley hadn't married Lord Ashley until long after the book was in print, and so there was no actual Lady Ashley at the time Hemingway was writing about the character. The suit was eventually dismissed, but not before a great deal of correspondence had passed back and forth between the author and the legal department at Charles Scribner's Sons, and between Scribner's and Lady Ashley's attorney. It had no legal basis, and neither the writer nor his publisher was at fault, yet the system had to run its course.

You can be careful and still be careless. In 1932, MGM changed the name of Rasputin's assassin in *Rasputin and the Empress*, fearing the assassin, a member of the Russian imperial court, would sue the filmmakers; the assassin sued anyway. He was proud of his deed, and humiliated to find himself eliminated from the cast of characters. Then Rasputin's daughter tried to take the studio to court for maligning her father's character!

The moral is, take whatever precautions you need to feel secure, but understand that being careful, or even innocent, is no guarantee that you won't have to defend yourself against legal action. (I prefer to invest the time I might have spent calling Information on my writing.) In fact, given the frequency with which renowned writers are taken to court, odds are the more successful you are, the more likely it is someone will pick you as the target for an easy buck. When it happens, consider yourself a hit—and use some of those royalties to retain a good lawyer.

A publishing contract can be as terrifying at first sight as an IRS audit, and with good reason; it's harder to read than Form 1040. Compared to what publishers expect you to sign now, the quaint things they sent me back in the 1970s look like a Model T Ford parked next to a Stealth bomber. New technological markets have added pages, and every time a publisher or a writer is sued in a high-profile case of libel or copyright infringement, the lawyers tack on another clause to protect their corporate clients, even if it mainly duplicates what's already there. Care to hedge your bet on living off your royalties? Invest in a company that manufactures staples.

Also an agent.

Yes, I know the catch-22: Can't get a publisher without an agent, can't get an agent without a publisher. Which is bull. For tips on how to snare one or both, read chapter twenty-one: Fifteen Percent of Your Life.

It's an agent's duty to protect you and your work and to secure the best deal. It's his or her deal, too, don't forget. Other duties include listening to your concerns and providing explanations and advice. (Generally speaking, the more things that are scratched out of the contract, the better for you.) It may surprise you to learn how many concessions you can get just by asking, and how often it's just a matter of scribbling in a new line and initialing it. This is the time to make changes, before both parties have signed. Any second thoughts will come with a lawyer attached.

That's why it's important to have expert guidance at the start. Market that first book yourself, if you like—that's my advice, although it's not often taken—but once you have a publisher's interest, turn over the negotiations to an agent. This is what gladiators are for.

* * *

Fiction Fact

No roundup of literary anecdotes is complete without a Dorothy Parker story. Reviewing a novel for The New Yorker, *she wrote: "This is not a book to be put down lightly. It should be thrown with great force."*

* * *

Fifteen Percent
Of Your Life

* * *

TWO QUESTIONS, nearly as old as the agent-writer relationship
(which, truth to tell, isn't very old):

1. Do I need an agent?

*No; despite what you've been told, and even despite what an
editor may have said the last time you had a manuscript rejected.*

2. Should I have an agent?

You'd be a fool not to.

Okay, elaboration is in order.

I placed my first book with a publisher before I had an agent.
Jimmy Carter was in office, and George Lucas was still trying to figure out how to make an action-figure look like Luke Skywalker on
camera. But times weren't all that different.

Then as now, publishers were more likely to take seriously those submissions that came their way through a recognized author's representative. It subtracted one step from the screening process and gave the manuscript a leg up out of the slush pile.

Oddly enough, though, even when no agent was involved, an unknown and unpublished writer could reasonably expect to hear back from the editor in six weeks or less. Today, even when the new writer is fronted by a well-known agent, a year of silence is not unusual.

More on that later.

The point is, I got the book published with no one fronting for me but the firm of what I like to call Underwood & Noggin, meaning my typewriter and my own lively ego. And when I submitted my next book to the same publisher, I was lucky enough to have found an honest editor who liked my stuff, and who told me candidly that the new book was too good for that press, and sent me a list of three agents she felt could place it properly.

Two of those agents rejected the manuscript. The third sold it to Doubleday, and many books after that until his death twelve years later.

It's still possible to land a publisher without an agent. However, the dynamics of self-preservation have changed.

As always, put your best foot forward. First impressions are important, and with no other evidence upon which to judge you, strangers will form positive or negative opinions based on your appearance. Dressing well eliminates unfavorable snap judgments. Similarly, when you submit an outline and sample chapters to a publisher, the pages should be neat and free of typos and misspellings. A professional-looking package is far more likely to get a second look than a sloppy one, and may help overcome whatever misgivings the editor may have about reading something that was not submitted through an agent.

I assume the writing itself is the best you can do at this point in your passage. If it isn't, you have no business wasting the editor's time. If it is, it will go a long way toward eradicating prejudice against unagented manuscripts; but not if a sheaf of stained, thumbed-through, dog-eared pages discourages the editor from reading it at all.

If you use a typewriter, there's no excuse for that except laziness; if you use a computer or a wordprocessor, there's no excuse at all. Take a little time and come off like a professional.

All this was true when direct submission was more common, of course, but it's more important than ever now that publishers can draw the "unagented" card and spare himself the effort of coming up with another excuse to bounce an uninviting package.

Self-preservation, too, has become a primary concern. In the old days, it was considered bad form for a writer to send the same book to more than one publisher at a time for consideration. That was when you could expect to hear back promptly, and if the answer was no, to rework the material or pack it off to another publisher. As with every other industry, the gears in publishing grind more slowly in reverse ratio to the rise in rapid-fire technology, and you can lose a year of your life only to be rejected and have to start the process all over again.

This is criminal neglect. The only way around it is to submit the material to two or more publishers at a time, keep records of where and when it was sent, and follow up with polite letters after four to six weeks asking about the status of the submissions. And for God's sake, don't *tell* any of these editors you've submitted the work else-where; they've no right to know that, and it takes the blush off the rose, giving them another reason not to extend themselves, in case a rival publisher has locked up the book already.

Don't worry about an editor from one house having lunch with an editor from another, comparing notes, and concluding they're being two-timed. Any business gossip they share will involve work in production instead of what's in their slushpile. The only thing you're risking is getting an offer from more than one publisher. This is called an auction, and for writers it's a *good* thing. But even if they all reject you, you've cut many months off the hang time.

I know; practically every publisher you've looked up in *Writer's Market* says it doesn't consider "unsolicited' (i.e., unagented) manu-scripts. That's just a dodge to encourage talentless amateurs to both-er agents instead of editors and reduce the over-the-transom traffic. Every publisher worthy of its imprint employs at least one editor who hopes to discover the next Tom Wolfe or Mary Higgins Clark. When such a writer appears, heralded by good prose in a professional package, no disclaimer in *Writer's Market* or elsewhere will prevent that editor from making an offer.

So why have an agent at all?

As late as the turn of the last century, it was the publishers who asked that question. W. Somerset Maugham was one of the first professional writers to engage a representative, and he was roundly badmouthed by publishers, who felt the decision violated the spirit of the "gentlemen's agreement" they said ruled their profession. This was the same argument advanced by sweatshop owners against labor unions. Maugham got a better deal, and the age of writers representing themselves drew to a close. Which brings us to the first answer to the question:

1. **An agent can get you a better deal.** Agents represent writers for a living, not for a lark, and unlike writers who represent themselves, they do it full time. They know what the book is worth on the current market, know which publishers are most likely to be interested in it, and know most of the editors they'll be negotiating with. Furthermore, as disinterested (not uninterested) professionals, they aren't afraid to walk away from an offer they consider unsatisfactory. (Face it: You'd jump at a handful of magic beans.)

2. **An agent understands publishing contracts.** My earliest contracts at Doubleday were three feet long, printed on both sides, and could be understood by one of those monkeys that have been taught to converse in sign language. Back then, that publisher didn't concern itself with motion-picture rights, and audio and electronic publishing hadn't been invented. The last contract I signed ran eighteen pages single-spaced and contained more compound sentences than a Gabriel García Márquez first draft. I'm thankful to have an agent with a thorough grounding in contract language who keeps up on all the legal challenges involved with each new development in this ever-mutating industry. Many agencies retain contract attorneys, whom they pay out of their

fifteen percent fee, spread out over all their clients. I'd have to hock a close relative to retain one on my own for an hour.

3. **An agent is a punching bag.** Not literally, of course; although I had one for a week that I'd have liked to try out my left jab on. Publishers can be dense, and even the best editor can make a mistake and strike a passage out of your work that would bring on world peace and make reality TV vanish. But if you vent directly at them, you can destroy your reputation for cooperation and jeopardize your option.

   Agents are a great place to lodge all your complaints, and when you want to get your message into your publisher's ear, are adept at translating a four-letter vocabulary into the professional language of a stern memorandum. They have been known to hold their clients' heads and hands as well, and present shoulders to cry on. It's not in the job description, although it goes with the territory, so remember this at Christmas.

4. **An agent does all the things you don't want to.** Or haven't time for, which amounts to the same thing, if you're serious about writing. This one would sway me even if all the others didn't. Agents don't stop working for you once the book is sold and the contract signed; it may even be said that that's when their work truly begins. The best ones reserve rights from the contract and peddle them elsewhere like parts from an automobile. These may include foreign rights, which involve dealing with agents and publishers in countries and territories outside the U.S.; motion-picture, theatrical, electronic, audio, large-print and other reprint editions; and a cornucopia of T-shirts, games, and action figures related to the original work. Such rights are defined as subsidiary, and each comes with its own contract to be negotiated.

   Then there is the business of keeping track of term licensing agreements and applying for reversions when they run out, so that the book may be sold again elsewhere or a new deal arranged with the original publisher; after which the cycle begins all over again. Having an agent, for me, means paying someone to look after all these things so I can concentrate on my writing. At fifteen percent, you won't find a better bargain.

So how do you get an agent? If you've interested a publisher in your book, you should have no trouble lining up an agent to close the deal. The prospect of a paying client is a great icebreaker. But whether you begin your shopping at that point or prefer to work through an agent from Square One, the procedure is the same as if you submitted directly to a publisher, with *publisher* crossed out and *agent* written in.

Writer's Market and *Literary Marketplace*, leviathan publications compiled annually and available in most libraries and bookstores, list agents along with publishers, with contact information, tips on what they're looking for, and the names of some of their famous clients. Make a list of those most likely to serve your best interest, put together an outline and sample chapters, and send them to the agents on the list, along with a cover letter explaining your situation. Submit to more than one at a time, and follow up with polite reminders if you go four to six weeks without hearing back (earlier, if you have a publisher interested). Some things about this business don't change. The only difference here is you're sending the material to someone you hope will represent you instead of straight to the horse's mouth.

Most literary agents ask their clients to sign contracts, which fortunately don't require engaging yet another agent to interpret. They normally run one or two pages, laying out the agency fee (usually fifteen percent; *do not agree* to anything higher), an agreement to cover costs of postage, copying, and purchasing extra copies of the published book to submit to subsidiary markets (these should never amount to more than a few dollars), and an escape clause (very important) allowing either party to dissolve the professional relationship with an exchange in writing. It's a simple form, protecting both parties.

A cautionary note. The majority of literary agents are scrupulous professionals, but you should know that, barring an understanding to the contrary, the agent you sign with will retain the right to represent the works you place through him or her in perpetuity. Even after you've implemented the escape clause and place all your future work yourself or through another agent, the original agent continues to act as custodian of all the material you sold through him or her—paying you royalties and advances as they come in, of course, but acting as your agent-of-record for those works as long as they remain in private domain. That's why this chapter is titled "Fifteen Percent of Your Life."

I was blessed with one agent who when we parted company was gracious enough to surrender these rights to me without being asked, but that's extremely rare, and hardly to be expected even when you ask. I still receive royalty statements on books sold by my first agent, who's been dead sixteen years, submitted with scrupulous regularity by the heir to the agency. It's more pleasant all around when these separations are cordial.

Although I'm happy to employ someone to haggle and crunch the numbers, I like to keep my hand in from time to time by marketing my own short fiction and nonfiction. Agents as a rule are just as happy not to interfere in this area, as fifteen percent of properties that seldom sell for more than a few hundred dollars is poor compensation for the time spent. The contracts rarely run longer than two pages, are easy to understand, and are usually nonexclusive; meaning you can resell the stories after they appear without having to ask for a reversion of rights. To make sure I retain this privilege, in my agent contracts I add the words "excluding short fiction and short nonfiction" to the phrase "all rights inherent in ray literary work," and initial the emendation. It's up to you whether this is important, but don't complain to me when a hundred dollars for a short-short story shrinks to eighty-five by the time you get the check.

The agent-author relationship is a marriage, and regardless of how long it lasts, part of it is for life. As with mating, the best in the world may not be right for you. A lot of high-power names on the client list may mean that a lot of good work is getting done, but it doesn't mean there will be any left for you after all those huge egos have been massaged. On the other hand, a small, low-profile agency may offer you the care and attention you deserve and still demonstrate just why it's small and low-profile. And avoid like the Pit any agent who refers to his or her "stable" of writers, talks of "hiring" and "firing" clients, or in any other way behaves as if you work for the agent instead of the other way around. I know a romance writer whose policy is to fire agents whenever they tell her no more can be done for her than has been done. She's gone through a lot of agents, with all the hassle that involves; but as her income is in seven figures, I doubt she has many regrets.

* * *

Fiction Fact

During the 1920s, Edgar Wallace planted name-brand products as essential clues in his mysteries, then collected as much as ten times the sale price of the stories from manufacturers for the advertising. This may be the first instance of product placement in history.

* * *

A Prayer for the Short Story

* * *

LET'S GET SOMETHING STRAIGHT right off the bat: The short story has been on its way out since the day it was invented.

Edgar Allan Poe, the form's greatest practitioner, managed to avoid starvation only by peddling copies of the magazine in which his stories appeared. Those copies were his sole payment.

At the height of his popularity, Ernest Hemingway had to promise Charles Scribner two novels in order to persuade him to accept a collection of his short stories.

The Broadway musical based on James Michener's 1947 collection *Tales of the South Pacific* made him a millionaire. Meanwhile, the collection itself has yet to sell enough copies to pay royalties to the author's estate.

The short-story audience is small and select and always has been. Back when reading had little competition from other forms of entertainment, the greater public preferred to lose itself in fat novels by Dickens, Thackeray, and the Brontës, and even now, in our microwave world, the harried airport traveler will shell out thirty bucks for four hundred pages of Dean Koontz rather than part with $4.99 for a paperback anthology of short stories by modern masters. The market for the form has dwindled to a handful of collections, each bound by a theme, and a smaller number of diehard magazines specializing in fiction. Yet the form survives, if for no other reason than that the struggle to do so has made it as tough as gnarled wood, with a root system ten times the size of what appears above ground.

I have no time for people who say they don't read short stories. Further conversation invariably unveils their barren minds, and life's just too short to waste time talking to an idiot. The only negative review I read of one of my collections, *General Murders*, was written by an ex-convict, recruited by a Detroit newspaper to present the criminal perspective, who opened his piece by announcing he didn't like short stories. I doubt he worked in the prison library.

The short story is often perceived to be easier to write than a novel because it's shorter, and so it's difficult for those who write them to receive respect, even from their novelist colleagues. In a space-saving measure, the same annual convention of mystery writers and fans that honored Edward D. Hoch, who writes short stories exclusively, eliminated the names of short-story writers from its newsletter. Yet several of the novelists whose names appeared there declined when invited to submit stories to an anthology, explaining that they'd never written one and wouldn't know how to begin.

Their instincts were sound. William Faulkner once said he couldn't write poetry, so he tried writing short stories, and when he found he couldn't write short stories, he wrote novels. The work is intense, and unlike the rambling structure of the book-length manuscript, will not hide imperfections. The short story is to the novel what the exquisite miniature is to the sprawling mural. Characters demand to be defined in a couple of sentences, rather than paragraphs, and the writer needs to know where he or she is going before the writing begins. Telling a complete and satisfying story in under ten thousand words is like making love in an elevator and having to finish before the car reaches the top floor. It's no job for the writer who likes to dither around with interior monologue and detailed landscapes.

Once you've submitted to the discipline of a short story, a novel seems like a tropical vacation.

"How appealing," you yawn. "More work, less pay."

Not true. Although a first novel brings in a minimum advance of five thousand dollars, it's for months of work, with no guarantee that the advance will be paid off by sales and go into royalties. At a scale of five to ten cents per word, a ten thousand-word short story will clear five hundred to a thousand dollars for a week's work or less, with the opportunity of being picked up for reprint. Many years before John Lutz found success in Hollywood with *Single White Female* (adapted from his novel, *SWF Seeks Same*) he took a year off from writing books to devote his full time to writing short stories, which continue to reward him with surprise checks years later, just in time to pay a utility bill.

Stories I sold more than twenty years ago are routinely salvaged for anthologies, which pay a hundred here, two hundred there, with prorated royalties on top of those sums once sales go into the black. "Dr. and Mrs. Watson at Home," a little farce I wrote in 1987 to entertain friends who share my interest in Sherlock Holmes, paid two hundred dollars when Martin H. Greenberg accepted it for an anthology, *The New Adventures of Sherlock Holmes*; to date, it's netted me more than seven hundred dollars in royalties. Not too shabby for an afternoon's work.

The late lamented *Armchair Detective* once asked me to submit a story. I was busy with a book at the time, but since I never turn down a market for a short story I said I'd get to it after I made my publishing deadline. A few mornings later, I awoke from a dream with an entire short-short story (1,000 words or less, generally) in my head. I suspended work on the book to see how it played out, and at the end of three hours, I read what I'd written, liked it, and sent it to the magazine, whose editor sent me a check for five hundred dollars. One hundred sixty-six dollars and change per hour is a good wage by just about anyone's standards, and I expect to make more when the story is reprinted.

Since magazines and anthologies commonly buy first-serial or nonexclusive rights only, you don't need to apply for a reversion in order to resell your work; a time-consuming process in the book world. The problem, of course, is that there aren't as many short-story markets as there were fifty years ago, when drugstore racks groaned beneath the weight of slick and pulp magazines that published short fiction for every taste and all the writer had to do was work his way down the list until he'd made a sale. But the market has not disappeared. In the mystery field, *Alfred Hitchcock's Mystery Magazine* and *Ellery Queen's Mystery Magazine* are still healthy after nearly half a century, and at any given time, a new start-up appears to compete with them; while it lasts, it's a showcase and a source of income. *Asimov's Science Fiction* is a staple of its genre. *Glimmer Train* publishes "literary fiction," whatever that may be, and the literary and "little" magazine market has introduced many a powerhouse talent from John Dos Passos to John Irving, albeit for as little as a half-cent per word or, just as in Poe's time, copies of the magazine. Place them at the bottom of your list, but by all means include them. You never know where a bit of exposure may lead.

Why bottom? Because if you sell a story first shot out of the box to the *Lilliput Journal* in return for copies, you'll wonder for the rest of your life what might have happened if you'd sent it to *The New Yorker* instead. The same wisdom applies to peddling a novel. Writing is the only profession where you start at the top and work your way down. The worst an editor will say is no, and they're so used to doing that they won't resent you for making them do it again.

Anthologies are the widest and most enduring market for short fiction. Martin H. Greenberg, a preternaturally prolific editor, assembles them in double digits annually, with Ed Gorman, Bill Pronzini, Charles L. Grant, and J.N. Williamson close behind. Frequently, national best-selling writers such as Mary Higgins Clark and Jeffery Deaver lend their names to collections, with the task of soliciting stories and obtaining rights handled by editors. The Mystery Writers of America, the Western Writers of America, and the Romance Writers of America weigh in regularly with anthologies of new stories written by members, which is as good a reason to join up as any.

Commonly, stories are collected to coincide with a specific theme: Christmas, time travel, Victorian, etc. If you can work such an element into a story, you might just be God's gift to a harried anthologist trying to fill out his or her book. I once wrote a Western story I was proud of, only to learn when it was finished that the market for short Western fiction was going through one of its periodic droughts. I put the manuscript in a file, and when I heard that Bill Pronzini was looking for material for an anthology called *Christmas Out West,* I reread the story, which happened to take place during winter, inserted a single reference to Christmas Eve, and made the sale. "The Death of Dutch Creel" was subsequently picked up for an audio anthology for as much as I was paid the first time out.

A good story can always be refitted or recycled for a particular market. Before I was published anywhere, I wrote a story set during the Turko-Magyar wars of the fifteenth century. Now, there never has been a huge demand for fiction about obscure periods in world history, but I didn't know that at the time, and put the story away after numerous rejections. Later, after I'd established myself, I updated "Marduk's Bride" to the nineteenth century, moved the action from the Carpathian Mountains to the Chihuahua desert, changed the adversaries to Mexicans and Indians, and used it to top off a collection of Western stories published by the Ohio State Press under my name. Martin H. Greenberg then bought the reworked "Mago's Bride" for *The Greatest Western Stories of the 20th Century,* which was later reissued in audio. I wound up with three checks for a story I'd given up on years earlier. (Similarly, in 1977 I dug out a failed allegory, found in it the seeds of a good crime story, and made my first short-story sale ever, to *Alfred Hitchcock's Mystery Magazine.* Never throw anything away.)

In order to interest publishers, anthology editors line up commitments by well-known writers whose names on the covers help sell the books in stores, but they like to include good stories by relative newcomers as well. You'll know you've arrived when your name appears on the cover instead of being lumped in among the "... and others."

The friendliest market for new writers is the writing contest, sponsored in the hundreds by universities, writers' organizations, newspapers, and regional creative writing programs. Most of them offer cash prizes and publication, and many well-known writers began their careers in that venue. (*Ellery Queen's Mystery Magazine's* Department of First Stories, which monthly showcases the work of writers who have never before been published, has provided an audience for a host of successful new voices in American fiction.) Consult the various writers' magazines and your local periodicals for announcements of upcoming contests. Whenever you begin to suspect that publishing is a closed shop, remember that the next generation of Sara Paretskys, Peter Straubs, Ursula K. Le Guins, and Elmer Keltons have to come from somewhere.

The short story is not just a novel told at briefer length. It's a different art form, just as the five hundred-plus-page "epic novel," with its sprawling backdrop and army of subplots, is more than just a 75,000-word book pumped up on steroids. With some exceptions, short stories feature a small cast of characters and cover a short period of time. Because more happens in ten pages than in the first hundred pages of a novel, the work is usually more intense. For me, two pages of a short story take as much out of me, physically and psychologically, as the five finished pages I try to get in per day when writing a novel. I seldom begin a short story without knowing how it will end. Otherwise I'll ramble, and contrary to what you may have heard, novels that began as short stories and morphed into something larger are seldom very good. Rather, they smear what might have been a dynamite twenty-page plot over three hundred pages of dreary self-examination. "The Lottery," which made Shirley Jackson a permanent fixture in American Literature textbooks, depends entirely on its methodical buildup to a devastating twist that could not be sustained beyond a dozen published pages. At eight, it's unforgettable. Similarly, stories best told with plenty of flesh on their bones come off shallow and half-baked when compressed into the short form. Despite short-story master Jack Ritchie's boast that in his hands, "*Les Miserables* itself would have become a novelette. Possibly even a pamphlet," the result would have been quite different from the one Victor Hugo achieved.

Some years ago I bought a collection of short stories in a used bookstore, on the flyleaf of which a previous owner had written:

"Nothing in this book qualifies as a short story. A short story should run no longer than ten pages, with a 'snapper' at the end." Whether this was the owner's personal definition or one impressd upon him by an English teacher, it was erroneous, as well as too tidy. Although it applies to "The Lottery" and everything written by O. Henry, it excludes all the seminal work of Ernest Hemingway and Flannery O'Connor, and disqualifies most of the writers working in today's short story field. I would certainly hesitate to call fiction published at fifteen pages or less anything but a short story, and a diet too rich in Tomato Surprise is both tedious and severely lacking in nutrition.

A short story is a slice of life, whether it takes place in a rundown flat occupied by a married couple who would sacrifice their most prized possessions for the happiness of the relationship or a group of interplanetary explorers searching for the meaning of life on a deserted asteroid. If it manages to stir readers even while leaving them perplexed as to its meaning, and if you can finish it in one or two sittings without immediate need for a chiropractor, it's a successful short story. (There is an argument in favor of anything running longer than thirty published pages but less than fifty—the breakpoint for the novella, or novelette—being called a "long story," but I've yet to find enough people to agree with me to get it into the official lexicon.) Poetry used to have to rhyme in order to be considered poetry; but art is notoriously hostile to easy categorization. A short story is short. It tells a story. What could be simpler?

It is, as I said, intense work, and because flaws are harder to conceal in a piece that can be read from start to finish with few or no breaks, when I finish writing what I consider a good short story, I feel a sense of accomplishment beyond what I feel when I've written a novel. Often, when a short-story idea strikes me like a good left hook, I suspend work on the book in progress to see it through, or write on the book in the morning and the story in the afternoon, after a short rest to recharge my batteries. And as weekend projects go, it beats cleaning out the garage.

If the market were as broad as it was half a century ago, I sometimes think I would give up writing novels entirely (very tempting when I'm in the doldrums or working with a difficult copy editor) and write short fiction exclusively. Since the income depends on outright sales more than royalties based on copies sold, I could make my tax accountant happy and estimate my earnings with a greater degree of accuracy, based on how many stories I could expect to write and sell during the coming year, as opposed to guessing based on last year's 1099s.

So what does this prayer for the continuing existence of the short story have to do with a book about writing the popular novel? Again, the answer is simple. If you really enjoy writing, and artistic satisfaction is your Holy Grail, the short story is the medium for you. I strongly recommend you try it. Good short story writers make the best novelists.

* * *

Fiction Fact

In On Writing, *Stephen King recalls that he wrote the first pages of* Misery, *a nightmare story about the dark side of being a popular author, in a London hotel on a desk that had belonged to Rudyard Kipling. When he went back to the concierge to thank him, the man replied: "Kipling died there, actually. Of a stroke. While he was writing."*

* * *

Poetry:
A Requiem

* * *

NOT SO LONG AGO, poetry was popular fiction.

This raises the question of whether poetry *is* fiction.

It is. Whether it's inspired by history or biography or autobiography or the imagination, any form of expression that depends upon stylization to make its dramatic point is fictive. Paul Revere, who was far more at home with a silver engraving tool in his hand than a set of reins, has become a romantic figure through the poetry of Longfellow, and Lizzie Borden's infamous "forty whacks" did not prevent her from being acquitted of double murder.

Even less open to argument is poetry's past popularity. From the ballads of an itinerant troupe of singer-poets operating under the Homer franchise circa 1000 B.C. through the beloved doggerel of Edgar Guest in the first quarter of the twentieth century, it seemed every man, woman, and child of every class embraced the whole of human experience set in verse.

Today, only long-suffering students and the odd dilettante who smells of old newspapers bother with the stuff sneezed out through publishing, triple-spaced, with margins as wide as the Zuyder Zee—also extinct. So how did we get from the love sonnets of Shakespeare to Gary Snyder's ode to the joys of urinating in the presence of a waterfall, and consequently a big ho-hum from the reading public?

My theory is poetry stopped rhyming.

Whenever an enterprise abandons its signature style, it loses its identity, and soon after its intrigue. About the time American motorists found themselves unable to distinguish between a Ford and a Cadillac, they turned to Japan and Germany to serve their personal transportation needs. It certainly had nothing to do with safety, as a Toyota crumples like a Bud Lite can when it rear-ends a Jimmy at five miles per hour. You can at least tell the two apart.

Similarly, when a group of self-appointed pundits declared that rhyming was not only unnecessary to poetry but a useless ornament, readers turned their backs on slim volumes of blank verse and discovered James Bond.

This retreating tide has done nothing to wash away Shelley, Byron, Tennyson, Poe, the Brownings, Kipling, and even Whitman, whose blank verse in the time of Swinburne arid Dickinson had at least the virtue of innovation; they sell as well as they always have, probably better. But it certainly has contributed to the preponderance of postmodern poets who subsidize their self-publishing from their salaries as bank tellers, postal carriers, and telecommunicators.

Until a few years ago, some of the original mystique still clung. Regional writers' conferences abounded with keynote speakers who tossed aside their capes and broad-brimmed soft black hats to cast their rounded vowels out over the heads of rapt listeners munching arugula and washing it down with house wine; but that was the generation that read Robert W. Service and Ogden Nash hot off the press, and remembered the bewildering brilliance of William Butler Yeats. Their successors would rather ask Anne Rice and Elmore Leonard how many hours they work and whether they compose in longhand or on a word processor.

Rhyming in its heyday was a discipline, not a gimmick. In masterful hands it carried its own music:

Which, while I forded, —good saints, how I feared
To set my foot upon a dead man's cheek,
Each step, or feel the spear I thrust to seek
For hollows, tangled in his hair or beard!
—It may have been a water-rat I speared,
But, ugh! it sounded like a baby's shriek.

More than a century and a half after it was penned, Robert Browning's *Childe Roland to the Dark Tower Came* still manages to cast a weird spell, like a witch's cant, and not for its disturbing images alone; while formless stanzas written by a graceless vulgarian like Gary Snyder forty years ago grow fainter by the day. Readers with less than even a marginal interest in poetry may recoil from what the poet is saying, but must respond to the hypnotic effects of rhythm and rhyme. Conversely, a stark word-picture of someone pissing is necessarily one-note, and just annoying.

The nihilistic beat poets of the 1950s, and the later generations who have imitated them, effectively killed poetry as a medium of mass entertainment. This was their aim, as they interpreted wide popularity as pandering. Movies, popular prose, and rock 'n' roll (whose lyrics rhymed) poured into the vacuum, and too many years have passed to reverse the flow. No major publisher accepts poetry, even through agents. What volumes of verse they continue to issue have been written by hands long dead.

This is a sad state of affairs, not only for admirers of poetry, but for fans of good prose as well. Some of our finest writers of fiction (James Dickey, *Deliverance*; Jim Harrison, *Legends of the Fall*) perfected their word skills writing and publishing poetry. With the exception of advertising, which long ago discovered the visceral effects of *free*, *fresh*, and *power*, no other form depends so completely upon the writer's understanding of the emotional and sensual content of every word in the text.

William Faulkner's famous quote of how he came to write novels begins with his confession that he tried to write poetry, but couldn't. Poetry is a demanding discipline. Once you've mastered it, you can write anything.

Without having read Faulkner's attempts at poetry, I suspect they were a lot more successful than mine. I spent a good part of my high school years filling notebooks with epic ballads, which for humanitarian reasons I eventually burned. I'm not even a good judge of poetry, and have turned down invitations to serve as one; although great poetry announces itself quite loudly, and bad poetry at the top of its lungs, I could never separate good from mediocre, as I can with most prose. But my youthful efforts weren't wasted. They taught me to respect words, and not just their definitions, but how they are perceived by readers. *Alibi*, for instance, is a perfectly respectable term, defined as evidence that a person suspected of a certain deed could not have committed it; but years and years of exposure to the sneering question, "What's your alibi?" have turned it into an instrument of willful misdirection. No dictionary recognizes that definition, but we do. Poetry understands that. It's an emotional medium.

Whether you rhyme or not, writing verse is excellent practice for the writing that will capture the attention of readers and editors. If you're good at it—and it's the nature of this demanding mistress that you will know soon enough if you are—by all means, send it to literary magazines and the small-press publishers who specialize in modest print runs and realistic expectations. But don't pin your career to poetry alone. You won't make a living at it, and if your ambition is to reach a wide audience (and if not, why are you reading this book?), you won't find it through poetry. However, if your prose becomes popular, you may someday be in a position to twist a publisher's arm and get him to bring out a volume of your poetry for a readership far larger than it would ever have found on its own. At the very least, you'll have had the pleasure of twisting a publisher's arm, which is a kind of poetry in itself.

* * *

Fiction Fact

In The Godfather Papers and Other Confessions, *Mario Puzo reports that his wife said she has no idea when he wrote* The Godfather, *as every time she walked past his office he was snoozing on the couch.*

* * *

The Golden Cage

* * *

WHILE ATTENDING A MYSTERY CONVENTION too many years ago, I shared an elevator with a woman who told me she wished I would give up writing Westerns so I could devote myself to mysteries full time.

I thanked her for her interest, and added: "If I did that, you wouldn't like my mysteries."

I wasn't being flip.

How often has someone recommended a writer to you, then cautioned you to read his early work, which is his best?

I find this ineffably sad. In the perfect world, a writer should get better, not worse, as he or she develops the craft. Whatever the wear and tear of age and familiarity take away from the bloom of first discovery, wisdom and the confidence that comes from practice should replace with interest. But too often writers grow bored and complacent. Like actors who have been repeating the same lines night after night for the weeks and months of a long-running

Broadway show, they merely go through the motions, without inflection or emotional investment. They've stopped having fun; and so, eventually, do their readers.

The signs aren't hard to spot. At one extreme, the books grow slimmer, the margins wider, and the print so large you can poke a fist through the hole in the Os. Handed an anemic, hurried manuscript, the printer is driven to such space-filling tricks in order to add heft to the end product and justify the fat cover price. At the opposite extreme, the writer, once known for his or her lean style, tries to fill the void with unnecessary adjectives, meaningless action, and paragraph upon paragraph of eyeball-rolling introspection, until you need a block-and-tackle just to hoist the book down from the shelf. This is the equivalent of fat Elvis huffing and puffing and bending the boards once trodden by the rangy hound dog of 1956.

Perversely, the decline may not be reflected in the writer's standing on the sales list. Like voters who continue to re-elect the same public servant long after he's been exposed as a corrupt fraud, large blocks of readers keep on buying the work of worn-out name authors, out of habit or fear of the unknown and untried. But the writer knows what's happening. He's lost the only vote that counts: his own.

When this book first came up for discussion, someone suggested a subtitle promising lessons on how to write a best-selling novel. I explained that since I'd never written a best-selling novel, I wouldn't know where to begin. This confession surprised some editors, who assumed that because my name has been around since man learned to walk upright, I must have cracked the venerated *New York Times* list many times. My sales have always been respectable, although not spectacular, and I've supported myself and my family for many years writing fiction full-time. At this writing, I've published fifty-one books, with three more scheduled to appear next year, and a couple of hundred short stories. I'm proud of everything I've written, and although I could bring new wisdom to much of my early work, I can say that I've done my best every time, and enjoyed myself in spite of the hard work and setbacks involved. I look forward to each new project with the same excitement—and stimulating fear—that I felt when I sat down to write my first short story when I was fifteen.

My secret is no secret. I almost never write the same kind of fiction twice in a row.

My first agent—never a man to use a euphemism when bluntness was so close to hand—called my approach to writing "pissing all over the lot." I prefer the phrase "literary crop rotation."

Farmers know that a field that has been devoted to growing the same crop season after season will eventually produce unsatisfactory results. Certain plants leech valuable nutrients from the soil, leaving it barren. Before the deterioration progresses too far, the farmers plant a less demanding crop in their place, or let the field lie fallow while they work another. By the time they rotate the original crop back to that field, the soil is refreshed and ready to perform at maximum strength. If, as I attempted to explain to the woman at the mystery convention, I wrote one mystery after another, or one Western after another, I would soon deplete the field and raise nothing but dust.

As it is, when I've been away from the mystery for a while, I'm ready once again to deal with clues and motives and the contemporary urban scene; and when that book is finished, I'm just as eager to return to the Western and remind myself that horses have to be fed and news travels slowly because there is no Internet. The first hundred pages of one of my best Westerns, *City of Widows,* zipped along on greased rails because publishing commitments had kept me away from the form for two years. Conversely, by the time I finished *White Desert*, which took place in the Canadian territories during the winter of 1882, I was so sick of horses and snow that I plunged into an Amos Walker novel set in Detroit in June 1999 the same day I sent off *White Desert*. I'm happy with the way both books turned out.

My first agent's implication was I'd have found a bigger audience faster if I'd chosen either the mystery or the Western and stuck with it. But in the next breath, he said that since I seemed to enjoy both genres, he wouldn't dream of advising me to forsake one for the other. He was right. I still enjoy what I do, and I'm pretty sure I've found that broad audience, even if it took a little longer than if I'd kept my head down and hoed the same long row.

The writer who makes his first great strike in one area, and who fears to step outside it at the risk of losing his readership, has sentenced himself to life inside a golden cage. It may contain all the comforts he could ever ask for, but it's still a cage, and in time he'll grow to resent it and want to break out. By then, his audience and his publisher won't let him. The late Frederic Bean, a celebrated author of Western fiction, became restless near the end of his life and crafted a compelling murder mystery in which all the suspects were members of a wealthy ranching family in modern-day Texas. His publisher packaged *Eden* as a Western, in a desert-tan cover with no twentieth-century features in sight, to exploit his reputation and avoid confusing readers conditioned to expect another of Bean's frontier historicals. The effect was to disappoint fans of his traditional Westerns and fail to place an impressive debut mystery into the hands for which it was intended. Alternating between the two genres before he was so effectively pigeonholed by his publisher's publicity department might have prevented this.

Before the stunning success of his first novel, *Hondo*, Louis L'Amour wrote hard-boiled mysteries for the pulps, and late in his career he published novels set against the backdrop of Medieval Europe and America post-Vietnam, but because of the great body of his work, his name will forever be synonymous with the West of rugged lawmen, outlaws, and Indians on horseback.

The golden cage isn't a new development. In the 1890s, Arthur Conan Doyle—not yet Sir Arthur—threw Sherlock Holmes off a cliff in "The Final Problem," seeking to bury the popular character who threatened to overshadow what he considered his more serious work. An outraged public badgered him into reviving Holmes a dozen years later, and although he was knighted ostensibly for his epic nonfiction book about the Boer War, few would argue that he would have been so honored had not King Edward VII been a fan of Sherlock Holmes. Today, Doyle's reputation rests squarely on the shoulders of the World's First Consulting Detective; yet he forbade the name from being mentioned at his family dinner table because it upset his digestion. Not a happy canary.

Another good reason for writing in more than one genre is the tendency of every genre to go soft from time to time. Everything passes through cycles, and regardless of their tenacity, Westerns, horror, and science fiction have been especially vulnerable to the caprices of the marketplace. The mystery and the romance have been on top for a long time and show no signs of slipping, but let's not fool ourselves that they won't reach their saturation point. When that happens, it pays to have your feet in more than one boat, lest you go down with either one. Writing is writing, after all, and demands the same skills no matter what your subject.

There's no reason why your U.S. marshal can't abandon his horse and board an airliner, or your love-struck governess can't stop pining for her master of the hounds and get her Ph.D. in forensic pathology. Stephen King is probably secure no matter what happens to his horror colleagues, but just in case he isn't, he could be just as scary hunting serial killers as werewolves. Broaden your résumé.

Many writers, like the incredibly prolific Erle Stanley Gardner, have prevented reader confusion by publishing their experimental work under a pseudonym; those who bought and borrowed books written by A.A. Fair knew better than to expect one of Gardner's Perry Mason mysteries. John P. Marquand chose to write literary fiction and thrillers under one name, but he's best remembered for creating the enigmatic Japanese detective Mr. Moto, whom he dismissed in public as his "bastard child."

Michael Avallone wrote tough crime novels and Westerns under the name Ed Noone, sex-changed himself into Edwina Noon for romances, and banged out dozens of movie and TV tie-ins under his own name. Isaac Asimov, who has them all beaten for sheer body of work, produced science fiction, fantasies, and mysteries using so many *noms de plume* that bibliographers are still trying to ferret them all out—apart from some three hundred books "by Isaac Asimov." All of these writers enjoyed long, fulfilling careers.

I've never used a pseudonym. I always felt that if my name didn't appear on my books, I might subconsciously fail to do my best work. There are many good reasons for pseudonyms, but the best argument in their favor is the opportunity to explore a variety of types of fiction once your own name has been compromised by what your readers have come to expect. If the idea of using an alias makes you uncomfortable, you're best off testing your wings in more places than one before the door slams shut on that golden cage. You'll remain alert for all the challenges, and those who have seen you in flight will recommend your latest work right along with your earliest.

* * *

Fiction Fact

Jack Ritchie, master of pared-down prose, once quoted the shortest story he had ever written:

When it was all over, only two people remained on the face of the earth. After twenty years, the older man died.

On reflection, Ritchie said, "I think I can still cut it a little."

* * *

Real Stuff

* * *

GOOD FICTION IS REINFORCED WITH TRUTH. I tend to stop reading whenever a writer demonstrates ignorance or disregard for any of the following, crucial to his or her genre:

* When you fire a laser outside the earth's atmosphere and destroy an enemy starship, it doesn't go "phoom" or "kachow" or make any other sort of noise; nor does the starship erupt in flame. Sound and fire don't exist where there is no oxygen.

* Real-life cops love it when a hooker asks them point-blank if they're police and they say no and she solicits them, thinking they can't arrest her if they failed to ID themselves when asked. It isn't against the law to lie to a cop, or for a cop to lie back. I like to think crime-story writers are aware of this when I read this type of scene, but since they never make this point, I suspect they're as ignorant as the hooker.

* You hang witches. You burn werewolves.

* Sheriffs are county officials. There has never at any time been a "town sheriff."

* It's okay for the hero in a romance to rough up the heroine and force himself on her. In real life, the reader who finds this unbearably sexy in a book will call a cop and throw your ass in jail.

* I've never heard anyone say, "How dare you," in my life, outside of a soap opera.

* Fog—even the thick, ocher "London particular" of Victoria's time, doesn't muffle sounds; in fact, sounds carry much farther in damp air than at other times.

* Bullets are what come out of the barrel of a firearm, and are dug out of victims. Cartridges are what you load into the other end. I'm tired of professional shooters buying "a box of bullets." And ...

* It takes a village idiot to use a revolver and leave telltale shells behind at the scene of a shooting. Since shells remain in the cylinder after firing, he'd have to eject them deliberately. Only automatics and semiautomatics eject shells automatically. And ...

* I don't know what those snipers with the some-assembly-required rifles expect to hit when the last thing they do is put on the scope. A scope has to be sighted in during target practice to make sure the bullets line up with the crosshairs, after which you put glue on the set-screws and leave them alone. Too late for that when you're setting up in the empty room across from the generalissimo's reviewing stand.

* I have trouble buying into suspense in a tale of time travel. Why doesn't the good guy just go back a few minutes and ambush the bad guy from behind?

* For that matter, I know for a fact no one will ever invent a time machine. History says nothing about yutzes running around medieval France with cameras.

* The fast-draw Western holster, tied down and lubricated with grease, is a fiction. How would you keep your revolver from slip-

ping out while you're on horseback, except with a hammer-thong; which is another fiction? And doesn't slipping a thong over the hammer spoil the point of having a fast-draw holster in the first place?

* Why do vampire hunters get such a late start? By the time they reach the coffin with their stakes and mallets, the undead gentleman is always up and waiting. I'd set the alarm clock for 6:00 a.m., have a nice breakfast, go out, do the job, and be back in time for lunch.

* During sex scenes, romance heroes seem to take off everything but their socks. The studs in old-time stag films didn't take theirs off either, but no one was looking at them.

* Next time you hit your detective on the back of the head, consider that every time a blow knocks someone unconscious, the victim has suffered a concussion. You only get so many before you end up in the Sam Spade Home for Old Sleuths, muttering at the wallpaper.

* Same whenever a bullet strikes someone in the shoulder, which is a network of nerves, muscles, ligaments, and bone. If you want to shoot someone without causing lasting damage, the buttocks are best, but when they make a movie out of your book, the musical score will make more use of the wa-wa horn than a bluesy saxophone.

* There has never been any such thing as a Mafia hit woman. The mob is not an equal opportunity employer.

* If your criminals discuss a criminal act over a telephone—any sort of telephone, and especially a cordless or cellular phone—I'm going to expect them to be arrested on page 10.

* Lynch mobs almost never took the time to twist a noose into the conventional thirteen coils. A simple square-knot does the job when you're drunk and in a hurry.

* There must be two kinds of ghosts: The ones who walk through

walls and the ones who pick up objects and people and toss them around. I don't see how one could do both.

* Restrain your eighteenth-century gentleman from smoking in an open coach. It's hard enough lighting a cigar under such circumstances with a match, and just about impossible when the match hasn't been invented yet.

* Murderers in books talk too much, especially when the only evidence against them is circumstantial or they've got the hero tied up and are planning to kill him anyway.

* Shouldn't aliens piloting spaceships wear protective helmets on their enormous exposed brains?

* * *

Fiction Fact

Playwright George S. Kaufman was known to pace the floor behind the last row of seats during performances of his plays. One night he slipped out to the local Western Union office and sent the following telegram to the actors:

AM WATCHING THE PLAY FROM THE BACK OF THE THEATER. WISH YOU WERE HERE.

* * *

Five Things
Your Teacher Never Told You
* * *

I HAVE GREAT RESPECT FOR TEACHERS, some of whom served as my earliest mentors and cheering sections. I think it likely there are far more people out there who can do but can't teach than can teach but can't do. Anyone with musical talent can sing or play an instrument, but it takes a special empathy to bring out the best from others with talent.

However, the best teacher who ever lived cannot hold your hand through life, or prepare you for all the obstacles that will come your way. I can't, either, but here are five considerations that probably didn't come up in Composition 101:

1. **Believe good reviews ignore bad reviews.** The conventional wisdom is to assign equal value to both. However, since it's more fun to dish someone than to praise him, and journalists are by and large lazy, you're better off discounting negative commentary and drawing what encouragement you need from the positive press.

Recently, a reviewer for a national magazine told me his editors insist that at least one line of criticism appear in every good review. This is the same as a judge instructing a jury to find the defendant guilty on at least one count of the indictment. Compound this situation with the tendency, now longstanding, for publications to depend on freelance reviews submitted by nonstaffers, regardless of their experience or whatever personal axes they have to grind, and you'll realize that giving bad reviews any consideration at all is a waste of good writing time.

If, however, all your reviews are bad, you might consider taking another look at your work, or updating your résumé.

2. **It is better to be politically incorrect and still be read in a hundred years than to be politically correct and forgotten in five.** Censorship is not new. Galileo was tortured for claiming the earth revolves around the sun instead of the other way around, and four hundred years later the New York Port Authority destroyed copies of James Joyce's *Ulysses* smuggled in from Europe because of its sexual content. That was persecution from the religious Right, and we can take heart from the fact that the penalties became less severe with each succeeding generation. Now that it comes from the socially diverse Left, the worst you can expect is a shrill howl.

Every great writer was condemned in his or her time for not writing "uplifting" fiction. Not one writer to whom each was compared unfavorably is still in print. Recently, the Library of America released two volumes of fiction denounced in the 1950s as paperback trash, including novels by Jill Thompson, Chester Himes, and William P. McGivern. At this writing, no plans are on the horizon to reissue Lloyd C. Douglas' preachy *The Robe*. Society has a way of catching up with realists and discarding romantics.

The First Amendment to the Constitution guarantees us all the right to offend. No law protects us from being offended. One sure way of rendering your fiction bland and pointless is to avoid upsetting anyone. (Compare the entertainment value of the

Smurfs to Bugs Bunny.) Had the P.C. Police been sworn in during previous literary eras, Shakespeare's Othello would have been white, Stevenson's Long John Silver would have invested his piratical ambitions in a prosthetic leg, and a few intense sessions with a counselor would have saved the marriage of Max deWinter and Rebecca.

The point of all social unrest is respect. This includes the right of every member of every minority and majority and both genders to be a vicious bastard. (Illegitimate children, don't write me.) If they were all heroes there wouldn't be anything for them to do.

3. **If you can't do it right, do it wrong.** I learned this one while building extra shelves to hold my personal library. My paternal grandfather, whom I never met, was a master cabinetmaker, but none of his genes passed down to me. When I finally realized I would never be good enough to rabbet a joint, and that even a bent nail will hold together a set of shelves sufficient to my purpose, I felt an enormous sense of empowerment. No one would ever admire my carpentry, but the books stayed in place.

Sometimes, despite all your best efforts, you're not up to the task as you envisioned it. In even the most positive situations, there is little resemblance between the scene you've pictured and the one that winds up on the page before you. (If it doesn't fall below the original, you aren't reaching high enough.) I'm convinced this frustration is more responsible for writer's block than anything else. Make it as good as you can, but learn to let go of your first ideal. Later, when the pain has receded, and you've forgotten whatever effect you were going for, you'll be impressed by how well you did.

A metaphor can go only so far. I'll never be impressed by my woodwork. However, I realize now that my grandfather was probably never satisfied with his, but learned to settle for being almost satisfied—enough, anyway, to allow a bed he built to be entered in the 1908 Paris Exposition and win first prize. I think whatever pride and attention to detail I put into my writing I inherited from him. Letting go was something I had to learn for myself.

4. **Never respond to critics.** I've seen this from both sides, as a writer who's been reviewed, kindly and cruelly, and as a some-time reviewer for *The Washington Post* and *The New York Times*. The author of a biography I gave a thorough pasting in the *Post* went so far as to organize a letter-writing campaign to the news-paper, denouncing me as all kinds of a charlatan. All I could think about was the paying work he wasn't getting done.

They have no right to your time. If they praise you, take it in your stride. Don't go out of your way to thank them; they might get the idea they were too kind, and shaft you later. If they con-demn you, why give them the satisfaction of knowing they hit home? Your words will outlive theirs, even if it lasts only two weeks on the racks. You've already won the argument.

If you feel so incensed you must lash out, remember that once you set a precedent, it will be that much more difficult to keep silent the next time a critic takes your work in vain. You must choose carefully the hill you're prepared to die on. Raise your criteria, and you raise your pain threshold. There's a wonderful feeling of freedom in being able to laugh off attempts by small-minded cranks to get your goat. Writing well is the best revenge.

If it helps, consider that all most people remember is your book got mentioned. The jerk gave you press, and you gave him zilch.

5. **Booksellers are your best friends.** Be polite to publishers, but remember they don't know the first thing about selling books. Owners and managers of bookstores do. They have to, because no corporate white knight is likely to charge in and save them from bankruptcy. Most of them are big readers, and if they like you and your books, they'll handsell them thus: "Well, if you enjoy John Grisham, you'll *love* ..." They know what their cus-tomers want, and their customers trust them. This is plain good business. If every publishing board contained one retired book-seller, we'd all be wintering on the Riviera.

There is no substitute for personal contact with the people who sell your books. If you are not a totally reprehensible personality, even a brief meeting will cause your bookseller to take more notice the next time one of your titles crosses his or her counter, and expend more effort on your behalf than if you had never met. All the postcards and promotional key chains in the world won't even come close.

This is a good thing to keep in mind when a signing doesn't go well. It will happen to you—it's happened to national best-selling writers, and it sure as heck has happened to me. Either the weather, or a big football game, or inadequate publicity, or nothing anyone can figure out will place you behind a stack of your books in a store that does good business every other day of the year, with no one to talk to but the occasional salesclerk and no one to sign for. It's a blow to the ego, and if you're any more insecure than a hunk of granite it will make you wonder if you ought to look for another line of work. But those two hours weren't wasted, because you showed up and made a bookseller happy.

I found myself in a mall bookstore in Dallas the night *Seinfeld*'s last episode aired, and tumbleweeds were the only things wandering the corridors; everyone else was home watching the tube. On another occasion, with everything apparently working in my favor—a rainy Saturday in spring, when the world goes to the bookstore to kill the afternoon, and Mother's Day coming up, when loving sons and daughters are desperate for a gift as personal as a signed book—I still managed to sell only two copies, one of them to the bookseller. On both days, I went ahead and signed the stock, with the understanding that the clerks would put "Autographed Copy" stickers on the covers and display them prominently, and later learned that the books had sold out within the next two weeks. And by being cheerful and not complaining, I made friends of the only people who count when it comes to selling books. Cast your bread upon the waters, and save the grumbling for when you're alone.

Fiction Fact

Raymond Chandler was suspended from his Hollywood contract for refusing to remain faithful to a novel he was adapting for the screen. The novel was The Lady in the Lake, *by Raymond Chandler.*

* * *

The New Mainstream

* * *

AMERICA'S IS A JUNK CULTURE. Its symbol should be an immigrant of indeterminate national origins polishing a battered coffeepot on his sleeve for resale. Our artistic specialty is reclaiming and reinventing media cast off by other cultures and returning them to circulation as our own. As a result, our homegrown artists have been involved in a two hundred-year struggle for recognition and respect, even in their own country. Especially in their own country.

While Nathaniel Hawthorne and Louisa May Alcott sought attention from across the Atlantic by behaving and writing as Europeans, dozens of scribblers who couldn't care less if their prose survived the coarse paper it was printed on earned their rents writing about highwaymen and pirates and Indian trackers—figures of entertainment identified with by an audience conditioned by history to distrust authority. Often anonymous, just as frequently pseudonymous, these writers introduced guerrilla tactics to an orderly field, and if we measure their success in terms of sales, won the day.

I'm not convinced that any other unit of measurement applies. That which reaches the greatest number of people exercises the greatest influence. While it may have taken *Moby Dick* a century to catch up to *Peck's Bad Boy* in sales, it's the size of Melville's readership that has determined his importance, and not just the opinion of a handful of academics who happened to discover him just when everyone else did. Edgar Allan Poe, Jack London, and Dorothy Parker have all endured scorn in literary circles for slightness of theme and the transparency of their methods, yet their work can be found in every library and chain bookstore in the Western hemisphere; fresh evidence that it's the bookseller, and not the critic, who is the final arbiter of literary immortality. Since the cultural revolution of the 1960s, which untaped original movie posters from dormitory walls and put them in archival frames and moved Depression glass from the flea market to the display case in the drawing room, first editions by Dashiell Hammett and Raymond Chandler, dismissed in their prime as pulp detective writers, have been bought by collectors for more than both men earned in their lifetimes, and a first state of Edgar Rice Burroughs' *Tarzan of the Apes* can expect to outearn the complete works of Henry James at auction. Where does culture stand when a Babe Ruth baseball card accrues more value in seventy years than the first three hundred years of a Shakespeare first folio?

William Shakespeare was phenomenally popular in his time. If he hadn't been, his friends and associates would not have been so eager to invest in a published edition of his plays and sonnets, a project intended as much for profit as to commemorate a late friend's genius. Melville became popular decades after his death because the swashbuckling melodramas of Rafael Sabatini paved the way for a deeper rumination on the conflict of sea and self. Ned Buntline's dime novels of frontier adventure, and Buffalo Bill Cody's over-the-top dramatizations in the arena, founded a genre that festooned Owen Wister, Zane Grey, Dorothy Johnson, Luke Short, Louis L'Amour, Cormac McCarthy, Larry McMurtry, Lucia St. Clair Robson, and Jane Smiley with garlands nearly as long as Wild Bill Hickok's and Annie Oakley's. Kurt Vonnegut, Ursula Le Guin, and Robert Heinlein cast aside the tawdry trappings of pulp science fiction to question the meaning of human endeavor in an increasingly automated world. The widely reviled restrictions of the category romance shaped the early careers of Tami Hoag, Nora Roberts, and Barbara Taylor Bradford, each of whom commands an audience as large as Charles Dickens' at his peak. Who's to say they won't still be read and revered when that handful of writers now fighting over the shrinking territory of the academically sanctioned "literary novels" are forgotten? Millions of readers don't simply vanish. They're mortal, but seldom mute, and their preferences reverberate through generations.

Whenever I pick up a copy of the *National Review*—rare event, as dentists and barbers tend to provide their waiting customers with magazines most people actually read—I witness these aging *literati* bitch-slapping each other in print and picture Daffy Duck, dangling from a morsel of pulverized rock and declaring, "I, Duck Dodgers, claim this planet in the name of earth!" (with Porky Pig hanging on for dear life to Daffy's ankle, saying, "B-b-big deal!). As I said away back in chapter one, the old-school mainstream novel that defied category is on the critical list, and although most bookstores maintain a large section devoted to general fiction, the majority of the titles— shorter, perhaps, by a hundred pages, and packaged traditionally— could be shelved under Mystery or Western or Science Fiction or Horror without confusing a single consumer. Many of the authors began in those venues and brought their readers with them when they jumped the fence, and the rest are at least aware of the conventions of the various forms. Genre is the new mainstream.

Not everyone who writes in genre will make that leap. No matter how well the thing is done, the Western writer who never changes his characters' dusty trailclothes and sprinkles his dialogue with "I reckons" and colorful cornponisms isn't likely to share Tony Hillerman's hallowed halls, and the romance writer who doesn't chafe at her editor's demands for a happily-ever-after ending every time won't clink cocktail glasses with Danielle Steel. Mainstream's a scary place, and however it may seem at first to resemble the country you left behind, it's a Bizarro world, as unpredictable as an earthquake or a drunken driver. You'll need to abandon some equipment you've grown to depend on.

I've mentioned there is a point at which romantic mystery acquires enough of the elements of the classic whodunit to be considered a mystery with romance, and fantasy-science fiction becomes either fantasy or science fiction, without qualifiers. Although the point is hard to see, it's not difficult to tell when it's been passed.

The movie *Alien* is emphatically horror, for all its futuristic space-travel trappings. The transformation takes place the moment the embryonic monster bursts from the belly of the stricken astronaut. From that point on, the story is a battle for survival against the unspeakable, with weapons that would not be unfamiliar to the nineteenth-century readers of Bram Stoker and Mary Shelley.

Major League—if I may pursue the cinema analogy—is a sports comedy; *Bull Durham* is a romantic comedy with sports. In the first, Tom Berenger's pursuit of his ex-wife Rene Russo are limited to two scenes, while the rest of the story follows the misadventures of a team of incorrigibles pursuing the league championship. In the second, the baseball scenes revolve around Kevin Costner's obsession with Susan Sarandon. In neither case is the audience left in confusion as to what it's watching; it knows by the preponderance of certain images. Those images were selected by the writers, producers, and director, who knew what they were after before the cameras began turning. In the multimillion-dollar business of Hollywood, no one can afford to stumble forward, chasing this or that theme and counting upon divine inspiration to show the way.

It's cheaper, of course, for us writers of books. If our initial vision doesn't pan out, we can scrap the first hundred pages and gallop off in another direction. But why waste the paper and time, not to mention creative energy? While it isn't necessary to know precisely how the story will end when the writing begins, or each specific step that will lead there, it saves a lot of wear and tear on the imagination to go in with a definite idea of the kind of story you're writing; and if you haven't done so before the last page, you're going to pile up rejection slips like Fargo snow. Publishers are terrified of half-castes.

There are many mysterious romances. They contain everything one looks for in a mystery, including a central crime, alibis, red herrings, and menacing characters on both sides of the law. But you know it's a romance, because the mystery is always secondary to the love interest. Romantic mysteries abound as well, but whether the courting couple winds up together at the finish is less important than solving the crime.

This doesn't mean that a hasty roundup of suspects and motives in the closing chapters, after a hundred pages of throbbing passion, will fool the mystery fan that he's found a new P.D. James. I'm reminded of the novelty "perfect country song," in the last chorus of which the singer's mother is run over by a train just after she's released from prison. Only a dunce would take this for anything but a clever satire. The same wisdom applies to the plucky heroine who seduces a dozen witnesses in her pursuit of the solution, then returns to Mr. Right. Romance writers demand *romance* and category romance readers will have fidelity, or go back to the bookstore for a refund. But they won't have to, because no category romance publisher would agree to buy the manuscript.

When one of my first Westerns was in processing, I was appalled when the editor insisted I trim a racial slur from the speech of a bigoted character. I was naïve enough to think censorship was dead. (The phrase "politically correct" had yet to be coined.) The brutal truth was the Western line I was writing for sold most of its copies to libraries, and the editor was unwilling to risk offending sensitive librarians. I made the change—not because I agreed with his assumption that all librarians are little old ladies with their white hair in a bun, but because I realized I'd pushed the envelope as far as it could be pushed with that particular publisher.

Later, once my Westerns had been reviewed favorably and brought in respectable sales, I found myself free to flout most preconceptions and allow all my characters to be themselves, however odious or admirable they may be, and regardless of the social or economic consequences. (Needless to say, I was no longer with the same publisher.) Today, I'm often told by people who say they "never read Westerns" that they read mine. I consider it a great compliment, because I know what kind of Western they're talking about.

With *The Bridges of Madison County*, Robert James Waller smashed every previous publishing record by turning the traditional romance on its head. His heroine had the temerity to commit adultery with a complete stranger, then return to her faithful husband without regret for her infidelity. The ending is bittersweet; both the principals sacrifice the love of a lifetime for the sake of the status quo. No category publisher would have given it a second look, and the slimness of the volume put the lie to the industry belief that a novel had to weigh in at a pound or more in order to sell more than fifteen thousand copies. (The editor friend who recommended it to me cautioned me to obtain a copy right away, because it probably wouldn't be around for long.) But Waller managed to tap into the same core readership that yearned to be swept away by the passion that comes but once in a lifetime, while attracting less idealistic readers who refused to accept that love conquers all. Here was one writer who trampled all over the tipping point. Yet he could hardly have been unaware of the emotions that put the category romance out ahead of every other genre for twenty years. His success revived the mainstream romance as written by Margaret Mitchell and the Brontë sisters before her, paving the way for significant literary talents like Annie Proulx (*The Shipping News*) as well as lesser, but no less successful lights, such as Nicholas Sparks (*Message in a Bottle*). These are love stories with no easy answers, and endings are as likely to be tragic as rosy.

Not counting the hopeless hacks, there isn't a writer working in category who doesn't aspire to grab the double brass ring, earning huge sales and the respect of the critical community. David Guterson's *Snow Falling on Cedars* is a case in point. Nominally a murder mystery, this tale of Japanese-Americans forced to give up their homes and relocate to FDR's concentration camps during the Second World War is also an interracial love story, but in the final analysis it's a novel about a monstrous atrocity committed by a government at war with fascism. It provides all the suspense of the classic whodunit, exploits the passions of readers who have ever experienced or wished to experience an all-consuming love for another human being, and exposes the tragic hypocrisy of a dark moment in American history. It's also beautifully written. When Raymond Chandler wrote that it's every good writer's dream to exceed the limits of a formula without destroying it, he might have had Guterson in mind, had Guterson been born when Chandler wrote those words. At the same time, it's likely that Chandler's own publisher would have rejected *Snow Falling on Cedars* as "not exactly a mystery," and that Ernest Hemingway's publisher would pass on it as "too much like a mystery."

That's how much mainstream has changed. I envy you to be beginning your career in such a friendly climate.

* * *

Fiction Fact

Oscar Wilde once said, "I was working on the proof of one of my poems all the morning, and took out a comma. In the afternoon I put it back again."

* * *

Recommended Reading
* * *

BOOKS ARE WISDOM, and while neither one writer nor one book can pretend to contain all the answers to all the questions, the miracle of paper and print brings every scrap of human experience and intelligence within the reach of every writer, beginner and veteran.

These choices are subjective, but they are not all mine alone. Those I know personally teach, inspire, and entertain; and they tell no lies. The rest come with the imprimatur of sources I trust and admire.

INSTRUCTIONAL

Early in my career, I was often frustrated and irritated by the conflicting advice I read in writers' publications. One well-known expert insisted I should use fresh crisp paper for all my first drafts, to inspire me to do finished work; another, writing under the same masthead, said to scribble my rough drafts on the backs of discarded sheets, so as not to let the waste intimidate me from revising and rewriting until I attained perfection. Had I not been very young and therefore certain of my genius, I might have given up entirely.

Of the following, some have come my way for comment, others were projects I participated in personally; still others carry recommendations from people I'd be a fool to ignore. All seem to me to be free of the doomsday arrogance that plagued me when I was first groping my way toward publication.

Braun, Matt. *How to Write Western Novels*. Cincinnati: Writer's Digest Books, 1988.

> A best-selling and respected writer of westerns for many years, Braun provides an insightful analysis of the form, and of writing in general. Even if you never intend to write a western, you will benefit from these lessons.

Burack, Sylvia K., ed. *How to Writer and Sell Mystery Fiction*. Boston: The Writer, Inc., 1990.

> The legendary publisher and editor-in-chief of the oldest continuing magazine for writers gathered a pantheon of world-famous mystery writers to share the secrets of their trade. Bloody good stuff.

Chittenden, Margaret. *How to Write Your Novel*. Boston: The Writer, Inc., 1995.

> Chittenden, a veteran of romance, mystery, and mainstream writing, offers bright, positive advice and a tantalizing peek into her working method.

Grafton, Sue (with Jan Burke and Barry Zeman), ed. *Writing Mysteries: A Handbook by the Mystery Writers of America*. Cincinnati: Writer's Digest Books, 2002.

> Grafton is the author of the multimillion-selling alphabet mysteries featuring detective Kinsey Milhone (*A is for Alibi* through *Q is for Quarry*, to date). Assisted by fellow seasoned mystery writers Burke and Zeman, she apprehended a mob of

suspense experts, gave them the third degree, and shares with us their various *modi operandi*.

Levin, Donna. *Get That Novel Started! (And Keep It Going 'Til You Finish)*. Cincinnati: Writer's Digest Books, 1992.

Levin's a cheerleader with a whip, getting you off the couch, into a chair, and lashing you mercilessly from Chapter One through The End. A good swift kick in the behind, but with strokes.

Nolan, William F. *How to Write Horror Fiction*. Cincinnati: Writer's Digest Books, 1991.

Part of Writer's Digest's Genre Writing Series, this is a basic how-to guide to a form that depends absolutely upon coaxing the right reaction from readers. The suspense techniques it teaches are equally useful in every other area of fiction.

O'Conner, Patricia T. *Woe Is I: The Grammarphobe's Guide to Better English in Plain English (Expanded)*. New York: Riverhead Books, 2002.

I could only touch on this crucial subject in "Gears and Pulleys." The word on this one is it serves up a semester's worth of college-level instruction without the mumbo-jumbo. This one might have spared me the misery of diagramming sentences.

O'Conner, Patricia T. *Words Fail Me: What Everyone Who Writes Should Know About Writing*. New York: Turtleback Books, 2000.

One of the things I like about how-tos is their titles lay it on the line.

Rendell-Smock, Sharon, ed. *Hooking the Reader: Opening Lines That Sell*. Rearney: Morris Publishing, 2001.

You know by now how I feel about hooks in general; but the ones here, quoted from among a score or more of writers' favorites, are fun and stimulating. They make you want to write one of your own.

Seidman, Michael. *Living the Dream: An Outline for a Life in Fiction*. New York: Carroll & Graf, 1992.

> Seidman has edited for most of the major publishers in New York, probably because he tells it like it is, regardless of the consequences. An irreverent, entertaining, and highly informative rundown on the state of writing for publication today, with good and bad writing examples quoted and clear explanations of why some work and some don't.

Truss, Lynne. *Eats, Shoots & Leaves: The Zero Tolerance Approach to Punctuation*. New York: Gotham Books, 2004.

> I'm no fan of "zero tolerance" or the fascist thinking behind it, but I'm one with Truss on the importance of precision in this area. English purists with a well-developed sense of irony are rare, and hers entertains, instructs, and draws the sting from a thorny subject. If you're curious about the title, try it without the misplaces comma; Truss is quoting from a book about pandas.

Wainger, Leslie. *Writing a Romance Novel for Dummies*. Indianapolis: IDG Books Worldwide, 2004.

> I know a lot of smart romance readers who would take exception to this title; but of course it refers to writers, not their audience. Those familiar with the "Dummies" franchise know they can expect a coherent introduction to a complex subject in clear, simple language laced with large doses of common sense.

Walsh, Bill. *Lapsing into a Comma: A Curmudgeon's Guide to the Many Things That Can Go Wrong in Print-And How to Avoid Them*. New York: McGrawHill/Contemporary Books, 2000.

> I'm torn between wishing this business were more efficient and being grateful that it doesn't place more faith in cold figures. A book that shows writers how to skirt its Pickwickian pitfalls without upsetting the status quo is destined for a place in my heart—or rather, the heart of my library.

Williamson, J.N. *How to Write Tales of Horror, Fantasy & Science*

Fiction. Cincinnati: Writer's Digest Books, 1991,

> Williamson, a leading writer and editor of horror, fantasy, and science fiction anthologies, has worked closely with the best in these genres. These reflections are as close as any of us is likely to come to thoughtful shoptalk with King, Koontz, Bradbury, Heinlein, and Le Guin.

WRITERS SPEAK

I'm a lifelong enthusiast of busman's holidays. Whenever I'm not writing, I'd as soon curl up with autobiographies, journals, letters, and essays by writers I admire as sit down to a home-cooked meal. Their thoughts, so beautifully and poignantly expressed, challenge me to be a better writer than I am, just as a good tennis player plays better against a champion.

Chandler, Raymond (Dorothy Gardener and Kathrine Sorley Walker, ed.). *Raymond Chandler Speaking*. Boston: Houghton Mifflin, 1962.

> "… when I split an infinitive, goddamn it, I split it so it will stay split, and when I interrupt the velvety smoothness of my more or less literate syntax with a few sudden words of bar-room vernacular, that is done with the eyes wide open and the mind relaxed but attentive."
>
> At times crusty, often philosophical, always startlingly coherent, Chandler's private and public thoughts on life and the craft of writing are as fresh and entertaining as his groundbreaking detective fiction. This "wit and wisdom" collection also contains "Ten Percent of Your Life," his essay on working with agents, from which I borrowed the title (adjusted for inflation) for my own take on the subject.

Chandler, Raymond. *The Simple Art of Murder*. Boston: Houghton Mifflin, 1950.

> The title essay is indisputably the best known in detective fic-

tion history, and one of the most frequently quoted in literature, "Down these mean streets a man must go who is not himself mean, who is neither tarnished nor afraid," ranks just behind the Twenty-third Psalm for recitation from memory; yet every line of Chandler's polemic on the American vs. the British school of mystery writing is a polished gem. This volume includes four Chandler stories and his famed introduction to *Trouble Is My Business,* in which he wrote, "When in doubt have a man come through a door with a gun in his hand."

Chandler, Raymond (Frank MacShane, ed.). *Selected Letters of Raymond Chandler.* New York: Columbia University Press, 1981.

These letters, collected here for the first time, are the source of many of the passages quoted in *Raymond Chandler Speaking.* From 1937 until just before his death in 1959, they document a life spent almost entirely at a typewriter. Part autobiography, part lecture, part gossip, they present a unique, gimlet-eyed perspective on the first half of the twentieth century and writing for the pulps, Hollywood, and posterity. Warning: once you open it to check a specific reference, you'll find yourself still reading an hour later. It's like potato chips.

Fitzgerald, F. Scott (Larry W. Phillips, ed.). *F. Scott Fitzgerald on Writing.* New York: Charles Scribner's Sons, 1985.

This slim volume gleans nuggets of pure gold from Fitzgerald's letters, conversation, and essays, applicable to every writer's situation. It's comforting to learn that the crystalline style familiar to readers of *The Great Gatsby* and "The Diamond as Big as the Ritz" came only after great struggle, and that the author worked as hard to attain that free flow as any of us, and harder than most. To daughter Frances: "It is an awfully lonesome business, and, as you know, I never wanted you to go into it, but if you are going into it at all, I want you to go into it knowing the sort of things that took me years to learn."

Fitzgerald, F. Scott (Matthew J. Bruccoli, ed.). *The Notebooks of F. Scott Fitzgerald*. New York: Harcourt Brace Jovanovich, 1980.

It's impossible to place a value on this glimpse into a great writer's working method. It's like being able to open Fitzgerald's brain and see all the moving parts at work. Divided, as originally, into such categories as "Descriptions of Girls," "Jingles and Songs," "Titles," and "Vernacular," this is the repository from which he drew the components of the Great American Novel.

Forster, E.M. *Aspects of the Novel*. New York: Harcourt, Brace, and Co., 1927.

The author of *Howard's End* and *A Passage to India* treats us to a series of lectures he delivered to students at Trinity College, Cambridge, England, in 1927. "The Story," "People," "The Plot," and "Pattern and Rhythm" are only a few of the subjects covered in this crash course in an Ivy League education on the art of fiction. The morning coat and detachable collar he wore while speaking may be out of style, but the lessons are timeless. A tough find, well worth the quest.

Hammett, Dashiell (Richard Layman and Julie M. Rivett, eds.). *Selected Letters of Dashiell Hammett, 1921-1960*. Washington, D.C.: Counterpoint, 2001.

In *The Simple Art of Murder*, Chandler gave complete credit to Hammett for raising the mystery to the level of literature. Hammett's fiction supports that claim, and these letters-to friends, publishers, producers, family, and the formidable Lillian Hellman, his lover and intellectual companion of many years, tell *how* he wrote, with engrossing details of his career as a Pinkerton detective and his battles with tuberculosis and the House Un-American Activities Committee. His life, like Hemingway's and Jack London's, reads as compellingly as any of his novels and short stories.

Hart, Moss. *Act One: An Autobiography*. New York: Random House, 1959.

This is one of the most entertaining autobiographies I've ever read. Hart, a brilliant comedic playwright (*The Man Who Came to Dinner, You Can't Take it With You*, and many, many others), spins the hilarious, touching tale of his battle to succeed, his collaboration with the great George S. Kaufman, encounters with the giants of the Algonquin Round Table, and the grueling, riveting struggle to turn one-third of a good play into his first great Broadway success. Fascinating and inspiring.

Hemingway, Ernest (Larry W. Phillips, ed.). *Ernest Hemingway on Writing*. New York: Charles Scribner's Sons, 1984.

The most important writer of the twentieth century shares his thoughts on the craft his name has become synonymous with. Chapter titles include "What Writing is and Does," "The Pain and Pleasure of Writing," "Advice to Writers," and "Working Habits." Some of it's tough love; but he never asks anything of anyone else he didn't ask of himself.

Hemingway, Ernest. *A Moveable Feast*. New York: Charles Scribner's Sons, 1964.

It's fictionalized; but what fiction writer's autobiography isn't? Everything he writes about writing is gospel. A powerful glimpse at the early life in 1920s Paris of a future eagle testing his stubby wings. Warning: You'll be tempted to catch the next flight abroad and scribble in some sidewalk cafe over a piece of cheese and a jug of cheap red wine.

London, Jack. *Martin Eden*. New York: Macmillan, 1908.

This one is fiction, but only because of the downbeat ending. Martin Eden is the young Jack London, condemned to toil at inhuman manual labor to avoid starvation, stealing precious minutes to write. No writer in history ever faced greater rejection or enjoyed more stunning success. (Why, he asks, do people invite you to dinner only after you succeed and can afford to buy your own?)

Johnson, Ben (Walter Raleigh, ed.). *Johnson on Shakespeare*. London: Oxford University Press, 1908.

> Boswell's crusty curmudgeon only pretends to write about Shakespeare in these pithy, iconoclastic essays; in a rare display of humility, he's letting us all in on his own theories of writing. Another hard-to-find jewel.

King, Stephen. *Stephen King's Danse Macabre*. New York: Everest House, 1981.

> The best (are there any others?) one-volume critical history of horror fiction ever published, with flashes of insight into King's own method and theories of writing to a specific effect, which is to scare readers out of their socks. This is where he makes that notorious admission about going "for the gross-out" when he can't frightens, but he redeems himself with his thought-provoking take on the classics of his genre.

King, Stephen. *On Writing: A Memoir of the Craft*. New York: Charles Scribner's Sons, 2000.

> In case you were disappointed not to find this charming, essential book in the section on instructional guides, I saved it because it's as much an absorbing and ruthlessly honest autobiography as it is a helpful tool. From his (justifiable) childhood terror of doctors to his addiction to drugs and alcohol to his near-fatal encounter with a reckless driver, King is so unsparing of himself that anyone would be a fool to argue with the truth of his writing theories. If you like his books, you'll love *On Writing*, and if you don't like them, you'll like him after you've read this one.

Perkins, Maxwell E. (John Hall Wheelock, ed.) *Editor to Author: The Letters of Maxwell E. Perkins*. New York: Charles Scribner's Sons, 1950.

> He only discovered Fitzgerald, Hemingway, Thomas Wolfe, Marjorie Kinnan Rawlings, and James Jones. From 1914 until his death in 1947, Max Perkins, of Charles Scribner's Sons, was the gold standard of American editors. He threatened to quit if the editorial board refused to take a chance on the unknown

Fitzgerald, gently browbeat the pugnacious Hemingway into soft-
ening his language for wider consumption, and did everything but
enter into a full-scale collaboration with Wolfe to trim his ele-
phantine manuscripts to human scale. These letters were written
by the same hand that shaped the first half of the American literary
century.

Poe, Edgar Allan (T.O. Mabbott, ed.). *"The Philosophy of
Composition." Selected Poetry & Prose of Edgar Allan Poe.* New
York: Random House, 1951.

Any collection that contains this essay is worth having. Poe's
lucid, methodical observations on writing apply now as they
did more than 150 years ago, and his beautiful, hypnotic style
is as well suited to them as to his stories and poetry. He was a
savage critic of his contemporaries at a time when candid criticism was considered ungentlemanly, but he wrote according to
the same standards by which he judged them.

Puzo, Mario. *The Godfather Papers & Other Confessions.* New York:
G.P. Putnam's Sons, 1972.

The author of *The Godfather*—the novel and the three classic
films it inspired—conducts us on an entertaining, catty, self-
deprecating tour of his life from family schmoe (chooch is his
term) to best-selling writer and Oscar winner. My favorite passage: Watching a Hollywood producer revising a script while
conversing on the telephone, Puzo remembers a Russian peas-
ant-soldier he saw nailing a plundered bathroom faucet to a
fence post and turning it on, expecting water to come out. "He
thought writing came from the pen."

Steinbeck, John. *Journal of a Novel: The East of Eden Letters.* New
York: Viking, 1969.

All the time he was writing *East of Eden*, the future Nobel laure-
ate wrote letters intended for his close friend and editor, Pascal
Covici, which he eventually presented to Covici in a wooden
box he carved himself. They contain a lot of kvetching about

---

how rotten the writing is going, serious doubts about his talent, and all the other plagues that visit us all throughout an extended and ambitious project; and all the time he was writing *East of Eden*! I challenge you to witness this self-flagellation by a giant without feeling better about yourself and your work. (As for me, I couldn't even carve the #$%* box.)

Steinbeck, John (Robert DeMott, ed.). *Working Days: The Journals of the Grapes of Wrath*. New York: Viking, 1989.

Same basic thing, and this time he's only writing one of the three or four best American novels.

Wallace, Irving. *The Writing of One Novel*. New York: Simon & Schuster, 1968.

Here, Wallace, one of the best-selling novelists in history, provides us with a detailed, book-length outline of *The Prize*, a page-turning fictional account of the race for the Nobel Prize, from conception to completion. He lets us in on his research, his notes, his working outline, his cast of characters, and their function to the plot, and he does so with the same attention to detail and pace that he applies to his fiction. Few writers have the self-confidence to remove the panel from their creative machine and show us the gears. It's my guess *The Prize* enjoyed a brand new run on *The New York Times* list after this book appeared.

Welty, Eudora. *One Writer's Beginnings*. Cambridge: Harvard University Press, 1983.

One of the ornaments of modern literature, and a pillar of Southern American writing, Welty is as frank and clear about her own early life and work as she is about any of the characters she created. A Cinderella story, with grits in the glass slipper.

Wharton, Edith. *A Backward Glance: An Autobiography*. New York: Curtis Publishing Co., 1933.

Wharton, a keen observer of her era, its people, and their customs, turns that same sharp eye on herself. It's difficult to conceive now how great the odds were that women faced in the late nineteenth and early twentieth centuries when they decided to publish. A realistic, sometimes whimsical, and determinedly non-strident account of the challenges she accepted—and conquered for all time when *The Age of Innocence* claimed the Pulitzer Prize.

Winokur, Jon, ed. *Advice to Writers: A Compendium of Quotes, Anecdotes, and Writerly Wisdom From a Dazzling Array of Literary Lights*. New York: Pantheon, 1999.

> The title says it. Wit, counsel, and object lessons from sources ancient and modern. Great for dipping into at random or reading straight through.

Wolfe, Thomas. *The Story of a Novel*. New York: Charles Scribner's Sons, 1936.

> Max Perkins had to tell him when *Look Homeward, Angel* was done. We'd never have known that if Wolfe hadn't told us in this ninety-three-page wonder, the briskest thing he ever wrote; Perkins was too modest, and respected his writers too much, to take credit for his part in the project (although he did once describe it as "like slapping a girdle on a hippopotamus"). Wolfe had cause to regret his candor later, when Bernard DeVoto and other critics took it to mean he was worthless without his editor. His humiliation eventually led to a break with Perkins and Scribner's. That's sad, but it's hard to feel anything but exhilaration while poring over this blueprint of the soul of a poet.

BIOGRAPHIES AND APPRECIATIONS

Obviously, writers' lives fascinate me, and judging by the questions I'm asked about my personal life when I speak at schools, libraries, and writers' conferences, I'm far from alone. Writers are, of course, uniquely qualified to write about other writers, and with very few exceptions their books are free of the condescending attitude so many biographers adopt toward their historical subjects.

Since the so-called cultural revolution of the 1960s, a new hybrid has appeared among writers' biographies. Part life story, part fan publication, these books approach the characters and events created by well-known writers as if they were as real as their creators; and why not? Writers are mortal, but their characters live on, to be born all over again whenever a new generation discovers them. Ask Sherlock Holmes and Scarlett O'Hara.

These are some of the most readable and stimulating biographies and character appreciations I've come across in a lifetime of collecting. They make me want to write, and I hope they do the same for you.

Bennett, Mildred R. *The World of Willa Cather.* Lincoln: University of Nebraska Press, 1961.

> Decades before Larry McMurtry and Cormac McCarthy, Willa Cather discovered and exploited the monumental theme of the American frontier that was overlooked by so many writers of the shoot-em-up school typified by Max Brand and Frank Gruber. Bennett's biography explores the life of the author of *My Ántonia, O Pioneers!,* and *Death Comes for the Archbishop* (Cather's masterpiece), and visits the sites of her books to paint a vivid picture of the environment that inspired her genius.
>
> Western writing, long considered a male bastion, has given us Dorothy M. Johnson (*A Man Called Horse, The Man Who Shot Liberty Valance*), Lucia St. Clair Robson (*Ride the Wind, Ghost Warrior*), and Jane Smiley (*A Thousand Acres*). The World of Willa Cather reminds us that it was a woman who established its full potential.

Berg, A. Scott. *Max Perkins: Editor of Genius.* New York: E.P. Dutton, 1978.

> Perkins' reputation grows with each passing generation of timid, forgettable editors with no passion for books. Berg's page-turning style makes an adventure story out of a sedentary life spent almost entirely in a chair behind a desk piled high with manuscripts. A funny, touching, and crackling narrative of Publishers' Row throughout the first half of the twentieth century, and the perfect companion to Perkins' *Editor to Author.*

Engel, Joel. *Rod Serling: The Dreams and Nightmares of Life in the Twilight Zone.* Chicago: Contemporary Books, 1989.

Rod Serling's picture should appear in the dictionary next to the definition of *driven*. Most of us remember him as the sardonic narrator of TV's groundbreaking series *The Twilight Zone*, but Engel steps behind the camera to give us a three-dimensional picture of one of the angry young men who founded television drama. Like Ray Bradbury and Richard Matheson (both of whom scripted some of the series' best episodes), Serling used the sci-fl/fantasy form to make political and social statements that might otherwise never have gotten past the censors of the McCarthy era, and did it in such a way that the themes and the stories still resonate. He was an artist constantly in motion, simultaneously writing and producing his program, adapting his original teleplays for the Broadway stage, screenwriting, and publishing short fiction, with one hand on a typewriter and the other feeding cigarettes to his face. His heart exploded at age fifty, and no wonder. This biography is as powerful as anything Serling himself ever attempted.

Farr, Finis. *Margaret Mitchell of Atlanta: The Author of Gone With the Wind.* New York: Avon Books, 1974.

The Hollywood treatment, and Vivian Leigh's problematic Southern accent, has clouded perceptions of Mitchell's *Gone With the Wind*, one of a handful of works vying for the title of Great American Novel and the greatest romance since *Wuthering Heights*. Farr's detailed, fast-moving biography blasts the myth that Mitchell was a talented amateur (she was an experienced journalist) and provides ample material to rebut the claim of the politically correct that book and author were racist. The many hours Mitchell spent researching the various Negro dialects of the antebellum South alone are enough to banish Alexandra Ripley's bland, cautious *Scarlett* to obscurity. A compelling book about the making of a book that in itself reads like a great novel.

Farson, Daniel. *The Man Who Wrote Dracula: A Biography of Bram Stoker.* New York: St. Martin's Press, 1975.

> It's impossible now to imagine a cultural environment in which there is no Count Dracula. Farson's biography offers thought-provoking insight into the life of an ordinary talent who rose above his own level to create a work as immortal as its ogreish subject, with psychoanalysis of the repressed Victorian mind and luscious gossip about such flamboyant acquaintances as Sir Henry Irving and Oscar Wilde. It's emblematic of the continuing influence of Stoker's creation that his biographer felt compelled to put Dracula in the title and give Stoker second billing.

Kaplan, Justin. *Mark Twain and His World.* New York: Harmony books, 1974.

> A complete collection of Mark Twain's writing would fill several walls of a good-size library, and his importance to our national identity ("I am *the* American") is larger than most of the cities he visited during his long life in the public eye. Twain, a.k.a. Samuel Clemens, is revealed here in all his triumph and deep personal tragedy, and his Gilded Age made to shine once again; a time both celebrated by Twain and changed forever with his writing. You can't get him into one volume, but Kaplan comes close here.

Lane, Margaret. *Edgar Wallace: The Biography of a Phenomenon.* London: Hamish Hamilton, Ltd., 1964.

> This well-written book (Wallace himself could not have been capable of it) is long out of print now, as is most of Wallace's own work, but it's worth tracking down if only for its rollicking narrative of an improbable life. Not a great writer by any standard, but certainly a clever and entertaining one, Wallace was fantastically successful throughout the 1920s and until his death in 1932, after which his appeal dropped off steeply. He's nearly forgotten now, remembered in the U.S. chiefly for the screenplay for the original *King Kong*, which he never lived to see, but he was one of the most relentless self-promoters of his or any other era. His story presents an object lesson for writers who

aim exclusively for a contemporary readership, with no thought of how-or if-future generations will receive them.

MacShane, Frank. *The Life of John O'Hara*. New York: E.P. Dutton, 1980.

O'Hara, who shot to fame with the appearance of his stunning first novel of small-town tragedy, *Appointment in Samarra*, committed the unpardonable sin (in critics' eyes) of becoming extremely popular in his own time, obscuring honest assessments of his great skill; for as we all know, true artists are always unappreciated in their own time and expire in poverty. A well-balanced, engaging book about a sensitive soul with a brawling Irish-American background, MacShane's is one of the best authors' biographies I've read. Skip Geoffrey Wolff's recent clumsy hatchet job, *The Art of Burning Bridges: A Life of John O'Hara*. Why a biographer should spend time researching and writing a book about a man he so clearly considers his inferior is a character puzzle only O'Hara could solve, although the book seems intended to head off this neglected writer's inevitable return to favor. MacShane's book is far better crafted, with no axe to grind.

Morgan, Ted. *Maugham: A Biography*. New York: Simon and Schuster, 1980.

W. Somerset Maugham's career was epic length. Beginning as a popular playwright in Oscar Wilde's London and ending with his death in 1965 as an elder statesman of the British novel, it embraced the whole of human experience from the height of Empire to the Beatles' invasion of America. His pose, in so many books and short stories (*Of Human Bondage* and "Rain" will long outlast these pages before you), is as the objective observer of mortal imperfection in all its forms, while in life he came to personify that same imperfection. However, Morgan never loses sight of Maugham's importance as a writer, and includes a sharp analysis of his best work. Like John O'Hara, Maugham was scourged by critics and his writing inferiors for the sin of popularity, but time has silenced their voices and amplified his. Maugham might have written this eminently readable biography himself, although he'd have taken care to disguise its subject's identity.

Nolan, William F. *The Black Mask Boys: Masters in the Hard-Boiled School of Detective Fiction*. New York: William Morrow and Co., Inc., 1985.

Nolan, author of one of the better biographies of Dashiell Hammett that appeared all in a bunch during the 1980s, treats us to a brief, two-fisted history of the pulp era and its acknowledged leader, *Black Mask Detective*, and capsule biographies of seven of its greatest writers: Hammett, Chandler, Erle Stanley Gardner, Horace McCoy, Carroll John Daly (inventor of the fictional private eye), Frederick Nebel, Raoul Whitfield, and Paul Cain, with a story by each as it appeared in the magazine.

This delightful book, covered by a bright yellow wrap reminiscent of the pulps' four-color covers, provides an accelerated education in that seminal period when America took back detective fiction from the British, and somewhere among the cracked skulls, bloody noses, discarded corpses, and women in bondage, managed to forge an authentic national language. A delicious guilty pleasure this, on a par with what it must have been like to snare the latest issue of *Black Mask* or *Dime Detective* from the corner newsstand and read it on the train home.

Pronzini, Bill. *Gun in Cheek: A Study of "Alternative" Crime Fiction*. New York: Coward, McCann, & Geoghegan, 1982.

Great sardonic fun. Pronzini, an icon among mystery writers and an omnivorous collector of pulp fiction, presents us with the flip side of Nolan's *Black Mask Boys*: The worst of the hilarious worst writing ever to appear in pulp detective magazines, books, and stories so horrendously bad they qualify as what Pronzini calls "alternative classics." Sample line, quoted from one alternative master: "She … unearthed one of her fantastic breasts from the folds of her sheath skirt." A stunning collection of bad examples to avoid. Followed, five years later, by *Son of Gun in Cheek* (Pronzini, Mysterious Press). You didn't think one volume could obtain all of the very worst, did you? But wait! There's more:

Pronzini, Bill. *Six-Gun in Cheek: An Affectionate Guide to the Worst in Western Fiction*. Minneapolis: Crossover Press, 1997.

> More alternative classics, this time from pulp Westerns. "On yore laigs, buzzard! ... Bust the breeze outa hyar onless you crave lead-pizenin'!" It's taken generations of Will Henrys, Dorothy Johnsons, Elmer Keltons, and Annie Proulx's to rescue the Western from the gutter this kind of writing kicked it into. (Pronzini's been threatening for years to issue *Raygun in Cheek*, taking the worst in science-fiction to task; so be warned.)

Riley, Dick, and Pam McAllister, eds. *The Bedside, Bathtub & Armchair Companion to Agatha Christie*. New York: Frederick Ungar Publishing Co., 1979.

> The Bedside series books are fast becoming a franchise to rival the Dummies. This one, one of the first, tells you everything you want to know about the bloodstained, cozy world of Dame Agatha's murderous gentry. Riley and McAllister assembled a sinister gang of writers to rifle through Jane Marple's knitting basket and Hercue Poirot's "little gray cells," helping us to all the thrills and chills we felt when we first discovered Christie. Read this back-to-back with Nolan's *Black Mask Boys* if you're at all confused about the basic differences between "cozies" and "hardboiled."

Starrett, Vincent. *The Private Life of Sherlock Holmes*. Chicago: University of Chicago Press, 1960.

> Starrett, an accomplished writer and poet, pioneered the concept of writing biographies of fictional characters; or rather, characters who left "fictional" far behind and now seem more real than their flesh-and-blood contemporaries. If you've ever felt an almost overpowering urge to board a horse-drawn han-

som cab in the London fog, then return to the coal-fire in your Baker Street flat to discuss the details of your latest mysterious case, this book will show you you're not alone. It led to the establishment of the Baker Street Irregulars (U.S.) and the Sherlock Holmes Society (U.K.) comprising hundreds (thousands?) of dedicated fans of the novels and stories published by Sir Arthur Conan Doyle who meet to hash over the plots, characters, and settings, and read and publish papers based on their scholarly research. You may want to try your hand at an "undiscovered" Holmes story of your own after an evening with Starrett.

Tropp, Martin. *Mary Shelley's Monster: The Story of Frankenstein*. Boston: Houghton Mifflin, 1977.

Part biography of Shelley, part literary critique, part detective story, Tropp's thesis tells the story of her world-famous story, explores its social and historical ramifications, and traces it to its scientific and chronological source. The scholarship is brilliant, and you will come away from it with a better understanding of the nature of horror and the power of fiction.

Van Ash, Cay. *Master of Villainy: A Biography of Sax Rohmer*. Bowling Green: Bowling Green University Popular Press, 1972.

From 1913 until his death in 1959, Arthur Sarsfield Ward, best known to the world as Sax Rohmer, creator of the evil Dr. Fu Manchu, wrote novels and stories of reeking Limehouse alleys, mysterious Egypt, extrasensory perception, and medieval and modern sorcery, and made the world like it. Van Ash's is the only biography of Rohmer to date, and likely the last we'll see until political correctness has died dismally and left us to enjoy a little harmless ethnic evil from time to time. The story of how Rohmer's friend Harry Houdini helped him escape from the trap set by one of his own mysteries is worth the effort it will take to search this book out, and there are many more anecdotes about the stuff of mystery and the posh life of the successful writer before the competition got too stiff.

Wilson, Andrew. *Beautiful Shadow: A Life of Patricia Highsmith*.
New York: Bloomsbury, 2003.

> Highsmith is one of the few writers who manages to disturb me
> every time I read her. Her fame is due to the Hollywood adap-
> tations of *Strangers on a Train* and *The Talented Mr. Ripley*, but
> despite the respective directing genius of Alfred Hitchcock and
> Anthony Minghella, the brooding Freudian quality that infests
> her writing has never translated to the screen. Wilson's authori-
> tative biography helps us understand the conflicted personality
> and boundless talent that haunts her work nearly a decade after
> her death. A masterful feat of literary detection.

Winn, Dilys, ed. *Murder Ink: The Mystery Reader's Companion*.
New York: Workman, 1977.

> Winn founded New York's Murder Ink, the first of many individu-
> ally owned and operated mystery bookshops that have since
> come to dominate independent bookselling. She got together a
> plethora of detective-story writers, detectives, and forensics
> experts to fill this compendium dedicated to the thriller-lover in
> all of us. Decidedly leaning in favor of the "cozy," and despite
> taking a couple of cheap shots at Chandler in favor of Hammett
> (as if one would prosper from the misfortune of the other), this fat
> volume is good for hours of hand-rubbing entertainment, while
> offering sound tips on writing mysteries and research about crime
> and detection in real life. Followed, two years later, by *Murderess
> Ink: The Better Half of the Mystery* (same editor and publisher),
> as if the male gender didn't share the first book equally with the
> distaff side; but who can complain about more fun?

INDEX